# Reaching the Hard to Reach

# Reaching the Hard to Reach
## Evidence-based Funding Priorities for Intervention and Research

*Edited by*

**Geoffrey Baruch, PhD**
*Director of the Brandon Centre for Counselling and Psychotherapy
for Young People, UK*

**Peter Fonagy, PhD**
*Freud Memorial Professor of Psychoanalysis, University College London,
and Chief Executive, the Anna Freud Centre, UK*

**David Robins, MPhil**
*Director of Grant Giving, John Lyon's Charity, UK*

John Wiley & Sons, Ltd

*Other Wiley Editorial Offices*

John Wiley & Sons Inc., 111 River Street, Hoboken, NJ 07030, USA

Jossey-Bass, 989 Market Street, San Francisco, CA 94103-1741, USA

Wiley-VCH Verlag GmbH, Boschstr. 12, D-69469 Weinheim, Germany

John Wiley & Sons Australia Ltd, 42 McDougall Street, Milton, Queensland 4064, Australia

John Wiley & Sons (Asia) Pte Ltd, 2 Clementi Loop #02-01, Jin Xing Distripark, Singapore 129809

John Wily & Sons Canada Ltd, 6045 Freemont Blvd, Mississauga, Ontario, L5R 4J3, Canada

Wiley also publishes its books in a variety of electronic formats. Some content that appears in print
may not be available in electronic books.

*Library of Congress Cataloging-in-Publication Data*
Reaching the hard to reach : evidence-based funding priorities for intervention and research / edited
    by Geoffrey Baruch, Peter Fonagy, David Robins.
        p. ;   cm.
    Includes bibliographical references and index.
    ISBN-13: 978-0-470-01941-2 (pbk. : alk. paper)
    ISBN-10: 0-470-01941-7 (pbk. : alk. paper)
    1. Psychotherapy–Great Britain.   2. Community mental health services–Great
Britain.   3. Community psychiatry–Great Britain.   4. Psychoanalysis–Great Britain.
I. Baruch, Geoff.   II. Fonagy, Peter, 1952– .   III. Robins, David, 1944– .
    [DNLM:   1. Mental Health Services–economics–Great Britain.   2. Adolescent–Great
Britain.   3. Child–Great Britain.   4. Health Priorities–Great Britain.   5. Preventive Health
Services–economics–Great Britain.   6. Psychotherapy–economics–Great Britain.
WM 30 R281 2007]
RC480.R4322 2007
616.89′14—dc22

                                                                                    2006023997

*British Library Cataloguing-in-Publication Data*
A catalogue record for this book is available from the British Library

ISBN-13 978-0-470-01941-2
ISBN-10 0-470-01941-7

Typeset in 10/12 pt Times by SNP Best-set Typesetter Ltd., Hong Kong
Printed and bound in Great Britain by Antony Rowe, Chippenham, Wiltshire
This book is printed on acid-free paper responsibly manufactured from sustainable forestry in which
at least two trees are planted for each one used for paper production.

# Contents

# About the Editors

**Geoffrey Baruch** is Director of the Brandon Centre for Counselling and Psychotherapy for Young People (the Brandon Centre) in Kentish Town, London. He is a member of the British Psychoanalytical Society, and is qualified in the treatment of adults and as a child psychoanalyst. He is the lead investigator for the first randomized controlled trial of multisystemic therapy in the UK. Between 2001 and 2003 he was a senior policy adviser to the child and adolescent mental health team, Department of Health, contributing to the *National Service Framework for Children, Young People and Maternity Services*.

**Peter Fonagy**, PhD, FBA is Freud Memorial Professor of Psychoanalysis and Director of the Sub-Department of Clinical Health Psychology at University College London. He is also Chief Executive of the Anna Freud Centre, London, and is a consultant for the Child and Family Program at the Menninger Department of Psychiatry, Baylor College of Medicine. He is a clinical psychologist, and both a training and supervising analyst in child and adult analysis for the British Psychoanalytical Society. He holds a number of important positions, which include co-chairing the research committee of the International Psychoanalytic Association, and fellowship of the British Academy. He has published over 300 chapters and articles and has authored or edited several books.

**David Robins**, MPhil is the Director of Grant Giving at John Lyon's Charity, and the author of a number of studies of disaffected and marginalized young people including *Tarnished Vision: Crime and Conflict in the Inner City* (OUP 1992).

# List of Contributors

**Eia Asen** is both a consultant child and adolescent psychiatrist and a consultant psychotherapist. He is the clinical director of the Marlborough Family Service in London. He worked for many years as a consultant psychiatrist in psychotherapy at the Maudsley Hospital, as well as being a senior lecturer at the Institute of Psychiatry. He qualified as a medical doctor in 1971 in Berlin. He has authored and co-authored seven books, as well as many book chapters and scientific papers, most of which relate to work with children and families.

**Dickon Bevington** is a consultant in child and adolescent psychiatry at the Darwin Centre for Young People in Cambridge, and with the Young Users Adolescent Substance Misuse Service in Cambridgeshire. He was previously consultant at Brookside Adolescent Unit in North East London. He arrived at medicine via anthropology, comparative religion, and philosophy.

**Jacqueline Cannon** is a counselling psychologist who has extensive experience of working in child and adolescent mental health services and in residential EBD schools. She works at the Brandon Centre as a member of a team delivering multisystemic therapy for families of persistent young offenders. She also contributes as a therapist to the Centre's interventions for parents of teenage children who have behavioural problems.

**John Cape** is head of psychology at Camden and Islington Mental Health and Social Care Trust, where he is professionally responsible for psychology services and practises as a NHS clinical psychologist. He conducts research on general medical practitioners' psychological management of patients, on psychological interventions in primary care, and on the organization of psychological services between primary and secondary care.

**Bob Foster** trained as a social worker and worked for social service departments for 20 years in child care and adult mental health before becoming, in 1997, Joint Strategy Manager of the Leicester, Leicestershire and Rutland Child and Adolescent Mental Health Services (CAMHS), which became one of the first CAMHS beacons. As the Child Health Programme lead for Leicestershire Health Authority he continued to chair the CAMHS partnership, and also led the children and families programme of the Leicester Health Action Zone. In 2003 and 2004 he was the Implementation Lead for the Department of Health's target to achieve comprehensive CAMHS, and set up the national CAMHS support service. Presently he is concentrating on developing the mapping and information tools developed in the role more widely across children's services.

**Anna Higgitt** is a consultant psychiatrist working with and providing clinical leadership to a community mental health team in West London. This is a post she has held since 1988. She also works as a senior policy advisor in the mental health branch of the English Department of Health, a post held since 1997.

**Pamela Jacobsen** was a research assistant at the Centre for Outcomes Research and Effectiveness (CORE) at University College London, and worked on the enhanced care study for depression. She graduated with a BA(Hons) in experimental psychology from the University of Oxford in 2004, and is now training as a clinical psychologist at the Institute of Psychiatry.

**Paula Lavis** is the Policy and Knowledge Manager at YoungMinds, a post she has held since 1998. She also works for the National CAMHS Support Service (NCSS) and assists with the development and maintenance of their website. Prior to this, she worked as an information specialist at the Royal College of Nursing, and assistant librarian at the Institute of Psychoanalysis.

**Judy Leibowitz** is a consultant clinical psychologist. She worked for some years in South West London Mental Health Trust as head of adult mental health psychology services. Since 2001 she has been working in Camden as Primary Care Mental Health Development Coordinator and is based in the Public Health Department of Camden Primary Care Trust. She manages the Primary Care Mental Health Workers in Camden and has been involved in a number of projects to evaluate their roles. She is also the Suicide Prevention Lead for Camden Primary Care Trust.

**Irwin Nazareth** is Professor of Primary Care at University College London. His research interests include: the physical and psychological management of people with severe mental illnesses in primary care; the management of unexplained medical symptoms; the psychological and health service consequence of physical illnesses such as cancer; the evaluation of interventions designed to change professionals' clinical behaviour in primary care; the evaluation of the under-treatment of depression in primary care; and the early diagnosis and detection of depression in primary care practice. He works as a part-time general practitioner in London.

**Stephen Pilling** is Director of the Centre for Outcomes Research and Effectiveness (CORE) at University College London where he works in mental health-focused health service research. He is also joint director of the National Collaborating Centre for Mental Health, which produces clinical practice guidelines for the National Institute of Clinical Excellence. He works as a clinical psychologist for Camden and Islington Mental Health and Social Care Trust. He has previously worked in a range of clinical services and has managed borough-wide mental health services and been a consultant advisor to the UK Department of Health.

**Benita Refson**, having previous experience in business and finance, trained at Regent's College London and the Westminster Pastoral Foundation, to become a qualified counsellor. She worked in the voluntary sector for several years with agencies offering counselling to young people. In 1994 she was the trustee responsible for establishing the Place2Be as a registered charity supporting children's emotional well-being in schools. As chief executive, she has been responsible for the development and growth of the Place2Be since the inception of the charity, growing it from 2 to 106 schools in the last 12 years. She works in a voluntary capacity and has three children and four grandchildren.

**Jemma Simmons** graduated from her undergraduate degree in 2003, and has since been working as an assistant psychologist at the Centre for Outcomes Research and Effectiveness (CORE), University College London. She provided the clinical intervention for a randomized controlled trial looking at providing an enhanced care management approach to treating depression in primary care.

**Peter Wilson** is a child psychotherapist who trained at the Anna Freud Centre in the late 1960s. He has practiced in a number of child and adolescent clinical settings in the London area, providing individual and family therapy, consultation, supervision and training. His positions of seniority have included Senior Clinical Tutor, Institute of Psychiatry, Director of the Brandon Centre (a psychotherapy and counselling centre for young people), and Director of YoungMinds, the national children's mental health charity. He has served on numerous committees and enquiries in relation to national developments in child and adolescent mental health service provision. Following his retirement from YoungMinds, he now spends much of his time lecturing, consulting, supervising child psychotherapists, and serving as the clinical adviser to the Place2Be, a voluntary organization providing counselling in primary schools. He is married with three grown-up children and enjoys playing jazz piano.

**Richard Wistow** is Senior Research Associate at the School of Applied Social Sciences, Durham University. For the last three years he has worked on Department of Health-funded projects mapping mental health services in England, particularly focusing on services for children and adolescents. Prior to this, he worked on a study of supported employment for people with learning disabilities. He has published articles based on this study, and is a co-author of the national mental health service atlas. He is also a member of the Tier 4 Policy Implementation Guidance Development Group.

**Miranda Wolpert** is Special Clinical Advisor on Child and Adolescent Mental Health to the Care Services Improvement Partnership; Director of the CAMHS Evidence-Based Practice Unit, Department of Psychology, University College London; and chair of the CAMHS Outcome Research Consortium (a collaboration between Child and Adolescent Mental Health Services across the UK, with the common aim being to implement routine outcome evaluation across their services and analyse the results in common). A clinical psychologist by background, she has a long interest in trying to support an 'evidence-based' approach to the development of both professional practice and service development in relation to child mental health.

# Foreword

**Professor Michael Edwards, JP, BSc(Econ), PhD**
Former Chairman of John Lyon's Charity and Joint Chairman of
Governing Bodies of Independent Schools

John Lyon's Charity was established by Royal Charter in 1578 and is a part of the Harrow School Foundation. (John Lyon was the Founder of Harrow School.) 'Reaching the Hard to Reach' was the title of a conference supported by the Charity, which was held at the Anna Freud Centre in Hampstead in October 2004. The conference explored methods of providing mental health services for children and young people. As a Trustee and a former Chairman of the Charity's Grants Committee, I have maintained a special interest in this area of the Charity's work and I was delighted to chair the conference. This book is based largely on the conference proceedings, and as you will see, the participants included leading figures with an international reputation from both the statutory health services and from the voluntary sector.

The main purpose of the conference was to inform the Charity's funding policy against the background of the Government's National Service Framework for Children, which maps out the future direction of child and adolescent mental health services. In this new context, the conference discussed the most effective ways of targeting private funds. There is a special role for the voluntary sector in pioneering initiatives that aim to reach those young people who fail to make use of the statutory services.

Evidence of unmet need is all around us. In a society of busy citizens pressed by work commitments, financial obligations, the desire for betterment, or driven by the lure of hedonistic lifestyles, people can have children and then not know what to do with them. There is an unprecedented absence of the kind of emotional and psychological support that was once available to children growing up in close-knit communities, and provided through extended family networks of parents, grandparents and other relatives, as well as friends and neighbours. It is not surprising that much of the Charity's support for families today takes the form of funding for after school clubs, nurseries, play schemes, and a variety of domestic support and mentoring services that involve professionals and volunteers who are trained in parenting skills.

Since 1994 the Charity has distributed over £1.5 million to enable young people to be offered treatment programmes ranging from individual psychotherapy to counselling in schools and family therapy. But what therapeutic approaches should the Charity support in the future? An expensive course of psychoanalysis based on the classic Freudian model devoted to an exploration of the life of the mind, may not appeal to young adults living in a society where inner life is something to be exposed and trivialized for popular consumption. Many will not comply with the old treatment methods, preferring the quick fix of obliteration through drugs, rather than the slow and painstaking process required in psychoanalysis. Not surprisingly, some of their parents and teachers will welcome the advances in the cognitive neurosciences, which have led to the design of behaviour-modifying drugs for children diagnosed with Attention Deficit Hyper-activity Disorder. Others will disparage the 'talking therapies', and feel that what is required to bring troubled children to their senses is a tough love regime of team building, outdoor pursuits and games.

Perhaps private foundations can be most helpful when they fill the gaps in state provision and back new approaches; for example the creation of non-clinical spaces for treatment appropriate to the needs of young people. There should be support for programmes where young people feel safe, and their privacy is protected; where they can receive flexible, but structured and purposeful, help from qualified professional therapists and counsellors. Such approaches are outlined in this collection of essays, which is to be welcomed not least for the very high quality of the contributions. Above all, no quick fixes are offered. For in the face of the often enormous and desperately complex issues presented by troubled young people today, this careful modesty of aspiration is especially welcome.

# PART ONE

# Policy and Research Background to Working with the Hard to Reach

# CHAPTER 1

# The Early Social and Emotional Determinants of Inequalities in Health

Peter Fonagy and Anna Higgitt

## BACKGROUND

This book is about how one may approach young people traditionally defined as hard to reach. Social inequality is a key determinant of both morbidity and response to treatment; this chapter will address the issue of the biological mediation for some of these social determinants. We will introduce a theme that runs through a number of the other chapters in this book, concerning the influence of the early child–caregiver relationship, which has the potential to place critical limitations on the child's chances of healthy development via biological, as well as social processes. This chapter will focus on physical as well as mental health, as social inequality sadly concerns both.

It is widely acknowledged that the society in which we live and work has a powerful influence both on our own health and well-being, and on that of the population of which we form a part (Blane, Brunner & Wilkinson, 1996). In the last 20 years an understanding has begun to emerge of the possible biological pathways by which the social environment contributes to the development of disease. In the closing decade of the twentieth century it surprised many to learn that the biggest risk factor for coronary heart disease (CHD) is neither cholesterol nor smoking, but rather the nature of an individual's work, the control they have over their job, and the social support they have available to them (Marmot, Ben-Shlomo & White, 1996; Marmot, Bobak & Smith, 1995). Even more interesting is the increasing body of research suggesting that the risks for many chronic diseases in adult life are set very early—during the first decade of life, or even *in utero* (Barker, 1990; Power & Hertzman, 1997). A relatively recent study reported questionnaire responses of 17 421 adult health plan members with Kaiser Permanente, who were routinely asked for information on adverse childhood experiences while being assessed for medical and physical problems (Felitti, 2002; Felitti et al., 1998). Exposure to several adverse early experiences, when adjusted for age, gender, race and education, was associ-

*Reaching the Hard to Reach: Evidence-based Funding Priorities for Intervention and Research.* Edited by G. Baruch, P. Fonagy and D. Robins. © 2007 John Wiley & Sons Ltd.

ated with a doubling of the risk of ischaemic heart disease, cancer, stroke, and diabetes, and a fourfold increase in the risk of chronic lung disease.

Awareness of these facts has been implicit in most medical research over the past
century; such studies often went to great lengths to statistically control for, or match
for factors such as social class, education, work conditions, and gender. Of course
these conditions are strongly correlated with health, and if uncontrolled could over-
whelm any source of variability when under scrutiny. The emphasis on the role of
medicine and lifestyle factors as major determinants of health has caused most
investigators to ignore the social factors and to focus instead on currently fashion-
able areas such as healthcare, smoking, high fat diets, and exercise (MacIntyre,
1997). These preferences have to be understood in terms of the psychological issues
that lie at the root of health inequalities. Weight, smoking, and exercise are emi-
nently under individual control and are therefore consistent with the culture of
individuation in which Western, particularly US, society currently lives (Rothbaum
et al., 2000). The emphasis we place on personal preferences from childhood as part
of a process of separation–individuation, which we conceive of as ubiquitous and
unassailable, naturally leads to a perception of health and sickness as a consequence
of personal choice, and under the direct control of the individual. Evidence for the
cultural and social determination of physical and mental health should lead us to
reflect on an all-too-well-prepared predisposition to assign causal significance to
individual lifestyle or habit.

There is a gradient in health outcome running from the most to the least advan-
taged members of our society (Marmot, 2006; Wilkinson, 1996, 2000); such health
outcomes are not specific to any particular cause. Inequalities in health are a mani-
festation of the social determinants of health. It does not necessarily follow that
social causes have social solutions; aspirin will relieve a headache even if the cause
is poverty. Thus, it is likely that an understanding of the pathways of health inequality will offer the possibility of policies that might directly contribute to addressing
social inequalities in health. Social engineering is unlikely to be a viable way to
address the social gradient problem. The essence of prevention is to find a point
along a causal path that allows the possibility of cost-effective psychosocial manipulation and intervention. This implies intervention in childhood and finding those
who are 'hard to reach'.

## THE BURDEN OF CHILDHOOD MENTAL DISORDER

Most surveys agree that about 10% of children and adolescents suffer from mental
illness severe enough to result in functional impairment. According to a World
Health Organization report (World Health Organization, 2001), by the year 2020
childhood neuropsychiatric disorders will rise by over 50% internationally. At that
point mental disorders will become one of the five most common causes of morbidity, mortality, and disability among children and young people.

Childhood mental disorders reduce the quality of children's lives as well as diminishing their productivity in later life. A recent analysis of one of the large-scale
longitudinal studies (Kim-Cohen, Caspi, Moffitt, Harrington & Milne, 2003) indicated that 75% of those who met criteria for one of 17 mental disorders at 26 years

of age had a disorder diagnosed by the age of 18, 57% by the age of 15. Thus, a third of those treated for depression at the age of 26 had diagnosable mood disorder symptoms in childhood. Others had conduct problems—oppositional behaviour or conduct disorder. Three or four times as many young people with conduct problems in childhood or adolescence had substance use disorder at 26 years of age compared to those who do not have substance use problems. Antisocial personality disorder is also at least four times more common among those with conduct problems in childhood than those without. Over half of children or adolescents who have moderate or severe depression in childhood continue to experience problems later (Dunn & Goodyer, 2006). No other illness damages so many young people so seriously as mental disorder. The stigma of mental disorder continues to be a significant barrier to mental health treatment, notwithstanding efforts to increase public education for both young people and their parents.

We have recently become more interested in child mental health, and the chapter by Miranda Wolpert and colleagues (this volume) illustrates the way in which government initiatives over the past decade have both mirrored and stimulated this increasing concern. The drivers of the intense current interest are to be found in at least three types of scientific advances. First, progress in developmental neuroscience and genetics (e.g. Benes, 2006; Gunnar & Vazquez, 2006; Ozonoff, Pennington & Solomon, 2006; Rende & Waldman, 2006). Our increased understanding of brain functioning, both at molecular, cellular, and neural systemic levels, underscores the formative nature of early development and the complex interactions between genetic and environmental influences in creating a stable yet responsive personality structure that progresses along predictable developmental paths, but rarely pathways that completely preclude modification. Progress has also been made in behavioural sciences, particularly in developing techniques for assessing subtle changes in emotional and cognitive development so that we can better map the emergence of normative capacities and individual differences. Improved understanding of the emergence of social cognition, emotional regulation and attention has been of particular importance. Behavioural studies have increasingly focused on the roots of emergent cognitive capacities in the child's physical experiences (Carpendale & Lewis, 2006; Lakoff & Johnson, 1999; Tomasello, 2005). A third driver of the intense interest in child mental health has been progress in techniques for clinical treatment and prevention. This volume relates this progress in the context of populations that are traditionally considered hard to reach. The last decade has seen the emergence of a range of innovative strategies, and the emergence of an increasingly clinically-relevant evidence base (Fonagy, Target, Cottrell, Phillips & Kurtz, 2002b; Wolpert et al., 2002).

## WHAT IS 'HARD TO REACH'?

Material adversity in childhood is a risk factor for both physical and mental health, not just in childhood (Caspi et al., 2003) but also in adulthood (Marmot, Ferrie, Newman & Stansfeld, 2001; Poulton et al., 2002). The indicators of disadvantage are well known and include social, economic, and parental factors. Indicators of family social disadvantage are young parental age, educational level, lack of

availability of a social network, number of parents in the family, and parents' occupational status. Indicators of economic disadvantage include low family income,
poor family living standards including poor housing, and the presence of pollution.
Parental adjustment problems are another factor; the most important ones are illicit
drug use, alcohol dependence and a history of offending. A further indicator of
childhood and adolescent problems involve antenatal and perinatal problems such
as unplanned pregnancy, ex-nuptial birth, seeking antenatal care late in the pregnancy, smoking or alcohol use during pregnancy, and the need for intensive care
following the birth. Impaired early child-rearing has been repeatedly identified as
an indicator of later difficulties. Such potential problems include lack of breast-
feeding, failure to immunize, no dental visits, limited preschool education, maternal
emotional unresponsiveness, harsh, negative parenting, lack of special experiences
such as going camping, lack of organized leisure activities such as sports, dancing,
Cubs/Brownies etc. Finally family instability may also indicate childhood and adolescent difficulties. For example, frequent changes of residence, schools, or of parental figures—be that as a result of separation, reconciliation or remarriage—are all
linked to subsequent problems and difficulties. Family breakdown, i.e. a separation
of at least six months, a step-parent in the family, or high levels of parental conflict,
arguments, assaults, or sexual problems, identify the child as at risk and increase
the likelihood of mental health problems.

   None of these indicators will surprise anyone working with children and families
in trouble. Of particular importance, however, is the cumulative nature of these
types of risk. In one particular study—the Christchurch Study—children whose
families scored at the midpoint on all these risk factors were 100 times more likely
to have problems in adolescence than the average child (Fergusson & Lynskey,
1996). Adolescents who are depressed are likely to have been exposed to at least
three types of risks, such as disruption of friendships, loss of a parent, or family
conflict (Goodyer, Herbert, Tamplin & Altham, 2000). Studying this prospectively,
one in five children who have three or more risk factors are likely to get depressed
in the next twelve months. The point here is that risk is cumulative. What makes a
child or young person 'hard to reach' is not any one type of social problem but the
sheer number of such problems. A recent personally disappointing life event will
increase the risk of depression by a factor of nine if the child had been exposed to
two or more previous types of risks.

   The children who we struggle to reach are literally buried under social disadvantage. The more indicators of difficulties they manifest, the less likely they are to
be able to respond to our call inviting them to engage in a process of healing. This
social disadvantage has many of the qualities of an avalanche, one problem bringing
many others with it. Thus, teenage pregnancy is likely to be associated with low
family income, poor housing and consequent exposure to toxic chemicals, limited
exposure to preventive healthcare, a great deal of family instability—in particular
changes in family composition, and also with poor antenatal care and nicotine and
alcohol exposure during the neonatal period etc. 'Hard to reach' is a child buried
under the rubble of cumulative psychosocial risk. We may expect children to be
resilient to one or more of such stressors, but as risk compounds even the strongest
constitutionally must succumb. In designing programmes for the hard to reach we
have to bear in mind this risk process and intervene in ways that address multiple

sources of danger for these children concurrently. The services described in this book are all designed with these processes in mind. Taking help to the child rather than expecting the child to seek help is perhaps the single most important lesson that the cumulative nature of risk teaches us.

## A LITTLE HISTORY

One of the dramatic events in the history of the human race has been the substantial decline in mortality and consequent exponential growth in the world population in the last 500 years (Mustard, 2000). This was particularly marked following the Industrial Revolution (Fogel, 1994; McKeown 1988). McKeown (1988) examined why the mortality rates for the British population declined at this time and concluded that, despite all of the socio-economic turmoil, the decline was a consequence of the improvements in overall nutrition within the population. The gradual increase in prosperity led to the better production, importation, and distribution of food. Fogel (1994) reanalysed the data and backed up McKeown's conclusions. In addition he reported that one of the biggest effects was on children, as assessed by improvement in the mean height of the population. He noted that as mean height of the population increased, so did life expectancy. This provides additional support for the current emphasis on early intervention: improved quality of early life carries benefits into adult life in terms of a reduction in health risk, especially in relation to chronic diseases.

Importantly, Fogel pointed to a virtuous cycle in health improvement. He demonstrated that up to 50% of the economic growth of the UK following the Industrial Revolution was due to the better quality of health of the population. He also found evidence that when economies got into difficulties, the mean height of the population could decrease. This was associated with a later decline in the health status of the population, as estimated by life expectancy. Thus, not only do the conditions of early childhood set the conditions for health in later life but, conversely, the better the quality of the population produced by the improved childhood conditions, the greater the productivity of the society concerned.

The evidence for social gradients in health is ubiquitous. The risk of mortality (early death) and the prevalence and course of disease has been shown to increase with lower occupational status, lower income, and fewer years of education (Adelstein, 1980; Dyer et al., 1976; Marmot, Adelstein & Bulusu, 1984; Pincus, Callaham & Burkhauser 1987). Risk factors, as well as morbidity and mortality, demonstrate a social gradient. For example, blood pressure is higher in individuals lower in the socio-economic hierarchy (e.g. Matthews et al., 1989). These associations are all closely related to race, which itself is closely related to socio-economic status (SES) (e.g. Kahn, Williamson & Stevens 1991) while increasingly recognized to represent an additional independent risk factor (Whitfield, Weidner, Clark & Anderson, 2002). Over the past 20 years, socio-economic inequalities in health have widened, yet welfare provision and employment have undergone major positive changes (Pappas et al., 1993).

Some have argued that historic social change is afoot. There is a shift in the methods of production from manufacturing goods to creating intelligence that will create all the features of the product without needing the product itself. An example of this may be digital Internet radio software replacing, for most of our children, the actual radios we have always known. But these 'radios' do not exist as physical products; they are computer code, part of the silicon revolution. This is equivalent to the technical revolution that took place in the late 19th century when electricity replaced steam. At these times, 'total factor productivity' is supposed to be flat (David, 1991)—this has been the case for the last two years according to statistics from the Organization of Economic Cooperation and Development—and declines are to be expected in some sectors of society. The privileged can usually protect themselves from change, but the rest may be more vulnerable. At these historic moments it tends to be the child who suffers most. Hence addressing inequalities is particularly apt at this point in time.

## SOCIO-ECONOMIC GRADIENTS IN HEATH

Since Sir Michael Marmot's Whitehall studies (Marmot, 1995, 1998, 2006; Marmot & Shipley, 1996), it has been clear that a social gradient in health exists within what might appear superficially to be a homogenous working environment. Whilst life-style factors such as smoking, cholesterol levels and family history, explain up to 25% of the gradient, the biggest factor seems to be some aspect of the individual's position in the work hierarchy. Individuals in high-demand jobs with poor control (i.e. individuals with a high level of work-related pressure and a lack of control over such demands) have higher mortality rates than those in high-demand jobs with a high degree of control (Marmot, Bosma, Hemingway, Brunner & Stansfeld, 1997). These considerations apply to most of the major causes of death, including smoking and non-smoking related cancers, strokes, myocardial infarctions, gastrointestinal disease, suicide, and accidents. The Whitehall studies found that the blood pressure of all civil servants goes up when they go to work. In the case of the top civil servants, their blood pressure goes down when they leave work, which is not the case for those lower down the hierarchy. In this investigation adjusting statistically for known behavioural risk factors did not eliminate the social gradient in health. There is one clue in the Whitehall data that points to the importance of early social environment. We know all too little about the early life of the civil servant in Marmot's sample. However, one index, which tends to correspond to the quality of childhood, is height (Fogel, 1994). It is noteworthy that Marmot's top civil servants are on average a few inches taller than those at the grade below, who in turn literally look down on the lowest grades.

One of the motives for establishing the British National Health Service (NHS) was the belief that if the Government removed the financial barriers to accessing health care then inequalities in health across social classes would decrease (Beveridge, 1942). Interestingly, American researchers continue to express the hope that improved access to health care and prevention services will serve to reduce social inequalities in health (Whitfield et al., 2002). However, 30 years after the establishment of the NHS, the social class gradient in health, as measured by mortality, had widened considerably (Merrison, 1979). Life expectancy overall had improved, but the primary beneficiaries have been the upper classes. The Black Committee was part of the fall-out from the debate that followed (Black, 1980, 1982). The conclusion of this committee was that there had been changes in the socio-economic environment with, among other things, a negative effect on the well-being of mothers and children. There were recommendations to introduce programmes that would create more equitable social conditions for mothers and children if the Government wished to reduce the inequalities in health. This did not sit happily with the four consecutive Conservative governments. Between 1970 and 1993 the social gradient for both suicide and ischaemic heart disease steepened considerably (Drever, Whitehead & Roden, 1996).

In July 1997, Sir Donald Acheson was asked by the UK government to review and summarize inequalities in health in the UK. The aim was for him to identify priority areas for future policy development likely to offer opportunities for the newly-elected government to develop beneficial, cost-effective and affordable interventions to reduce health inequalities. The 39 policy recommendations that emerged can be categorized into four groups: (1) all government policies should be examined for their possible impact on health inequalities, with highest priority accorded to women of childbearing age, expectant mothers, and children; (2) socio-structural improvements, including unemployment, poverty, housing, and nutritional recommendations; (3) emphasis on reducing disadvantage, highlighting the role of health visitors, economic inequalities, day-care, and preschool education; and (4) access to health services recommendations.

The Acheson recommendations (Acheson, 1998) reconfirm the importance of early intervention. We were gratified as our submission on the influence of early childhood experience on later health was part of our contribution to the inquiry (Fonagy & Higgitt, 1997, unpubl. manuscript). While the emphasis in the recommendations on early intervention—much of which has been adopted by the UK government, was to be welcomed, we were somewhat disappointed by the absence of a coherent theoretical framework behind the original recommendations. Yet a clear theoretical framework is available. Much, if not all, of what we know about the social gradient in health status may be accounted for by a set of explanations derived from an attachment theory framework. In brief, we argue that the relationship representations created in the context of early experience generate biases in adaptation to the social environment. These in turn decrease or increase subjective and physiological stress, predisposing the individual to better health or to disease. This chapter will attempt to demonstrate that attachment research provides a good account of social inequalities in health. We shall briefly review aspects of the literature on attachment and social inequalities in order to demonstrate this case.

## A BRIEF INTRODUCTION TO ATTACHMENT THEORY

Attachment theory, developed by John Bowlby (Bowlby, 1969, 1973, 1980), postulates a universal human need to form close affectional bonds. At its core is the reciprocity of early relationships, which is a precondition of normal development in probably all mammals, including humans (Hofer, 1995). Attachment behaviour of the human infant (e.g. proximity seeking, smiling, clinging) is reciprocated by adult attachment behaviour (touching, holding, soothing), and these responses strengthen the attachment behaviour of the infant towards that particular adult. The activation of attachment behaviour depends on the infant's evaluation of a range of environmental signals, and results in the subjective experience of security or insecurity. The experience of security is the goal of the attachment system, which is thus first and foremost a regulator of emotional experience (Sroufe, 1996).

None of us are born with the ability to regulate our emotions. A dyadic regulatory system evolves where the infant's signals of moment-to-moment changes in his state are understood and responded to by the caregiver, thereby achieving their regulation. The secure infant learns that arousal in the presence of the caregiver will not lead to disorganization beyond his coping capabilities. The caregiver will be there to re-establish equilibrium. In states of uncontrollable arousal, the infant will come to seek physical proximity to the caregiver in the hope of soothing and the recovery of homeostasis. The infant's behaviour by the end of the first year is purposeful, and apparently based on specific expectations. His past experiences with the caregiver are aggregated into representational systems, which Bowlby (1973) termed 'internal working models'. Thus, the attachment system is an open, bio-social, homeostatic regulatory system.

The behaviour of secure infants is based on the experience of well co-ordinated, sensitive interactions where the caregiver is rarely over-arousing, and is able to re-stabilize the child's disorganizing emotional responses. Therefore, they remain relatively organized in stressful situations. Negative emotions feel less threatening, and can be experienced as meaningful and communicative (Grossman, Grossmann & Schwan, 1986; Sroufe, 1979, 1996). Anxious/avoidantly-attached children are presumed to have had experiences where their emotional arousal was not re-stabilized by the caregiver, or where they were over-aroused, through intrusive parenting; they over-regulate the affect and avoid situations that are likely to be distressing to them because the caregiver is relatively unresponsive to, or intolerant of, the need of the child; seeking proximity through crying and clinging is futile and independence is valued. Attachment behaviours are relatively deactivated and the infant maintains proximity by avoiding disclosing dependence on the caregiver. Anxious/resistantly-attached children under-regulate, heightening their expression of distress, possibly in an effort to elicit the expected response of the caregiver. There is a low threshold for threat, and the child becomes preoccupied with having contact with the caregiver, but frustrated even when it is available (Sroufe, 1996). At the root of such patterns may be an inconsistent responsiveness of the caregiver; the child cannot rely on the caregiver's consistent and reliable presence, and even when they are present anxiously anticipates the moment when they will be left again.

A fourth group of infants exhibit seemingly undirected behaviour, giving the impression of disorganization and disorientation, because the attachment figure is simultaneously a source of reassurance and fear (Main & Solomon, 1990). These are the infants whose capacity to respond appropriately to stress appears to be the most compromised. Not surprisingly, a history of prolonged or repeated separation (Chisolm, 1998), intense marital conflict (Owen & Cox, 1997), and severe neglect or physical or sexual abuse is often associated with this pattern (Carlson, Cicchetti, Barnett & Braunwald, 1989; Teti, Gelfand & Isabella, 1995). Infant studies have established clear links between hostile or unavailable caregiving and disorganized attachment behaviour in infants (Goldberg, Benoit, Blokland & Madigan, 2003; Lyons-Ruth, Bronfman & Parsons, 1999).

Attachment is powerfully influenced by its social context. Social inequalities, directly or indirectly, have been found repeatedly to predict security of attachment, with social advantage usually associated with secure attachment (Belsky, 1996; Murray, Fiori-Cowley, Hooper & Cooper, 1996; NICHD Early Childcare Research Network, 1997; Shaw & Vondraa, 1993; Spieker & Booth, 1988). In one study, for example, only 24% of infants from an inner city sample were found to be securely attached, while 32% were found to be insecure/disorganized (Broussard, 1995). This compares to 65% who are normally found to be securely attached, and 10% generally found to be disorganized, in middle class samples (van IJzendoorn, Goldberg, Kroonenberg & Frenkel, 1992). There is some evidence to indicate that the mother's attachment security may protect the child from some aspects of social deprivation, for example marital disharmony (Das Eiden, Teti & Corns, 1995). Conversely, insecure attachment in the mother has been found to be associated with abnormal levels of aggression in preschoolers (Constantino, 1996).

## The Attachment System as an Organizer of Social Relationships

Any relationship in which physical and/or psychological proximity of one individual to the other creates a feeling of security can be considered an attachment relationship. Bowlby's internal working model (IWM) provided an early concept of relationship schema models that posits that the properties of self–other relationship representations govern the social relationships of that individual (Bowlby, 1973, 1980). The IWM has its origins in infancy and is therefore profoundly influenced by experiences with the primary caregiver. The model guides affects and behaviour when a threat is perceived.

While not all adult relationships are affected by the attachment system, many relationships have aspects of attachment associated with them. Some studies demonstrate considerable concordance between assessments of attachment classification in parent–child dyads at various ages (Main & Cassidy, 1988; Wartner, Grossman, Fremmer-Bombrik & Suess, 1994).

Substantial continuity of secure-versus-insecure classifications from the ages of 18 months to 20 years has also been reported using the adult attachment interview (Hamilton, 2000; Sroufe, 2005; Waters, Merrick, Treboux, Crowell & Albersheim, 2000) and other methods of measurement (Grossmann, Grossmann & Waters, 2005). In the context of benign life experiences, early, sensitive caregiving appears to endure to adulthood as a representational model of attachment relationships (Beckwith, Cohen & Hamilton, 1999). Stability has been less remarkable in other samples (Grossman, Grossman & Zimmermann, 1999; Weinfield, Sroufe & Egeland, 2000). However, combining these studies is very revealing: security in infancy is associated with secure classification in adulthood in 52% of cases, while given insecure classification it is only 21%. Thus the odds ratio is 4.15. While it is highly unlikely that continuity is to be expected in the natural course of development, the deviation appears to be predictable. Stability appears to be in the insecure classification and it is powerfully moderated by life events. 60% of the participants in these studies who were classified as insecure as infants, and who remained insecure, experienced one or more major life events (including maltreatment, loss, etc.). Only 14% of those who in young adulthood were classified as secure having been classified insecure in infancy experienced such life events. The likelihood of developmental continuity probably depends critically on important mediating conditions in the ecology of the family life that are not yet known, and could not be monitored in these studies. It appears that early attachment insecurity combined with subsequent life events relates to a predicted classification of almost 100% for adult insecurity. Early secure attachment on its own offers limited protection.

Early variants of attachment are viewed as initiating conditions by Bowlby (1973), starting individuals off on pathways that probabilistically relate to outcome. Whether change or continuity characterizes a particular individual's development, change from a pathway of attachment security does not imply that early influence is lost. Sroufe's work demonstrated the ways in which even when change was clear, early patterns could be discerned in certain ways and in certain settings. When preschool teachers selected children who they felt had an inner core of self-worth, even though they were struggling, they were more likely to select children who had been secure in infancy regardless of low level of current competence (Sroufe, Egeland, Carlson & Collins, 2005a). Similarly, children were observed to be more likely to recover from behavioural problems if they had been secure early in infancy.

Attachment relationships play a key role in the transgenerational transmission of deprivation. Secure adults are three or four times more likely to have children who are securely attached to them (van IJzendoorn, 1995). This is true even where parental attachment is assessed before the birth of the child (Benoit & Parker, 1994; Fonagy, Steele & Steele, 1991; Radojevic, 1992; Steele, Steele & Fonagy, 1996; Ward & Carlson, 1995). Specific patterns of attachment behaviour also appear to be transmitted transgenerationally. For example, mothers who report role reversal with their mothers during the adult attachment interview are observed to engage in more role reversal with their toddler-aged daughters; while fathers who reported role reversals with their mothers behave in a congruent fashion only with their sons (Macfie, McElwain, Houts & Cox, 2005). A history of parental emotional rejection and adult attachment anxiety and avoidance correlates negatively with accurate identification of emotions in crying infants (Leerkes & Siepak, 2006). At the extreme end, personality disorder in the mother is strongly associated with disorganized attachment in infants and children (Heffernan & Cloitre, 2000; Hobson, Patrick, Crandell, Garcia-Perez & Lee, 2005; Weiss et al., 1996). Thus, probabilistically at least, attachment socially mimics genetics.

Findings in relation to attachment patterns in infants and their determinants appear to be stable across cultures. Parents across a wide-range of Western and non-Western cultures state preferences for infant and child behaviour that are characteristic of secure infants and children (Posada et al., 1995). A 'secure base script' may be identified in maternal stories about parent–child interactions in both Western and non-Western cultures (Vaughn, 2005). There is also a significant meta-cultural effect in relation to attachment security. Regardless of cultural background, securely-attached infants are more readily socialized into any particular cultural milieu than insecurely-attached ones (Ainsworth, Bell & Stayton, 1974).

Attachment is a construct with application throughout the lifespan. Mother–daughter reunion behaviour is predictable from attachment security, even when the mother is an older adult and suffering from dementia (Steele, Phibbs & Woods, 2004). There is evidence that older individuals are more secure and dismissing, but less likely to be preoccupied with attachment relationships than younger ones

(Zhang & Labouvie-Vief, 2004). Early relationships have long-lasting effects and are as useful in applications to older people as to young children (Cicirelli, 1989; Consedine & Magai, 2003). Emotional experiences in older groups appear to be influenced by early emotion socialization and this is mediated, at least in part, by attachment style (Magai, Consedine & Gillespie, 2004). While people appear to become more selective in their attachment relationships with age, there appear to be critical gender differences in attachment patterns in older adults that do not manifest in early childhood, favouring the greater personal involvement of women (Birditt & Fingerman, 2003). While there are cultural differences in the composition of close attachment relationships at older ages (say between the US and Japan), the way in which these relationships change from middle age to older age appears quite similar across cultures (Antonucci, Akiyama & Takahashi, 2004).

Current models of adult attachment vary. Most models posit four categories of attachment: (1) secure–autonomous; (2) dismissing–avoidant; (3) preoccupied; and (4) fearful–disorganized (Bartholomew & Horowitz, 1991; Brennan, Clark & Shaver, 1998; Crittenden, 1994; Crowell, Frayley & Shaver, 1999; Klohaen & John, 1998). Broadly, secure attachment is believed to be an internalized sense of being worthy of care, of being effective in eliciting care when this is required, and a general sense of efficacy and control in dealing independently with stresses. Dismissing attachment is rooted in a distrust of emotional and social support from others, while manifesting a superficially positive view of the self as an independent self-sufficient individual who can afford to treat others with a certain degree of coldness or even callousness as far as dependent relationships are concerned. Preoccupied attachment leaves the individual with doubts about their own capacity to cope with stresses and challenges, but a greater hope of being assisted by others; this is manifested as excessive care-seeking at times of stress, and greater than average fear of loss of support. Fearful or disorganized attachment is currently poorly described in the literature. It has been linked with unresolved trauma, histories of mourning, and/or childhood maltreatment (Hesse & Main, 2000). It is associated with interpersonal caution, suspicion, anxiety, self-consciousness, and confusion (Bartholomew & Horowitz, 1991; Griffin & Bartholomew, 1996).

In a reconsideration of the dimensions underlying adult attachment we have suggested that two dimensions underpin the fourfold classification (Stein et al., 2002): (1) an interpersonal interpretative capacity that defines the dimension between secure and fearful attachment; and (2) an interpersonal interactive strategy dimension that ensures maximal proximity given limited capacity for interpersonal interpretation, which differentiates dismissing from preoccupied strategies. At the secure end of the interpersonal interpretative dimension the individual is able to be flexible about the interactive strategy to be used to maintain proximity; as this capacity decreases the individual will be more and more rigid in terms of the strategies they perceive as being available to them for maintaining interpersonal proximity (Fonagy, 2003). Some experimental evidence supports the hypothesis that adults process relational knowledge corresponding to all three primary attachment styles, and that it is the relative availability and accessibility of specific relational knowledge that determines the overall self-reported attachment style (Baldwin, Keelan, Fehr, Enns & Koh-Rangarajoo, 1996). We have suggested that measures of attachment do not measure types, but rather strategies for regulating emotion under conditions of relationship threat (Hill, Fonagy, Safier & Sargent, 2003). At the extreme fearful end of the interpersonal interpretative mechanism dimension, the strategies are no longer clearly differentiable and might contain components of both dismissing and preoccupied strategies in individual combinations, reflecting the confused aspect of this attachment category. Even though the strategies might not be clear, they are held onto with remarkable rigidity.

## GENETIC, MATERIAL OR PSYCHOSOCIAL CAUSES OF INEQUALITIES?

Social disadvantage is not purely a social process. In fact it may be more constitutional or genetic than it is environmental. Behavioural genetics studies have demonstrated the high genetic component of social disadvantage. Basically, social disadvantage is curiously hereditary. For example, the congruence between identical twins is greater, in terms of psychosocial risk, than between fraternal twins (Plomin & McGuffin, 2003). How is this possible? Within a simple psychosocial model of environmental influences on development, we assume that traumatic and/or facilitative experience leads to either an unfavourable or favourable outcome. But environmental influences may be genetically mediated. The genetic characteristics of the parent may be instrumental in creating traumatic or facilitative experiences for the child, but it is the inherited genetic predisposition that is responsible for unfavourable outcome rather than the early traumatic experience. Studies of adopted children and twins have allowed us to monitor genetic influences (Caspi, Taylor, Moffitt & Plomin, 2000; O'Connor, 2006; Rose, Kaprio, Winter, Koskenvuo & Viken 1999; Rose et al., 2003; Rutter, Pickles, Murray & Eaves, 2001).

The impact of genes on behaviour is complex. We now know that most psychological disorders have a genetic origin. At any one time point, heritability has been estimated at about 50%. For example, Arsenault et al. (2003) have shown that probably at least 61–82% of antisocial behaviour occurring across situations is genetically determined. A longitudinal study of twins (71% of all twins born 1994–5 in England and Wales) showed that 82% of the variation in antisocial behaviour that was agreed on by all informants was due to genetic effects; 18% was due to specific social experiences not shared by the twins, such as maltreatment of one twin but not the other.

While genetic factors clearly account for why one person at any one time is likely to be mentally ill, they cannot account for the increase in certain types of mental illness. As recent studies demonstrate (Maughan, Rowe, Messer, Goodman & Meltzer, 2004), specific types of disorders are increasing rapidly in prevalence in the UK. These include eating disorders, depression, conduct problems, and delinquency. A dramatic example of this complexity is the occurrence of weight problems in childhood. Behavioural genetics studies show that weight is almost totally determined by inheritance. The relative similarity of identical and fraternal twins clearly demonstrates that while fraternal twins may share the same environment and 50% of genetic material, the similarity in their weight is about half that of identical twins. Yet if weight is entirely determined by genes, why are children getting, on average, 10% heavier with each decade?

Behavioural phenotypes, i.e. how a child behaves, are the product of complex interactions between genes and environment. Genetic and environmental influences are not additive; genes create a vulnerability to environmental influence. A recent study following over one thousand children in the Dunedin community found a powerful interaction between maltreatment in childhood and the disposition towards violence as a function of one gene, which influences monoamine oxidase activity (Caspi et al., 2002). Monoamine oxidase is involved in the breakdown of neurotransmitters that mediate the stress response. We may expect those individuals with the version of this gene that is associated with low monoamine oxidase activity to be less efficient in breaking down the stress-related neurotransmitters, leading to a more prolonged stress reaction. It turns out that these individuals are four or five times more disposed to violent behaviour when subjected to severe maltreatment than those who experienced no maltreatment. In those with the monoamine oxidase gene that signals more efficient breakdown of stress-related neurotransmitters, maltreatment increases the disposition towards violence, but this is a far smaller effect, only just reaching statistical significance (Caspi et al., 2002). A similar association was reported between childhood maltreatment of children between the ages of three and 11 years and adult depression, as a function of the short versus long allele of the 5-hydroxytryptamine transport protein gene. In the presence of sever maltreatment the short allele of this gene is associated with depression in almost 70% of cases. Those with the same degree of maltreatment who had the long allele of the gene were depressed in less than a third of cases (Caspi et al., 2003).

These studies raise a key question concerning the prevention of childhood maltreatment. The question will be taken up again in a separate chapter (Fonagy, this volume), but in the present context what is relevant to note is that all prevention programmes aim to modify risk factors for child abuse; with more or less success they are able to interrupt antenatal risk factors, aspects of dysfunctional parental behaviour, or both. The genetic findings reviewed above point the way to how future studies might be able to focus on specific genetically-vulnerable groups, rather than attempting a universal approach. Some have argued that the social gradient is an artefact—healthy individuals rise to the top of social hierarchies while sick individuals (or those showing prodromal signs) are downwardly mobile (Anderson & Armstead, 1995). Since educational status predicts the same social gradient as income or occupation, and this clearly does not decline with health status in mid-life, the reverse causality hypothesis is improbable. Further, it has been suggested that the link is due to underlying genetic factors (Adler, Boyce, Chesney, Folkman & Syme, 1993). However, adjusting for factors such as height, body mass index and cognitive flexibility, and all influences with substantial genetic weighting, fails to remove the association between health and SES. Known health behaviours (such as smoking and lack of physical activity) have strong associations with SES (Winkleby, Fortmann & Barrett, 1990), but controlling for health behaviour tends to weaken but not remove the social gradient (e.g. Marmot et al., 1995). Furthermore, health behaviour fails to explain the significant relationship between SES and health in children in whom such risk behaviour may not yet be developed (Langford, Watson & Douglas, 1968). How much of the relationship between health and inequality can be accounted for by material factors? Is the gradient a function of physical exposure to toxins or other material hazards, or simply of poorer access to medical services? First, while traditional factors associated with deprivation included factors that were potentially directly related to health (e.g. clothing, housing, nutrition, risky work places), current definitions appear to relate only very loosely to health (inability to entertain children's friends, buy children new clothes, go on holiday, and pursue a hobby or leisure activity). Differential exposure to more toxic chemicals and unsafe physical environments can only account for a very small proportion of the gradient in wealthy countries (Hertzman, 1995).

Second, it was hoped that the improvement in access to medical services would tackle the inequalities in health problem; yet if anything, it exaggerated it (Black, 1980, 1982). There exist differences in how individuals with chronic illness use healthcare systems, which relates to social status, but differences here once again fail to account for the gradient, as 'medically-avoidable deaths' represent a small proportion of total mortality (Wilkinson, 2000).

Third, while lifestyle differences may explain parts of the social gradient, most of the gradient in mortality remains after the contribution of social class differences to the behaviour of interest has been taken into account. It should be noted that not all studies agree on this point. For example, the West of Scotland Collaborative Study reported an association between psychosocial stress and unhealthy behaviour, but there was an association between stress and better health because stress was also related to social advantage (Heslop, Smith, Carroll, Macleod & Hart, 2001; Metcalfe et al., 2001). Further, the excess of heart disease among UK ethnic minority groups is not accounted for by occupational class and is strongly linked to socio-economic effects (Nazroo, 2001). Hemmingway and colleagues (Bosma et al., 1997) reported that differences in cardiovascular disease between South Asian and white civil servants could be accounted for by psychosocial factors (such as social support at home and at work, job control). However, even in this context, psychological variables such as ethnic identity and racism (racial harassment and discrimination) proved to be important components of ethnic inequalities in health (Karlsen & Nazroo, 2002a, 2002b). The Whitehall II Studies revealed that concern about financial security, rather than actual shortage of funds, was most strongly linked to health (Ferrie, Shipley, Stansfeld, Smith & Marmot, 2003).

Fourth, current indicators of deprivation appear to strike at the core of *social* exclusion. Those who are deprived have fewer opportunities to participate in highly valued social groups or activities. Related to this, those deprived are less able than the rest of us to undertake activities as they might wish, i.e. to experience life under their own control. Thus, deprivation is very unlikely to be absolute. In attempting to understand the social gradient of illness we are searching for indicators of relative deprivation. We are attempting to identify social accounts with the power to mediate a relationship between relative social position and health. There are a number of leading candidates: (1) social support/social integration; (2) control/mastery, particularly over the psychosocial work environment; (3) hostility; (4) parenting; and (5) biological pathways. We suggest that all of these factors may be simultaneously active, but all may be determined by differences in attachment quality in early childhood.

## SOCIAL ENVIRONMENTS AND HEALTH

The social capital of a society is a term that includes measures of trust, helpfulness, and group membership (Putnam, 1993). Numerous studies have demonstrated that the degree of income inequality in developed countries is closely related to mortality rates (Kaplan et al., 1996; Wilkinson, 1996). Kawachi and colleagues (Kawachi, Kennedy & Protrow-Stith, 1996) have provided some insight into how income inequality might affect trust in a society and, through this, the health of a nation. Looking at individual states in the US, it was demonstrated that states where income inequality was greatest had the lowest levels of trust (measured by questionnaire responses; for example, the extent to which a person is likely to trust a stranger). These states also had the highest mortality rates for a range of causes of death, including coronary heart disease, malignant neoplasms, cerebrovascular disease, unintentional accidents, and suicide.

It is widely accepted that the social support available to individuals in society influences their health status. Those who have the least support are vulnerable to a variety of disorders. More generally, there is variability in the degree to which an individual is embedded in a web of social relationships that provide intimacy, love and meaning, as well as a sense of belonging within a larger community. This (1) influences health outcomes over the life course; (2) influences disease prevalence, progression, mortality, and physical and cognitive functioning; (3) is biologically plausible; and (4) is amenable to intervention (Berkman, 2000). The kinds of ties considered under this heading include relationship to partner, family of origin, friends and colleagues at work, membership of voluntary organizations, and affiliation to religious organizations. Differential social support can account for disparities between the health risks associated with different neighbourhoods. In a survey of nearly 6000 adults, low neighbourhood social capital, having no personal social support (especially for men), and having no involvement in community activities, were associated with an increased likelihood of reporting poor health (Rainford, Mason, Hickman & Morgan, 2000). The theme here is of not feeling attached either to the community or to individuals.

Over the last 20 years, 13 large, prospective, cohort studies across a number of countries have shown that people who were isolated or disconnected from others were at risk of dying prematurely (Berkman & Syme, 1979; Farmer et al., 1996; House, Robbins & Metzner, 1982; Penninx et al., 1997; Schoenbach et al., 1986; Seeman et al., 1993; Sugisawa, Liang & Liu, 1994; Weblin, Tibblin, Svardsudd & al, 1985). For example, Blazer found that self-perceived impaired social support (including feelings of loneliness) (1) increased the risk of dying by 3.4; (2) impaired social roles and attachments by 2.0; and (3) lowered the frequency of social interactions by 1.9 (Blazer, 1982). The same associations apply to post-myocardial infarction and post-stroke survival (e.g. Case et al., 1992; Craig, Lynch & Quartner, 2000; Jackson, 1988), pregnancy outcome (Hoffman & Hatch, 1996), and most other life-threatening disorders. Cardiac reactivity to public speaking stress is moderated by the *belief* that the subject has access to social support, even if this is not the case (Uchino & Garvey, 1997). In African–Americans, laboratory stress tests demonstrated that cardiovascular reactivity was predicted by neighbourhood characteristics (Jackson, Treiber, Turner, Davis & Strong, 1999). Even the incidence of the common cold is related to social networks (Sege et al., 1997). The experience of social exclusion as a consequence of racial harassment and discrimination is also linked to health outcome. In a population survey, those who believed some or most British employers to be discriminating against them had 60% greater odds of reporting poor health than those who believed that few or no employers behaved in such a way (Karlsen & Nazroo, 2000). However, ethnic identity is not a simple construct. The Fourth National Survey of Ethnic Minorities, for example, developed a five-factor description (Karlsen & Nazroo, 2002c). These authors concluded that ethnicity as identity, in terms of self-description, self-presentation and behaviour, membership of ethnic minority organizations, and perceptions and experiences of racism, is important to the experiences of ethnic minority people. However, ethnicity as identity does not influence health per se. The socio-economic and other disadvantage suffered by those from ethnic minority groups may explain apparent ethnic inequalities in health (Karlsen & Nazroo, 2004; Nazroo, 1998).

But the most compelling evidence for the importance of social support comes from the natural experiment that took place in Eastern Europe in the closing decades of the last century. There was a sharp rise in mortality in these populations following the break-up of the communist block (Hertzman, 1992, unpubl. manuscript); in 1970 the differences between Nordic and European Union (EU) countries on the one hand, and the communist countries of Central and Eastern Europe on the other, were relatively small. By 1994 the gap in life expectancy at age 15 between Russia and the EU increased from four to 10 years. The difference is accounted for by cardiovascular disease and suicide. These causes of death account for the gradients between countries and within countries. Many have attributed increased mortality in Eastern Europe to stresses affecting behaviour, leading in turn to more alcohol consumption, increased smoking, poorer diets, and to other negative lifestyle behaviour. But the mortality changes were far too rapid to be explained by lifestyle changes alone. It was found that the groups most affected by these changes were single men (Watson, 1994). One possible explanation is that marriage provided the main source of support for men when other forms of social participation suddenly became weak. Thus, single men appeared to be the most vulnerable group, left with the least social support to help them cope with changes. But current social conditions appear to only partially account for health risk; accumulated social risk over the lifespan needs to be taken into consideration to account for differences in health status (Nicholson, Bobak, Murphy, Rose & Marmot, 2005).

There is other evidence consistent with this proposition. Recent studies found that Latin American immigrants to the US who broke their ties with their culture of origin more comprehensively (as marked by higher levels of language competence and educational attainment), were more at risk of strokes than controls that were less well assimilated (Ontiveros, Miller, Markides & Espino, 1999). Surveys and audits of the health (both physical and emotional) of refugees and asylum seekers indicate that there is a fairly consistent worsening of self-reported health problems in the first several months after arrival in the UK (Burnett & Peel, 2001). Some might argue that with access to healthcare from the NHS (free at the point of delivery), and having in many cases endured extreme hardship and even torture prior to arrival, there might be expected to be a reported improvement in health status. However, in line with Eastern European evidence, a marked lack of social support may be experienced by this group, in the context of them experiencing having no control over events (see below).

Evidence from the Whitehall Study indicates that the lower the individual's hierarchical position, the less he or she is likely to participate in social networks outside the family, and the more negative the degree of social support (Stansfeld & Marmot, 1992).

Why a person within a stable society should be isolated is not well understood by epidemiologists. This may be for personal or for social reasons. More pertinent is the far greater prediction obtained from a subjective sense of relationship availability, rather than measures of the actual social matrix. This implies that it is the internal working model of attachment relationships that predicts mortality rather than the physical presence of supportive individuals. There may be people around but they are not perceived as being available, or expected to be supportive. The perception of social support has been found to relate to cardiovascular reactivity in patients undergoing cardiac rehabilitation after myocardial infarction (Craig et al., 2000).

The ability to maintain intimate, enduring, and trusting relationships in midlife is probably acquired in early life. In attachment theory this is referred to as the 'prototype hypothesis'. For example, a substantial body of data suggests that at preschool and at age 10, more appropriate relationships evolve between children who were securely attached in infancy and their teachers and counsellors (e.g. Weinfield, Sroufe, Egeland & Carlson, 1999). Bowlby (1973) suggested that those with a history of secure attachment will have positive expectations regarding relationships with others. In adolescence those with a history of secure attachment are more likely to be rated as effective in a mixed gender peer group and to participate smoothly in a wider range of social encounters, for example to be looked to by others at critical junctures in small group discussions (Englund, Levy, Hyson & Sroufe, 2000). A further recent longitudinal study (Grossman, Grossman, Winter & Zimmerman, 2002) showed that maternal sensitivity to the infant in the first year appeared to significantly predict the quality of a partnership at age 22. Attachment in the first years of life, together with measures of peer relationship and supportive parenting, turn out to be extraordinarily good predictors of competence in romantic relationships, with 25–35% of the variance being predicted even over substantial periods of time (Roisman, Collins, Sroufe & Egeland, 2005; Sroufe et al., 2005a). Parental sensitivity may influence health outcomes by setting in motion the opportunity to maintain relationships later in life. This has been shown not just in the occurrence of illness but in adaptation to ongoing chronic disease. Patients with type 1 and type 2 diabetes whose attachment style was insecure (dismissing) were found to have significantly higher levels of glycosylated haemoglobin ($HbA_{1c}$), indicating poorer self-management of the disease (Ciechanowski, Katon, Russo & Walker, 2001). Their attachment style caused them to disengage from their health care providers, repeating the pattern of relationship that they are assumed—by attachment theory—to have developed as a result of an insensitive primary caregiver. This formulation was reinforced by the observation that the differences in $HbA_{1c}$ among the patients with dismissing attachment styles were most marked in cases where the patient rated communication with their provider as poor.

Thus social isolation may increase stress, but the reason that the individual finds himself or herself isolated is to be found in the early relationship with the caregiver. It is generally agreed that it is the combination of social stress and early attachment that provides the best prediction of recovery (Sroufe, Carlson, Levy & Egeland, 1999; Sroufe, Egeland & Kreutzer, 1990), because accounting for continuity of functioning as well as accounting for change entails considering both early history and ongoing support and challenges (Sroufe, 2005). There is no question that secure attachment is critical for engaging the world of peers; however, mastering the inevitable frustrations of symmetrical relationships and coping with the expectable conflicts of social interaction are well predicted by earlier peer competence, which in turn is strongly associated with a history of mother–infant attachment security. Attachment in infancy is probably a specific predictor of interpersonal trust and the emotional tone of social relationships (Sroufe, Egeland, Carlson & Collins, 2005b).

## CONTROL/MASTERY IN THE PSYCHOSOCIAL WORK ENVIRONMENT

The two dominant models in the field of psychosocial work environment are the demand/control model and that of effort/reward imbalance. In a number of reports, including the Whitehall Study, the demand dimension did not predict heart disease, but low control in the work-place was an important predictor and accounted for 50% of the gradient (Bosma et al., 1997; Hemingway & Marmot, 1999). A combination of height, coronary risk factors, and low control in the workplace, appear to provide a complete explanation for the social gradient in occurrence of coronary heart disease. Of note is the recent increase in lack of certainty about people's future employment. The studies of Whitehall civil servants indicated that self-reported morbidity and blood pressure level are significantly higher among those workers who had lost their job security, compared with those remaining in secure employment (Ferrie, 2001; Ferrie et al., 2001; Ferrie, Shipley, Stansfeld & Marmot, 2002b). Job insecurity relates to rapid rates of promotion and social class gradients (Marmot et al., 2001). Decreasing job satisfaction and control are reported as areas of concern by the interviewees, but financial insecurity also contributes highly to the self-reported health inequalities. Whereas the 'flexible labour market' may have benefits in direct economic returns, there may be ongoing costs to society in terms of health deterioration (Marmot et al., 2001).

The question raised by these findings (replicated under many conditions) is what makes an individual feel in control of their work or, for that matter, any other part of their life? Low control is mostly viewed as a characteristic of individuals. For example, in the Whitehall Studies reported above, it was those individuals who had reported job insecurity consistently over a two to three year period who had the highest level of self-reported morbidity (Ferrie, Shipley, Stansfeld & Marmot, 2002b). There is extensive data on the close relationship between sense of control and mastery and poor self-reported health (Bobak, Pikhart, Rose, Hertzman & Marmot, 2000). Recent evidence suggests a specific link between the ratio of effort to reward and drinking behaviour in men, which will directly influence health risks

(Bobak et al., 2005). There is even a reported relationship between the average scores for sense of control and mastery and coronary heart disease rates for a whole population: the higher the mean level of control the lower the rates (Ferrie, Shipley, Newman, Stansfeld & Marmot, 2005). Further, past job insecurity also predicts poor health, indicating that these effects cannot be accounted for simply in terms of the acute threat (stress) of unemployment (Ferrie, Shipley, Marmot, Stansfield & Smith, 1995; Ferrie, Shipley, Stansfeld & Marmot, 2002b). In fact a person's sense of their job's predictability, as indicated by an individual's view of their work situation as being 'just' versus 'arbitrary and unjust', has been shown to be an independent predictor of coronary health (Kivimaki et al., 2005).

Bowlby (1973) strongly predicted that secure attachment relationships would constitute a bedrock for self-reliance. Infants who could use their caregivers as a secure base for exploration would be more independent and masterful in later development. In the Minnesota Study, children with anxious attachment histories were observed to be more reliant on their teachers in a classroom setting, both at preschool age and at age 10, with very little overlap between those with secure and anxious histories (Sroufe, Fox & Pancake, 1983; Sroufe et al., 2005a). A greater sense of agency and control has been observed in children aged 17 with secure attachment histories (Elicker, Englund & Sroufe, 1992; Weinfield et al., 1999). Those with secure attachment histories are rated as being more flexible, able to bounce back after stress, and less likely to be thought of as becoming anxious when the environment is unpredictable or inhibited and constricted (Sroufe et al., 2005a).

Why should a child who is securely attached find the world more controllable than his anxiously-attached friend? The literature on control is abundantly clear that, once again, it is not the objective extent of control but rather the subjective experience of feeling in control that predicts health–sickness outcomes. The likelihood that individuals will feel themselves to be in control in a social context may be assumed to be linked to their attachment history. The best-known predictor of attachment security is maternal sensitivity (De Wolff & van IJzendoorn, 1997). A sensitive caregiver creates an illusion that the infant's intentions are followed by effective action. In other words, she generates a cognitive bias for mastery, which will predispose these individuals to seek situations where they are in control of their destiny, with the expectation that they will re-experience an earlier sense of being in charge.

Is this simply a way of equipping the child with rose-tinted spectacles, at least as far as control or mastery go? No—we believe that there is evidence for this bias in terms of the greater social popularity of these children, and therefore their increased opportunity for social control, and also in terms of their capacity for mastery over their own internal state; for example, there is good evidence that secure attachment at 14 months is a good predictor of the capacity to regulate emotion nearly two years later (Kochanska, 2001). Children who are insecure in infancy become more fearful in a frightening situation, more angry in a frustrating situation, and distressed in a situation intended to generate joy. The mother's sensitivity has been internalized and used in the service of self-regulation.

Empirical observations from the literature on attachment confirm that infants whose attachment is disorganized are likely to become overly controlling socially in middle childhood—a response that we can understand as an over-reaction to a subjective sense of internal lack of control (Solomon & George, 1999). Insecure parent–infant relationships are assumed to be mediated by an inadequate capacity for self-regulation, both of emotion and probably also of attention. We assume that the experience of not feeling in control internally generalizes to a feeling that the outside world is similarly out of control. It is notable that over the 11-year span of the Whitehall civil servant study, notwithstanding changes in the hierarchical position of individuals over the course of the study, grades at the beginning continued to predict health status throughout the intervening decade (Ferrie, Shipley, Smith, Stansfeld & Marmot, 2002a).

In brief, the sense of control in the workplace of physically healthy individuals does not come from their job characteristics—it comes from a cognitive bias that makes them selectively seek situations where they will experience a sense of mastery, or re-interpret social information to support their belief that they are in control.

## HOSTILITY

There are findings that strongly link the levels of hostility in cities (based on a Gallup survey) and the cities' mortality rates for coronary heart disease (Williams et al., 1980). Do cities with less trust and greater hostility have more people who are prone to heart attacks? We know that hostile personalities appear to have higher rates of coronary heart disease than those who are not hostile (Jorgensen et al., 2001; Knox, Adelman, Ellison & Arnett, 2000; Sloan et al., 2001). This is based on psychophysiological studies as well investigation of the so-called 'coronary-prone (or type A) personality' (Clark, Seidler & Miller, 2001; Myrtek, 2001). But such associations appear to exist with more than just coronary heart disease; violent crime across states, cities, or even districts within a city, correlates closely to age-adjusted death rates from natural causes. For example, a study in Chicago revealed a correlation of 0.9 (50% of shared variance) between homicide and all other causes of death, excluding homicide (Wilkinson, Kawachi & Kennedy, 1998). Importantly, property crime does not correlate with mortality.

In fact, violence (or at least early manifestations of highly aggressive behaviour) has been independently linked with a disorganization of the attachment system (Lyons-Ruth, 1996; Lyons-Ruth & Jacobovitz, 1999). The trigger for violence is often disrespect (Gilligan, 1997). Self-esteem—a sense of self-worth—is generally accepted to be strongly associated with early attachment security (Verschueren & Marcoen, 1999). In the Minnesota Study, preschoolers with secure attachment histories were consistently rated by teachers as higher in self-esteem, emotional health, agency, compliance, and positive affect, and this persisted to assessment at age 17.5 (Elicker et al., 1992; Weinfield et al., 1999). Those with a history of secure attachment are less likely to respond with aggression to being 'dissed' (disrespected).

However, if hostility is simply a stable trait of illness-prone individuals, then there is no reason for it to be related to specific environments. If hostility were a fixed attribute we would expect coronary and other risks to move with individuals between towns. Even allowing for selective migration, this appears not to be the case. Risk characterizes the city—migrants normally take on the epidemiological characteristics of their chosen location (e.g. Villarejo, 2003). Perhaps these links emerge because of an underlying association between particular personal histories and a proneness to respond with hostility to certain environments where the individual feels unvalued. In a study of 219 patients recruited from a coronary care unit in Scotland, patients recovering from myocardial infarction were interviewed at five and 15 weeks. Recovery from a first acute myocardial infarction was unrelated to a range of psychological factors such as depression and anxiety, but was strongly associated with self-esteem. Self-esteem in turn predicted the perception of relative deprivation; those who showed lower self-esteem perceived themselves to be less well off than others, but both self-esteem and perceived relative wealth also independently predicted recovery (Graham, MacLeod, Johnston, Dibben & Briscoe, 2000; MacLeod, Graham & Johnston, 2001). Furthermore, social support may have some role in modulating the relationship of hostility to behaviours that are adverse to health in some people (Allen, Markowitz, Jacobs & Knox, 2001), and its relative absence may put patients at risk of disease progression (Angerer et al., 2000).

Both violence and physical illness are associated with a sense of lack of worth. Certain communities generate among their members exactly that feeling—of being unvalued. Communities can probably trigger attachment-related experiences, such as a sense of being ignored, neglected, or devalued—in other words feelings of insecurity. Moving to a different place removes the reminder. Violence is community specific because the characteristics of the community interact with the personal histories of the individuals in those communities. Those whose attachment system is disorganized are most likely to become violent, and these disorganized attachment systems are more likely to be activated by communities with particularly low levels of social cohesion.


## PARENTING

Barker's group in the UK have provided strong evidence for the programming hypothesis for coronary heart disease (Barker, 1990). The *in utero* environment programmes the organ systems of the developing foetus, which affects the individual's likelihood of developing chronic disease later in life. This poses the question of whether the child's environment after birth also influences disease risk.

Studies with rhesus monkeys have identified a subgroup of highly reactive individuals whose heightened and prolonged activation of the hypothalamic–pituitary–adrenal (HPA) axis is associated with early death, as well as a lower position in the dominance hierarchy (Boyce, O'Neill-Wagner, Price, Haines & Suomi, 1998). While this vulnerability is clearly genetic, the cross-fostering of highly reactive infant monkeys to particularly nurturant mothers for the first six months of life reduces the risk of early mortality and, paradoxically, propels these individuals to the top of the social hierarchy (presumably explaining why the associated gene is retained in the rhesus monkey gene pool) (Suomi, 1991). Some of these infants had babies of their own and were observed to display maternal behaviour similar to their foster mothers rather than to their biological ones (Shannon et al., 2005; Suomi, 1999, 2005; Suomi & Levine, 1998). The implication from these studies might be that a biological vulnerability present in say 20–25% of the human gene pool is counteracted by better (more nurturant) childcare in families at less socio-economic risk.

Several studies of college cohorts from Johns Hopkins and Harvard suggest that parental relationships in early childhood characterized by warmth and closeness are related to disease 35 to 50 years later (Funkenstein, King & Drolette, 1957; Russek & Schwartz, 1997; Thomas & Duszynski, 1974). British birth cohort studies, while not measuring the strength of early relationships, have found associations with distal indicators of insecure attachment such as acrimonious parental separation (Wadsworth, 1991). The claim that it is all decided before birth, or even during the first years appears unfounded as far as the social gradient of disease is concerned. Studies of the 1958 birth-cohort demonstrate that an accumulation of advantage and disadvantage across the life-course generates the social gradient (Power, Matthews & Manor, 1998).

The importance of early emotional adjustment is borne out by the finding that the best single predictor of health in early adulthood in the 1958 British birth cohort study was teachers' assessment of children's behaviour at primary school (Power, Manor & Fox, 1991). It is also important to note that upward social mobility is more closely related to height at age seven than to adult height (Montgomery, Bartley, Cook & Wadsworth, 1996). The implication is that the success of tall people is nothing to do with their physical presence as adults, but is related to something in early childhood that affects their growth and later social mobility. These findings also place the parents in the frame once again. It is known that slow growth in childhood is strongly associated with family conflict (quite likely explicable in terms of the influence of stress on growth hormones) (Montgomery, Bartley & Wilkinson, 1997). The argument here is that individuals experiencing supportive early environments are more likely to be mobile because of their relatively well-functioning internal working models of relationships.

There is incontrovertible accumulated evidence for the association between quality of parenting and SES. A host of studies have found income to be positively related to adult psychological well-being, which in turn is strongly linked to positive parenting and positive parent–child relationships (McLoyd, 1990, 1998). Studies have shown that the risk of poverty for child development is principally brought about through the way in which economic hardship frustrates good parenting and increases the likelihood of family adversity (Rutter, Giller & Hagell, 1998). Disturbances in parenting have been linked to psychopathology in children and adolescents including such problem areas as anxiety, conduct problems, depression, and achievement at school (Conger et al., 2002; Elder & Caspi, 1988; McLoyd, 1989; Mistry, Vandewater, Huston & McLoyd 2002; Yeung, Linver & Brooks-Gunn, 2002). More recently, experimental evidence has been gathered to support this theory. The New Hope Project (Huston et al., 2001), an anti-poverty programme with a randomized controlled design, offered wage supplements, childcare facilities, and subsidized health insurance, as well as case management services to assist with job searches, to a randomly selected cohort of 50% of women with small children from two high poverty districts in Milwaukee. The study found strong positive effects on the academic achievement of boys, a decrease in their problem behaviour, and an increase in positive social behaviour relative to the control group. Although the effect was not found for girls, this experimental study clearly demonstrates that improving material resources translates into a reduced experience of stress for parents, and this yields improved functioning in the child.

There is accumulating evidence that maternal responsiveness can moderate the effects of social disadvantage. A study of 93 black mothers (Jackson, 2000) found that parenting moderated the impact of financial strain and lack of support, and even the impact of maternal depression to a certain extent. In another larger study (Laucht, Esser & Schmidt, 1994), a cohort of infants born with either biological or psychosocial risk (low birth weight or social disadvantage) was followed up to eight years of age. Early responsive caregiving was studied as a possible moderator. Behavioural problems (which we know from other cohort studies to be important markers of later health status) served as the dependent variable. The increased risk of behavioural problems in the socially-disadvantaged group was almost totally ameliorated at all ages by sensitive parenting. Notably, parenting could also ameliorate the effect of biological risk, but the two types of risk were independent of each other.

Parenting is likely to have several dimensions all of which, independently and and in combination, contribute to risk and social disadvantage effects; two have been repeatedly highlighted in the literature, namely warmth and social control (Baumrind, 1991). There is ample research evidence that indicators of warmth, such as perceived closeness to parents, can have salutary effects on psychological, social, and academic functioning (Cowen et al., 1997; Luthar & Becker, 2002; Wyman et al., 1999). The harshness of parental discipline is also an independent predictor of behavioural outcomes through indicators such as parental criticisms (Hodes, Garralda, Rose & Schwartz, 1999; Le Grange, Eisler, Dare & Hodes, 1992; Wamboldt & Wamboldt, 2000). In addition there are a range of well-known indicators of parental interactions with the child with powerful social gradients that have been shown to protect children from adverse health outcomes (Fiese et al., 2002; Luthar, 2003). These include factors such as: (1) the absence of after-school supervision by adults (Cauce, Stewart, Rodriguez, Cochran & Ginzler, 2003); (2) not having dinner with parents (Luthar & Becker, 2002); and (3) high expectations related to a child's performance (Hauser-Cram, Sirin & Stipek, 2003; Hebert, 2002). While traditionally these variables follow a social gradient of advantage, more recent studies suggest that by no means all parents with economic advantage behave optimally in relation to their children, particularly in terms of warmth, expectations, and availability (Luthar & Latendresse, 2005).

## BIOLOGICAL PATHWAYS

It could be argued that we do not need to know about the pathophysiological effects of smoking to reach conclusions about its health effects. However, the criteria for assessing causation developed by Bradford-Hill and the US Surgeon General had much to do with the controversy surrounding smoking and health. One of these criteria is biological plausibility. The argument was that without a plausible biological mechanism the causal nature of any epidemiological association must remain questionable.

It could be that the link between attachment and health outcome is via health behaviour. For example, the socially-isolated individuals in Alameda County were more likely to engage in high-risk health behaviour (e.g. smoking) (Berkman & Syme, 1979). But, as we have seen, health behaviour only partially accounts for the gradient seen.

The biological pathways of the stress response have been identified as the 'missing link' in the explanation of the social gradient of health (Lupien, King, Meaney & McEwan, 2001). The stress response prepares the body for muscular exertion; but as well as mobilizing energy for the muscles, the resources are reduced for a wide range of other bodily functions, which in terms of response to an 'emergency' situation, are non-essential. These include tissue maintenance and repair, digestion, immunity, growth, and reproductive functions (Sapolsky, 1994, 1996). Evidence has been accumulating that prior stressful life events and perceived stress can alter immune function (e.g. Kiecolt-Glaser & Glaser, 1995; McKinnon et al., 1989; Naliboff et al., 1991). For example, Cohen and colleagues (Cohen, Tyrrell & Smith, 1991) showed that the rates of both respiratory infection and clinical colds increased in a dose-response manner with increases in the degree of previously-reported psychological stress. Chronic elevation of the stress hormones contributes to the onset of immunosuppression and diseases such as hypertension, hypercholesterolaemia, and arteriosclerosis (Munck, Guyere & Holbrock, 1984). The relationship between SES and health has been suggested as resulting in part from differential exposure to stress. The social class gradient in health within both Lithuania and Sweden, as well as the differences in the gradient between the two countries, were related to higher basal cortisol levels and to an attenuated cortisol response to stress (Kristenson, 1998).

Secure attachment is believed to provide the foundation for emotion regulation. Attachment has been defined as the 'dyadic regulation of emotion' (Sroufe, 1996, p. 172), which is generally accepted to be the prototype for later self-regulation (Sander, 1970). Ample observational data confirm that secure infant attachment predicts both actual capacity and confidence in one's capacity not to fall to pieces under stress (Sroufe et al., 2005a). We believe that attachment may directly impact on the biological mechanisms hypothesized to link stressful social experiences to health outcomes. Spending one's early years in an unstimulating and poorly-supported environment, both emotionally and physically, will affect the structure and neurochemistry of the central nervous system in adverse ways (Rutter & O'Connor, 2004). For example, Parker and colleagues carried out a study of 7–32 months old Romanian children and reported that the early negative, midlatency negative and positive slow-wave components of event-related potentials, in response to either the mother's or a stranger's face, were greater in amplitude in the non-institutionalized than in the institutionalized children (Parker & Nelson, 2005a). In an event-related (brain) potential study of emotion discrimination the institutionally-raised Romanian group showed a similar decrease in responses (Parker & Nelson, 2005b). The findings provide support for a general cortical hypoactivation resulting from early institutional rearing (Marshall & Fox, 2004). The suggestion that early social deprivation (institutionalization) leads to some kind of general 'underpowering' of a child's brain is also supported by adoption studies (Chugani et al., 2001). Positron emission tomography (PET) scan data collected after an average of 5.5 years in adoptive homes indicates that the metabolic activity in several brain regions in these children is still reduced. Deprivation of early social interaction may deprive the amygdalar circuitry of vital experiences through which social and emotional stimuli are associated with internal states of pleasure and displeasure. Early social deprivation may thus contribute to a long-lasting development of cortical hypoactivation, as well as dysfunction in emotion processing and brain function (Cicchetti & Curtis, 2005).

There is accumulating evidence that when frightened by separation infants activate a specific system of neural circuitry (Caldji, Diorio, Anisman & Meaney, 2004; Kalynchuk & Meaney, 2003), which might lead them into proximity-seeking with caregivers to deal with stress (LeBar & LeDoux, 2003). Such a fear system probably comes to be co-ordinated with a distinct affiliation system that also motivates social contact—including shared affect—via a dopaminergic reward system (Insel, 2003). Oxytocin, which is a neuropeptide, is clearly implicated in the activation of attachment behaviour, along with dopamine, serotonin, vasopressin, and progesterone (Insel & Fernald, 2004). As social attachment requires that stimuli become linked to major information streams, early experience, including adversity, might affect attachment-related behaviour through corticolimibic pathways (Pollak, 2005). However there are multiple ways in which breakdowns in corticolimbic circuitry could affect an individual's ability to use information to guide behaviour, and it is unlikely that examination of any one brain region will reveal how various aspects of information become integrated into a response system that coordinates fear and attachment with the processing of major information streams.

There is accumulating evidence that enduring psychophysiological effects on brain organization and stress physiology may result not only from overt physical or sexual abuse, but also from self-reported emotional abuse, such as repeated hostile or emotionally unprotective responses from caregivers (Teicher et al., 2003a; Yehuda, Hallig & Grossman, 2001) Children from low socio-economic backgrounds have been shown to have higher salivary cortisol levels during the elementary school years (ages 6–10) (Lupien et al., 2001). This might lead to cognitive (e.g. memory, Heffelfinger & Newcomer, 2001 or attention) and socio-emotional (e.g. depression, Kaufman & Charney, 2001) deficits that may or may not be reversible. The children affected in this way will display problems early on in school, which will lead to more acute and chronic stress with both physiological and life-path consequences. Because of the intimate relationship between the central nervous system and the immune, hormone, and clotting systems, systematic differences in the experience of life will increase or decrease levels of resistance to disease. This will change the long-term function of vital organs in the body and, in conjunction with the differential stresses of daily living, will generate differences in morbidity and mortality. This hypothesis has come to be known as 'biological embedding' (Hertzman & Wiens, 1996). Similar arguments may be applied to the findings related to insulin-resistance syndrome. A three-year follow-up of over 400 randomly-selected healthy children indicated that this syndrome (possibly indicating later risk of coronary heart disease) is predicted by maternal perception of difficult child temperament and hostile child-rearing attitudes (Ravaja, Katainen & Keltikangas-Jarvinen, 2001).

Animal models document the effects of early (even prenatal) stress on a range of neurobiological systems including the HPA axis, the dopaminergic, noradrenergic and serotonergic systems (Bremner & Vermetten, 2001). A cascade of alterations have been identified (Teicher, Polcari, Andersen, Anderson & Navalta, 2003b): (1) exposure to stress early in life activates stress response systems, thus altering their molecular organization to modify their sensitivity and response bias; (2) exposure of the developing brain to stress hormones has a number of effects including alterations of myelination, neural morphology, neurogenesis, and synaptogenesis; (3) different regions of the brain differ in both their sensitivity and the timing of this sensitivity, which depends in part on genetics, gender, timing, rate of development, and density of glucocorticoid receptors; (4) there are enduring functional consequences, including attenuated left hemisphere development, decreased right–left hemisphere integration, increased electrical irritability in the limbic circuits and diminished functional activity of the cerebellar vermis; and (5) there are associated neuropsychiatric consequences and vulnerabilities leading to enhanced risk of the emergence of habitual modes of adaptation that increase the likelihood of a chronic experience of stress.

Early stress can have lasting effects, such as an increased glucocorticoid response to subsequent stressors (Fride, Dan, Feldon, Halevy & Weinstock, 1986; Stanton, Gutierrez & Levine, 1988). Stressed animals have been shown to be unable to terminate the glucocorticoid response to stress (Sapolsky, 1994; Sapolsky, Krey & McEwen, 1984), which could be related to decreased glucocorticoid receptor binding in the hippocampus (Makino et al., 1995). Additionally, adverse early experiences in non-human primates resulted in raised levels of corticotrophin-releasing factor (CRF) in the cerebrospinal fluid as well as long-term effects on behaviour (Coplan et al., 1996). Thus, prolonged early stress may decrease the development of glucocorticoid receptors in the hippocampus and diminish negative feedback regulation of cortisol, thus augmenting cortisol levels in the CRF. This results in enhanced production of adrenocorticotrophic hormone and corticosterone. Animal models also demonstrate that certain interventions may ameliorate the negative effects of early stress, indicating a degree of plasticity in the brain. Thus postnatal handling of rat pups has been shown to increase type II glucocorticoid receptor binding that persisted throughout life, along with increased feedback sensitivity to glucocorticoids (Meaney, Aitken, Bhatnager, van Berkel & Sapolsky, 1988; Meaney, Aitken, Sharma & Sarrieau, 1989; Plotsky et al., 2005). This has been hypothesized to be due to a type of 'stress inoculation' from the mothers repeated licking of the handled pups (Liu et al., 1997b). Early stress has been found to be associated with lifelong increases in the sensitivity of the noradrenergic system (Francis, Caldji, Champagne, Plotsky & Meaney, 1999; Vicentic et al., 2006).

There is emerging evidence to suggest that a molecular mechanism is involved in the mediation of the long-lasting modulation of hormonal stress responses, in terms of the down-regulation of hypothalamic corticotrophin-releasing hormone mRNA levels in rats handled daily (Avishai-Eliner, Eghbal-Ahmadi, Tabachnik, Brunson & Baram, 2001; Champagne, Weaver, Diorio, Sharma & Meaney, 2003; Kalynchuk, Pinel & Meaney, 2006). As far as the serotonin system is concerned, a variety of stressors have been shown to result in increased turnover of serotonin in the medial pre-frontal cortex (Inoue, Tsuchiya & Koyama, 1994; Pei, Zetterstrom & Fillenz, 1990; Zhang, Chretien, Meaney & Gratton, 2005) and in other areas including the locus coeruleus (Caldji et al., 1998; Kaehler, Singewald, Sinner, Thurner & Phillipu, 2000). Chronic electric shock stimulation produces learned helplessness associated with reduced release of serotonin (Petty, Kramer & Wilson, 1992). Brain ageing in animal models is increased by elevated stress reactivity and reduced by lowered stress reactivity (Dellu, Mayo, Vallee, Moal & Simon, 1994; Liu et al., 1997a). Other studies indicate that an increased capacity to metabolize serotonin during exposure to inescapable stress prevents learned helplessness (Ronan, Steciuk, Kramer, Kram & Petty, 2000). Early stress has also been shown to alter the molecular composition of the gamma-aminobutyric acid (GABA)–benzodiazepine supra-molecular complex, which results in the attenuated development of central benzodiazepine and high affinity GABA-A receptors in two structures involved in the co-ordination of the stress response centrally—the amygdala and the locus coeruleus (Caldji, Diorio & Meaney, 2000a; Caldji, Frances, Sharma, Plotsky & Meaney, 2000b; Caldji et al., 1998; Meaney & Szyf, 2005). Thus, animal models offer a rich set of potential pathways that could mediate between variability in early psychosocial experience and inequality in adult health status (Cameron et al., 2005). In conclusion, there are ample routes by which early stress may be seen to prime the mammalian brain to be more fearful, and to have enhanced noradrenergic, corticosteroid, and vasopressin responses to stress.

The evidence from studies of clinical populations derives from relatively extreme environments. These results have, on the whole, been consistent with findings from the animal investigations. The results from studies of adults with a history of childhood trauma have been consistent with long-term changes in the HPA axis (Bremner et al., 1997; Stein, 1997). Childhood sexual abuse remains frighteningly common in society, with population surveys of adults indicating that 6–62% females and 3–31% males report sexual abuse as children in the US (Finkelhor, 1986). The rates reported by those diagnosed as adults as suffering from borderline personality disorder are as high as 80%, indicating a possible causal role (Zanarini et al., 2002). Teicher, Andersen, Polcari, Anderson and Navalta (2002) suggest a possible explanation for these effects. Animal and human studies indicate that left-sided brain changes (recorded via electroencephalogram (EEG) and magnetic resonance imaging (MRI)) are associated with early abuse (e.g. Cicchetti & Curtis, 2005; Pollak, Cicchetti, Klorman & Brumaghim, 1997; Pollak, Klorman, Thatcher & Cicchetti, 2001). For example, a reduction in the size of both the hippocampus and the amygdala has been found; these are areas associated with memory and emotion. Additionally there is reduction in the size of the corpus callosum with a lessened integration of the functioning of the two halves of the brain. The lessened development of the left half of the brain could lead to a greater likelihood of memory being associated with the right (emotional) side. It is hypothesized that the lack of integration of the two halves of the brain could explain the tendency of those with bipolar disorder to swing from one view of people to another.

Teicher (2000) suggests that it is unlikely that changes in brain development brought on by, or related to, exposure to early stress are simply forms of 'damage' occurring in a brain that is unable to cope with the cascade of the stress response. It is far more likely that as the brain develops it adapts to the exposure of early stress by following this cascade as an aspect of an alternative developmental path. This suggests that the differences that have been reported between stressed and non-stressed individuals are actually evolutionarily selected changes in structure and function that make the individual better adapted given exposure to hardship at key periods of early development. Such modifications may be designed to adapt the individual to cope in superior ways to privation and deprivation in later periods of their lives. This model is highly consistent with the evolutionary model of attachment recently proposed by Jay Belsky and others (Belsky, 1999; Bjorklund & Pellegrini, 2000; Fonagy, 2003), which suggests that attachment serves the function of optimizing the individual to the kind of relationship environments they are likely to encounter in later childhood and adulthood.

Attachment security may have important biological associations and there is a complex relationship between the reactivity of the HPA axis and attachment. The human HPA system is highly responsive from an early postnatal period: increases in salivary cortisol in newborns have been observed in the course of a brief maternal separation (Larson, Gunnar & Hertsgaard, 1991), and several studies have demonstrated that insecurely-attached infants, particularly those with disorganized patterns of attachment, have increased reactivity of the HPA axis (Nachmias, Gunnar, Mangelsdorf, Parritz & Buss, 1996; Spangler & Grossman, 1993). Animal models of attachment have highlighted the significance of the mother–infant relationship as a regulator of the infant's developing neural system (Hofer, 1996). Studies of deprivation of caregiving include reductions in cerebellar dendritic branching (Floeter, 1979) as well as neurotransmitter and hormone function (Kraemer, 1992). Prolonged periods of maternal separation are stressful to rat pups because they reduce maternal licking and grooming (Anisman, Zaharia, Meaney & Merali, 1998). Thus, it may be argued that increased HPA activity is not part of an integrated physiological response such as the stress response, but rather it is an indication of the absence of the regulatory effect of the prior mother–infant interaction. Loss of the caregiver, at least within the animal model, reflects the withdrawal of a number of different regulatory processes that had been hidden within the infant's relationship with the mother. Experimental animal studies in which different elements of the interaction between mother and offspring are manipulated demonstrate that infant animals will show some of the HPA responses to separation but not others. Withdrawal of nutrient supply specifically affects the adrenocortical response, whereas lack of anogenital licking has its action at the pituitary level (Sucheki, Nelson, VanOers & Levine, 1995). The premature release from parental regulation of the child's responses has long-term effects on the subsequent development of the neuro-regulatory system and manifests for example in susceptibility to immobilization-induced gastric ulceration (Ackerman, 1980; Weiner, 1996).

The implications for humans are naturally far from straightforward. Hofer (1996) argues that inadequate early care leads to disturbance because of the failure of the normal smooth modulation and co-ordination of physiological function, affect, and behaviour into a coherent and stable diurnal pattern. Primate studies of early maternal deprivation demonstrate massive disorganization of innate social behaviour, which preclude the infant from experiencing the repeated amplifications and reinforcement of innate behavioural patterns that result in social norms becoming encoded in procedural memory. The development of autonomous function requires a transition from the interdependent mother–infant regulatory system to relatively independent self-regulation of physiological functions. This transition depends on the unfolding of genetically-programmed neurological development under the constant modification of social interactions (Schore, 1993, 2001). The processes of mutual engagement and interaction that serve to maintain proximity to the caregiver are also critical in ensuring attachment security and physiological self-regulation. The major difference between human and animal models might be that whereas in infant animals the source of the regulation is at the level of behavioural interactions, in the case of mother–infant interaction this also occurs at the level of rapid interchanges of subjective expectations (cognitive representations or models of relationships). Facilitation through social support may operate via the regaining of interactional regulators. An examination of HPA reactivity (measured by salivary cortisol) to the stress of an unfamiliar situation demonstrated that elevated cortisol response to elicited arousal occurred only in inhibited toddlers accompanied by caregivers to whom they were insecurely attached (Nachmias et al., 1996). Inhibited toddlers who were securely attached did not show these elevations, indicating that secure attachment may be a protective factor in the face of this vulnerability.

Seventy 15-month-old infants were studied in the process of adaptation to childcare over a five-month period (Ahnert, Gunnar, Lamb & Barthel, 2004). Security of infant–mother attachment was assessed before and three months after childcare began. On average, during the first nine days without mothers (the separation phase), salivary cortisol rose over the first 60 minutes following the mothers' departures to levels that were 75–100% higher than those recorded at home. But compared with insecure infants, securely-attached infants had markedly lower cortisol levels during the periods where mothers were present (adaptation phase) and higher fuss and cry levels during the separation phase; in addition, their fuss and cry levels were significantly correlated with their cortisol levels. In a recent study (Schieche & Spangler, 2005) of a sample of 76 toddlers, quality of attachment (secure, avoidant, ambivalent, disorganized) was assessed at 12 months; at 22 months the subjects were observed in a challenging task and salivary cortisol was assessed before and afterwards. In-line with previous findings, adrenocortical activation was found only in insecure infants with high behavioural inhibition, indicating the function of attachment security as a social buffer against less adaptive, temperamental dispositions.

It is not clear whether the attachment model suggests an early vulnerability—an early-established biological switch—or a latent vulnerability that is triggered in the individual in midlife leading to disease and death. The attachment model is a pathway model. Attachment style is assumed to work throughout the life cycle to expose the individual to greater risk and reduce the availability of psychosocial protection. This has a biological as well as a psychosocial parallel. Stress responses can be set differently throughout life by the differences of the early emotional environment (Liu et al., 1997a). For example, it has been suggested that social isolation per se is a chronically stressful condition, not just (as we have always known) for infants (Spangler & Grossman, 1993), but also for adults who may respond by ageing faster (Berkman, 1988). Animal studies have demonstrated that corticosterone response to stress falls off more slowly in old age (Sapolsky, Krey & McEwen, 1983). Social support in ageing moderates basal levels of several neuroendocrine factors (Seeman, Berkman, Blazer & Rowe, 1994). The capacity to cope with stressors is strongly related to cognitive capacities such as the capacity to exercise selective attention, which in turn is highly likely to be a long-term consequence of secure early attachment (Kochanska, 2001; Kochanska & Murray, 2000; Kochanska, Murray & Harlan, 2000). Thus the capacity to moderate the impact of stress by more adaptive socio-emotional capacities rooted in secure attachment relationships is likely to be present throughout the lifespan. On the other hand, the pattern of behaviour that together can be classified as dismissing attachment style (an insecure attachment pattern) is associated with poorer treatment adherence in patients with diabetes (Ciechanowski et al., 2001), with poor long-term health outcome a likely consequence.

## ATTACHMENT THEORY AS A COMPREHENSIVE, SINGLE FRAMEWORK FOR UNDERSTANDING INEQUALITIES IN HEALTH

The emotional insecurity that comes from not having experienced love and appreciation as a child leads directly to insecurities about social status and whether one is valued and respected as an adult. While the attachment and social literature have been artificially divided in the past, it is increasingly easy to link concepts derived from attachment theory and those from social epidemiology. In this chapter we have attempted to draw a parallel between the findings of epidemiological studies on social inequalities in health and attachment research. Briefly, we claim that the social gradient in attachment security lies at the heart of the social capital concept. The interpersonal social function is acquired in the context of a dyadic relationship, which is the basic building block of the social world. An insecure bond with the primary caregiver predisposes an individual to later relationships in which the expectation of being appropriately and sensitively responded to is lacking. In addition, when multiplied a thousand-fold to describe the social network of a community or a social system, then this system will possess the characteristics of insecurity— whether of an avoidant/dismissing or a resistant/preoccupied type.

Thus the claim for a comprehensive yet singular framework is being made on several levels: (1) at the biological level, we assume that insecure attachment results in an endocrinological vulnerability in the HPA system. Early over-activity of the system may make it hyper-responsive to a range of stressful stimuli, thus making individuals with a history of attachment insecurity more prone to the wide range of disorders with which the HPA system is currently being linked; (2) on a psychological (cognitive and emotional) level, we claim that individuals with a history of insecure, particularly disorganized attachment are liable to experience particular social contexts as more challenging than those whose attachment representations (or expectations of the other's behaviour) is not coloured by mistrust. Thus, secure individuals will experience themselves as in control in their work and in their family environment. They will be less suspicious or hostile in relation to their social encounters, and they will provide more sensitive parenting for their child, reflecting the way in which they were parented; and (3) at a societal level, we believe that the attachment context may be comfortably applied to entire communities or social groups. Thus for example, social systems can differ in terms of the general expectation that the system can provide safety in the face of threat. Undoubtedly the functioning of these systems is complex and is determined by many factors other than the proportion of individuals with secure attachment patterns who are part of the system. As insecure systems fail to provide a sense of safety in relation to threat, individuals in that system may feel little sense of belonging to it. Separation is therefore not an obstacle and geographical mobility, with all the adversities it brings, is likely to be high. The individual receives no sense of recognition in such a system and there may be a general devaluing of human relationships as helpful in meeting the challenges of life, although relationships may be exaggerated in importance as obstacles to coping and adapting. This sketch is offered for heuristic or illustrative purposes to indicate that bonding is a social process that may be usefully delineated at a number of levels of analysis.

## POLICY IMPLICATIONS

Evidence points to the importance of relationships, both early and late, intimate and distant. It follows that health-oriented policy should consider relationships too. The focus needs to be on the development of the healthy child. Increasingly, governments as well as charities have accepted, at least in principle, that the creation of access to conditions for optimal development of all children is society's, not just government's, collective responsibility. Within this approach, the developmental period covering preconception to age five has been thought of by some as the 'investment phase', while the period from age six to age 18 has been called the enhancement or remediation phase. We now recognize this to be a simplistic division as investment continues throughout development, and particular periods, for example the period immediately antedating puberty, may be considered just as much as investment phases as the first years of life. Therefore investment should not be limited to specific developmental periods, but should be further reaching— i.e. in terms of supporting families to provide nurturing environments. The two multisystemic approaches described in this volume are explicitly concerned with the question of how families may be effectively supported in adolescence. Returning to the theme of this volume—the hard to reach—a reduction of social inequalities must be the guiding principle for all social investment. Given what we understand now of the cumulative impact of risk, addressing issues of prevention and preventive intervention can only take place in conjunction with reducing social exclusion and increasing control and mastery.

It is a priority to identify current policies in the public or private sector that are destructive to factors that may protect children and may aggravate risks associated with social disadvantage. There are too many examples of this to list meaningfully, but merely for the purpose of illustration the following strike us as being particularly harmful. The relocation of employees, for example by private corporations, should be avoided at times that are critical for family growth and development; this would apply as much to the adolescent as to the early years. Similarly urban renewal policies should endeavour to preserve well-functioning, low SES neighbourhoods. Welfare policies should not enforce the attainment of work-related skills at the expense of caring for children and other dependents. There is scant evidence that current policies in either the public or private sector are mindful of the culture-specific attachment networks of ethnic minority groups. Initiatives may cut across traditional attachment processes with the best of intentions. For example, policies with regard to asylum seekers, however humane, are likely to undermine the attach-ment networks of asylum-seeking families.

In general, the pressure that individuals with roots in other cultures might come under to individuate and approximate to a stereotype of separateness and autonomy may create many more problems than it solves. The conflict between individual success, when set up in opposition to relatedness, represents a wider concern in our culture. For example, the incessant educational pressure on our children to compete and excel and win independently, in implicit or explicit competition against their peers, may well come at a price. Schools competing against each other and pressur-ing students to excel, at the expense of relational priorities, is likely to create the kind of pressures and stresses that can lead to an increase in the prevalence of depressive illness in school-age children. Counselling services such as the Place2Be, described in this volume, may serve a critical function in mitigating some of these competitive pressures. We might need further pieces of social engineering to create acceptable and desirable alternatives to an extended family system broken down by geographical mobility. Schools could become the foci of enhancement of related-ness for older children as well as younger ones. Schools that are too large, where children feel unknown and unrecognized, may break down the relatedness potential of these institutions. The media concerns about inappropriate behaviour by teachers and a pseudo-professionalism that can overtake any profession, makes teachers less effective foci for attachment needs than has been the case in the past. If we accept the general proposition of this chapter, namely that relationship experiences under-pin the functioning of several biological systems including the brain, then surely all social opportunities should be used to create opportunities for enhancing social intelligence and developing mental capacities that will further facilitate secure attachment in a virtuous social cycle.

For all the reasons we have discussed—genetic factors, early environmental influ-ences on brain development, and above all the risk-related barriers to prevention and treatment—those who are hard to reach will continue to provide a challenge for policy makers, funders and those who design and implement interventions. In this chapter we have provided an overview of some of the factors—biological and social—that come together to create this major challenge for our social and health-care systems. There is no alternative but to be imaginative in the ways we address this challenge. I have tried to argue that creating a relational perspective is the most useful way of bringing together these risk factors within a single accessible model that provides suggestions for intervention, both at the level of policy and practical programmes. The relational perspective is perhaps an implicit rather than an explicit theme of this volume. What holds these contributions together is a recognition that problems of inequality are profound and must be tackled in childhood, in the inter-ests not simply of those who have been disadvantaged, but for all of us who would benefit from our lives having a healthier and less strife-torn social context.

# CHAPTER 2

# What Evidence for Evidence-based Prevention?

Peter Fonagy

## INTRODUCTION

Over the past decade there has been an explosion of reviews of early childhood prevention programme research (Barnett, 1995; Bryant & Maxwell, 1997; Durlak & Wells, 1997; Hertzman & Wiens, 1996; Karoly et al., 1998; Mrazek & Brown, 2002; St. Pierre et al., 1995; Webster-Stratton & Taylor, 2001). These reviews generally report that few prevention programme evaluations have been adequately designed, particularly those for children under five. (Mrazek & Brown, 2002; Webster-Stratton & Taylor, 2001). But most programmes have not been evaluated at all, or the evaluations are so seriously flawed that no meaningful conclusions may be drawn. The present analysis is based on Chapter Three of a systematic review of the evidence for childhood and adolescent interventions, commissioned by the English Department of Health (Fonagy, Target, Cottrell, Phillips & Kurtz, 2000). It covers the trial literature to 2001–2002; the methodology for the review is described in the published report (Fonagy et al., 2002b).

## REVIEW OF EVIDENCE FOR SOME KEY TARGETS FOR PREVENTION INTERVENTIONS

### Reducing the Risks for Low Birth Weight Infants

Low birth weight infants (2500g or less) represent 7% of newborns in industrialized countries, and very low birth weight infants (1500g or less) make up 1% of births (Blair & Ramey, 1997). Among the associated risks are low IQ, behavioural problems, and low academic attainment, correlated with low SES, ethnic minority status, and maternal health behaviour problems. Three types of preventive interventions have been evaluated in controlled trials: (1) child-focussed interventions with sensory enrichment and tactile and kinaesthetic stimulation; (2) parent-focussed

*Reaching the Hard to Reach: Evidence-based Funding Priorities for Intervention and Research.* Edited by G. Baruch, P. Fonagy and D. Robins. © 2007 John Wiley & Sons Ltd.

interventions that aim to help socially-disadvantaged parents understand and meet the needs of biologically-vulnerable children; and (3) complex multi-systemic parent- and child-focussed interventions that encompass the child's need for stimulation, the parents' needs for training and support, and the parent–child couples' need to develop a secure relationship.

## Child-focussed Interventions

There are three controlled studies including various forms of sensory stimulation for low birth weight infants (Field et al., 1986; Leib, Benfield & Guidubaldi, 1980; Powell, 1974). In these studies, neonates in the experimental group received tactile and kinaesthetic stimulation (from the mother or a nurse) for 40 minutes to five hours each day for between 10 days and two weeks. These infants experienced a significant benefit in terms of their development. The average developmental advantage was 0.6 SD (standrad deviation) on the Brazelton Scale and 0.6 SD on the Bayley scale (only available in one study). In one study there was a small benefit in terms of infant growth. However, by six months the cognitive developmental advantage was only observable in middle class families (Leib et al., 1980); this advantage was counteracted by the adverse conditions that low SES infants are exposed to. The intervention appeared to have no impact on mother–child interaction or parenting skills.

## Parent-focussed Interventions

Three studies have examined the specific impact of parenting-training sessions, mostly in the hospital (Meyer et al., 1994; Parker, Zahr, Cole & Brecht, 1992; Rauh, Achenbach, Nurcombe, Howell & Teti, 1988). The impact of a parenting programme on weight gain was small (average effect size (ES) = 0.3), but training in parenting attitudes and skills appears to have a positive effect on cognitive and mental development. In two studies where cognitive development was measured on at least two separate occasions the impact of parenting training increased with the passage of time. The magnitude of the effect on cognitive development associated with 11 parenting sessions (seven in the hospital and four at home) increased from 0 at one year to 0.5 at two years, 0.8 at four years, and 1.0 at nine years (Achenbach, Howell, Aoki & Rauh, 1993; Achenbach, Phares, Howell, Rauh & Nurcombe, 1990). However, the effect of parenting training on psychosocial adjustment appears to be surprisingly low, even at six months. The study showed far greater impact on measures of parenting skills and maternal well-being (average ES = 0.9).

## Multi-systemic Interventions

Six studies tested complex multi-systemic programmes that focussed on both parents and children (Barrera, Rosenbaum & Cunningham, 1986; Resnick, Armstrong & Carter, 1988; Resnick, Eyler, Nelson, Eitzman & Bucciarelli, 1987; Scarr-Salapatek & Williams, 1973; The Infant Health and Development Programme, 1990; Williams

& Scarr, 1971). In these studies infants usually received additional daily stimulation and parents were visited at home and were offered special training in promoting optimal cognitive and psychosocial development. The home visits were quite extensive in some studies, and were supplemented with sessions in a child development centre. In the Infant Health and Development Programme, mothers were also trained in systematic problem-solving skills for resolving personal and parenting difficulties. Notwithstanding considerable input, the positive effects on weight gain was only evident in one of two studies, and on motor development in one of three studies. However, the positive effects on cognitive and mental development were evident in all six studies, and the magnitude of the effect, recorded at the one year follow-up, averaged an ES of 0.6. However, this medium-sized effect became less marked by three years. Infants most likely to benefit in the long-term appeared to be those who were heavier to start with ($\geq$2000 g) (Berlin, Brooks-Gunn, McCarton & McCormick, 1998), had no neurological impairments, came from poorer families, had higher levels of negative emotionality (Blair, 2002), and engaged well with the programme. These more intensive programmes were the only ones to have a significant positive impact on the psychosocial adjustment of the child during the first three years, with a mean effect of 1.0; thus indicating that the average infant from families included in such programmes fared better subsequently than 84% of the control group. It should be noted that there was a wide variability in drop-out rates across these studies, with lowest drop-out rates coming from studies that provided participants with transport and other incentives.

## Conclusions

From this review it appears that developmental delay in low birth weight infants can be prevented to some degree, most obviously in the area of cognitive development. Long-term data are scarce, but multi-systemic programmes with this high-risk group appear to have a positive effect on the infant's psychosocial development. The findings from the long-term outcome of complex multi-systemic interventions indicate diminishing improvements as a child reaches school age, but in one study at least the benefits for cognitive development from parenting training appeared to increase rather than decrease with age. A combination of low biological vulnerability and greater environmental disadvantage combined with high participation made positive response most likely.

## Reducing the Risk of Cognitive Delay with Social Disadvantage

The prevalence of mild intellectual disability in low SES groups is 10%, compared with 2–3% in higher SES groups (Neisser, Boodo & Bouchard, 1996). Fifteen studies have been carried out attempting to reduce this disadvantage. The studies fall into four categories: (1) those exploring the effect of home visiting aimed at helping socially-disadvantaged parents understand their children's needs for intellectual stimulation, secure attachment, and consistent supervision; (2) those offering nursery or preschool programmes aimed at compensating for an intellectually impoverished home environment; (3) those combining home visiting and preschool-based interventions; and (4) multi-systemic programmes providing extended support services for children and families, from infancy into middle childhood.

## Home Visiting Programmes

Seven studies evaluated home visiting (Campbell & Ramey, 1995; Gutelius et al., 1972; Jester & Guinagh, 1983; Karnes, Teska & Hodgins, 1970; Levenstein & Sunley, 1968; Powell & Grantham-McGregor, 1989; Ramey & Campbell, 1991; Slaughter, 1983). Although these programmes were diverse, and home visiting involved slightly different interventions across studies, we may conclude that intensive early home visiting that involves parent education and infant stimulation has the potential to prevent cognitive delay, and is associated with gains in intelligence and language development as well as superiority in scholastic attainment. Comparing across studies, it appears that those programmes that span the infant's first two years of life and include at least weekly home visits are most likely to be effective. The benefits of these programmes were clear for all ages up to and including middle childhood and adolescence, where data was available. The magnitudes of such effects were medium to large, with average effect sizes for the first five years around 0.8 for IQ test scores. The effect on language skills was somewhat lower (around 0.4) and reading and arithmetic attainment was between these two values (mean ES 0.6).

## Preschool Programmes

Three studies explored the impact of preschool or school readiness programmes (Karnes et al., 1970; Lee, Brooks-Gunn & Schnur, 1988; Lee, Brooks-Gunn, Schnur & Liaw, 1990; Raine et al., 2001). The programmes ranged in duration from eight months to three years, with children entering the programme at less than two to five years of age. The effects on IQ were small to medium, but in the one study that collected long-term data such effects were maintained well into middle childhood. In another study, nursery enrichment was associated with increased autonomic and central nervous system arousal and orienting at age 11.

## Combined Home Visiting and Preschool Programmes

There were six studies looking at the combined effects of home visiting and a pre-school programme (Andrews et al., 1982; Deutsch, Deutsch, Jordan & Grallo, 1983; Gray & Klaus, 1965, 1970; Jester & Guinagh, 1983; Johnson & Walker, 1991; Schweinhart, Berrueta-Clement, Barnett, Epstein & Weikart, 1985; Wasik, Ramey, Bryant & Sparling, 1990). This included well-known programmes, such as the Perry Preschool Programme and Project CARE. The findings indicate that all combined home visiting and preschool programmes lead to gains in cognitive abilities, and such gains appear to be maintained into adulthood wherever information is avail-able. However, the effect sizes are moderate, around 0.6 at age five and 0.5 at later ages. The impact on language skills was similar over the first five years, but appeared to disappear markedly in middle childhood (mean ES = 0.3). The effects were even smaller on reading and arithmetic attainment (ES = 0.2).

## Multi-systemic Programmes

There are two studies in the literature that looked at long-term multi-systemic interventions involving home visiting, preschool and additional tuition (Campbell & Ramey, 1994, 1995; Garber, 1988; Ramey & Campbell, 1991). Both these were long-term interventions involving weekly or fortnightly home visiting and regular preschool attendance during the toddler years. The effect sizes for intervention effects over the first five years were correspondingly large (mean ES = 1.5), only decreasing slightly in middle childhood (mean ES = 1.2).

## Conclusion

Multi-systemic programmes are clearly the most effective. Programmes including home visiting alone and home visiting combined with preschool intervention are somewhat more effective than preschool programmes alone, indicating the importance of family involvement. Longer programmes are clearly far more effective than short programmes. Across studies the following conclusions about early intervention programmes appear warranted: (1) the more comprehensive a programme, the more likely it is to be effective; (2) the more attention an individual child receives, the greater the likelihood of positive effects; thus small child–teacher ratios produce better outcomes as do more intensive interventions; (3) interventions that begin early, including those beginning in late pregnancy, are likely to have better effects; (4) the impact of short-term programmes rapidly dissipate; (5) programmes that involve children's families are more likely to be effective; (6) programmes that include maintenance components are more effective; (7) manualized, structured programmes are more effective than unstructured ones; (8) if staff are rigorously supervized they are more likely to be effective—experienced well-trained staff produce larger effects than untrained volunteers; and (9) programmes that are adjusted for the cultural context of the participants are more likely to be effective. In conclusion, broad, intensive, early, long-term, culturally-appropriate, family-based programmes that are manualized but fitted to the individual needs of the child, implemented by trained and supervized staff, are highly likely to prevent cognitive delay in socially-disadvantaged children.

## Prevention of Physical Abuse

The physical maltreatment of children is known to be associated with adverse consequences and transgresses the child's human rights; its prevalence is 1–10% (Browne & Herbert, 1997). There are at least 20 studies testing the effectiveness of a range of methods for the prevention of physical abuse. They aim to reduce stress on parents, increase support, enhance parenting knowledge and skills, and to promote child health so as to reduce the demands children place on vulnerable parents. The programmes entail home visiting, behavioural parent training, life skills training, stress management training, and the provision of paediatric medical care for children. In some studies these are offered in isolation, while in others complex combinations of programmes are offered.

## Home Visitation Studies

The effectiveness of home visitation was evaluated in eight studies (Affleck, Tennen, Rowe, Roscher & Walker, 1989; Barth, Fetro, Leland & Volkan, 1992; Barth, Hacking & Ash, 1988; Gray, Cutler, Dean & Kempe, 1979; Hardy & Streett, 1989; Infante-Rivard et al., 1989; Larson, 1980; Olds et al., 1998; Olds, Henderson, Chamberlin & Tatelbaum, 1986). In four studies the home visitation was by a nurse, and in four by para-professional women with parenting experience. Visitations occurred from four months to two and a quarter years. In some of the studies the visits started before the birth of the child. The visits provided social support, advice, and education about childcare. In some instances respite care was also offered. In all, a non-judgemental, supportive attitude on the part of the visitor was ensured, and modelling and encouragement of effective parenting were features. Across these studies the results are impressive. The risk of physical child abuse may be reduced by 50%; poor, unmarried teenage mothers are at greatest risk and benefit most. The likelihood of childhood hospitalization is reduced by 50%. The decrease in maltreatment was associated with a reduction in the type of early-onset problem behaviour that is normally assumed clinically to be a consequence of maltreatment (Eckenrode et al., 2001). The impact on parental well-being is small (mean ES = 0.93), and mothers' reports of the child's health and welfare show only small effects. Programmes where home visiting began prenatally are more effective, but no consistent differences emerge between programmes using nurses or para-professionals. Drop-out rates across these studies were surprisingly low (20%), even though some programmes lasted over two years. Drop-out rates are higher in non-experimental studies (approximately 40%), particularly in the absence of the regular supervision of home visitors and younger, non-hispanic mothers (McGuigan, Katzev & Pratt, 2003).

## Behavioural Parent Training

Six studies tested programmes aimed at improving practical parenting skills and addressing inaccurate expectations of infants and lack of awareness of the age-appropriate capabilities of young children, which is common amongst perpetrators of physical child abuse. Parents are helped to develop practical skills to understand the infant's preverbal and early verbal communications, and to acquire skills for meeting the infant's physical needs (Barth, Blythe, Schinke & Schilling 2nd, 1983; Burch & Mohr, 1980; Field, Widmayer, Greenberg & Stoller, 1982; Peterson, Tremblay, Ewigman & Saldana, 2003; Resnick, 1985; Wolfe, Edwards, Manion &

Koverola, 1988). These parent-training initiatives lead to marked improvements in parental well-being that were maintained to the follow-up (mean ES at follow-up = 0.7). Marked short-term improvements in parenting skills are reported (mean ES = 0.6), but these were not maintained to follow-up (mean ES = 0). In the most recent study, parenting efficacy and child anger continued to show some therapeutic benefit. Further, the average drop-out rate is 50%.

### Multi-modal Community Interventions

Three studies, all involving the provision of a range of healthcare, social and educative services, looked at the prevention of child abuse (Lealman, Haigh, Phillips, Stone & Ord-Smith, 1983; Lutzker & Rice, 1984; Marchenko & Spence, 1994). Across the studies the risk of physical abuse was 6% in the study groups compared to 17% in families who did not participate. These multi-modal community-based programmes reduce the risk of hospitalization by a factor of four in at least one study (4% vs. 19%). Most families completed the programme, and drop-out rates were low (6–27%). However, the long-term effects of the programme are not known.

### Conclusion

All of these programmes, including stress management and inpatient programmes that are not reviewed in detail here, modify risk factors for child abuse or reduce the risk of physical abuse, or both. Home visiting programmes, particularly those beginning before the birth of the child may be particularly efficacious in this regard, but do not impact on parents' self-reported well-being. Stress management training and behavioural parent training programmes bring about marked improvements in parental well-being, but these appear not to be maintained at follow-up. Multi-modal community-based programmes appear to combine the advantages of home visiting and behavioural parent training. These programmes also have low drop-out rates. Thus, programmes conducted on a group basis in community centres show the greatest potential in terms of the prevention of physical child abuse.

## Parenting Interventions in Divorced Families

The divorce of parents elevates the risk of academic, externalizing and internalizing problems in their children (Hetherington & Kelly, 2002). There were two previous quasi-experimental evaluations of parent-based post-divorce programmes (Stolberg & Garrison, 1985; Warren & Amara, 1984). Neither study resulted in any positive effects on the children involved.

A more recent study (Wolchik et al., 1993) reported an intervention using 70 divorced mothers who participated in a 12-session programme or a wait-list condition. Ten group and two individual sessions were held to address the support given for non-custodial, non-parent adults, contact with the non-custodial parent, and the quality of the custodial parent–child relationship. The programme benefited all participants but the greatest effect was seen with those who were at highest risk. There was a significant reduction in child behaviour problems. Improved quality of mother–child relationships accounted for 43% of the positive effects on the child, in terms of a reduction in the child's difficulties. A similar group, parent-training programme intervention was tested in a sample of 238 divorcing mothers with sons (Forgatch & DeGarmo, 1999). A behaviourally-oriented intervention produced a significant increase in positive parenting, which accounted for improvements in the adjustment of the children, as reported by teachers, mothers, and by the children themselves.

## Violence Prevention

There have been two distinctly different approaches to preventing conduct problems in childhood. The universal approach has been directed at a total population, typically of a school, to promote the development of social and emotional competence (see 'Emotion Education Programmes'). Other universal programmes have addressed teacher behaviour and school atmosphere (Kellam, Ling, Merisca, Brown & Ialongo, 1998; Reid, Eddy, Fetrow & Stoolmiller, 1999).

The second approach has been to identify young children at risk on the basis of what is known about the developmental pathway of conduct problems (Tremblay, 2000). Prevention trials have employed both child-focussed and parent training components. The Montreal Experiment (Vitaro, Brendgen, Pagani, Tremblay & McDuff, 1999) was a two year intervention, which found no effect of parent training and social skills training at end of treatment; however, at the three-year follow-up the boys included in the intervention were rated as less aggressive by teachers and were less involved in delinquency. The First Steps Programme (Walker, Irvin & Sprague, 1997) provided help in social skills building for high-risk kindergarten children and in-home consultation for their families on supporting adaptive child behaviour. Immediately post-intervention the effects were large (Brotman et al., 2003b), but long-term outcome was only reported in one study.

The most ambitious programme so far, the Fast Track Prevention Trial (The Conduct Problems Prevention Research Group, 2002a, 2002b), combined universal intervention (the PATHS curriculum) and targeted intervention in a multi-site study planned over 10 years. There was a clearly a significant intervention effect, but the reduction at the clinical level was only 10% (from 37 to 27%). The magnitude of the effect on teacher rating was small (ES = 0.27). With an intervention of this magnitude, greater differences might have been expected. Nevertheless, a 37% relative difference was achieved and the 10% reduction in prevalence is generally considered as large (Scott, 2003).

Violence prevention programmes have mainly concentrated on high-risk groups, based on the knowledge that within most communities the 10% of adolescents who exhibit violent behaviour account for as much as 70% of all violent acts (Loeber, Farrington & Waschbusch, 1998). A number of elementary school-based multi-component studies show that interventions were either increasingly (Farrell, Meyer, Sullivan & Kung, 2002, unpubl. manuscript; Stoolmiller, Eddy & Reid, 2000), or uniquely (Kellam, Rebok, Mayer, Ialongo & Kalodner, 1994; Metropolitan Area

Child Study Research Group, 2002) effective for high-risk children. Most of these interventions focussed on changing the behaviour and social cognition of young people in relation to violence. However, even if relative risk increases as a function of cumulative risk, the prevalence of a particular level of cumulative risk may be such that the largest cumulative risk is only experienced by a very small proportion of the population (Davis, MacKinnon, Schultz & Sandler, 2003). Thus, prevention programmes guided by identifying the most high-risk groups may not always have the greatest public health benefit in terms of reducing the problem outcome. The strategies that have offered the strongest evidence of violence prevention have been universal, family-based, early interventions (Howell, 1997; Yoshikawa, 1994, 1995). However, as a recent statistical modelling analysis (Cuipers, 2003) shows, in order to demonstrate a reduction in the incidence of new cases within the universal prevention design, literally tens of thousands of subjects would need to be randomized. Thus, in order to show statistical effects researchers have to focus on high-incidence groups with multiple risk factors. The limitation of this approach in the present context is that from current studies (August, Realmuto, Hektner & Bloomquist, 2001; Conduct Problems Prevention Research Group, 2002; Lochman and Wells 2002; Metropolitan Area Child Study Research Group, 2002), we do not know what the relative impacts are of universal violence prevention interventions for high- and low-risk youths, or selective interventions for high-risk youths relative to universal ones for low-risk youths (Tolan & Gorman-Smith, 2002).

## REVIEW OF EVIDENCE FOR SOME KEY TYPES OF GENERAL PREVENTIVE INTERVENTIONS

An alternative way of looking at the effectiveness of preventive interventions is in terms of the general prevention strategy used across a number of different risk targets. While there are many ways of grouping preventive interventions, I will consider only a handful in this volume:

- relation-based, early family interventions;
- attachment-focussed interventions;
- parent training; and
- kindergarten-based, early childhood emotion education interventions.

### Relation-based Early Family Interventions

Relation-based family interventions are amongst the most effective early interventions that underscore the importance of the family for child development (Cowan & Cowan, 2002) and belie behavioural genetics-based critiques with the traditional assumption that parents have a profound impact on the personality of their child (Harris, 1998). Of 34 studies, 17 report an improvement upon home observation, and 21 out of 27 report improved parenting outcomes (Kendrick et al., 2000). A good example of robust gains comes from the 15-year follow-up of the Elmeira Project where low SES, unmarried, nurse-visited mothers made fewer social service claims and had fewer arrests and convictions than controls (Olds et al., 1997). This programme has been successfully replicated in Memphis (Kitzman et al., 1997; Olds et al., 1998). Mothers participating in both of these programme appeared to create more facilitative environments and to make better use of community supports.

Perhaps the most carefully-crafted example is the UCLA Family Development Project (Heinicke & Ponce, 1999). The provision of a trustworthy relationship is assumed to improve the mother's functioning, and her relationship with her family of origin, partner, and her child. The intervention was manualized and executed by trained professionals. There were multiple benefits to a group of high-risk mothers randomized to the programme: increased support from the family of origin; less coercion in disciplining; higher prevalence of attachment security in the child; and a greater autonomy in problem-solving tasks. In particular, the most pernicious category (disorganized attachment) is reduced by almost two-thirds (Heinicke et al., 1999, 2000). There were further benefits at two years in terms of the mothers' sensitivity and support of their child's autonomy and task involvement, and their attachment security and task orientation (Heinicke, Fineman, Ponce & Guthrie, 2001). Evidence suggests that for relation-based, preventive intervention to be effective, multiple systems that interface with the family need to be engaged.

Evidence is currently being gathered that suggests that the long-term effects of early relational interventions may be via environmental influences that shape affective and behavioural regulation through the HPA axis, as has been shown in animal models (Brotman, Gouley, Klein, Castellanos & Pine, 2003a; Watamura, Donzella, Alwin & Gunnar, 2003).

## Attachment-based Interventions

Insecure—particularly disorganized—attachment is both a risk factor and a potential mediating factor (Solomon & George, 1999). Insecure and even disorganized attachment classifications are too common, even within normal samples, for secure classification to be of itself a sufficient criterion for a preventive intervention. However, as a range of adverse outcomes are uncommon in association with secure attachment, it is possible that the latter is an index of a protective mechanism and therefore may be a legitimate conceptual framework on which to organize preventive intervention.

It appears that even depressed parents can readily be helped to be more sensitive and less intrusive with their infant (e.g. Malphurs, Field, Larrain, Pickens & Pelaez-Nogueras, 1996). Such improvements in sensitivity appear to engender secure attachment; a brief, three-session sensitivity-focused intervention can treble the number of securely-classified infants, with improvements maintained to 42 months (van den Boom, 1994, 1995).

Two other programmes with mothers with depression have been shown to impact on early attachment relationships (Cicchetti, Toth & Rogosch, 1999). The Mount Hope Family Center Programme (Cicchetti, Rogosch & Toth, 2000; Toth, Maughan, Manly, Spagnola & Cicchetti, 2002) provided corrective emotional experiences for depressed mothers to address distortions in the mother's perception of the child, and thereby foster resilience in the infant. The programme substantially reduced the number of insecurely-attached infants so that the intervention group of depressed mothers were comparable to a non-depressed comparison group, which was maintained on follow-up at age four. The impact of this intervention is also evident in the more positive views expressed by the child of the parent and self (Toth et al., 2002).

A second comparative trial aimed at preventing the adverse consequences associated with maternal depression contrasted three brief interventions: a cognitive behavioural intervention; a psychodynamic, psychotherapeutic protocol; and non-directive counselling (Cooper, Murray, Wilson & Romaniuk, 2003). Compared with the control group, all three treatments had a significant impact on maternal mood at 4.5 months. Only psychodynamic therapy produced a rate of reduction in depression significantly superior to that of the control, but the benefit of treatment was no longer apparent by nine months post-partum. All three treatments had a significant benefit on maternal reports of early difficulties in relationships with the infants; counselling gave better infant emotional and behavioural ratings at 18 months, and more sensitive early mother–infant interactions (Murray, Cooper, Wilson & Romaniuk, 2003). The treatments had no significant impact on maternal management of early infant behavioural problems, security of infant–mother attachment, infant cognitive development, or any child outcome, at five years. Early intervention was therefore of short-term benefit to the mother–child relationship and infant behavioural problems. This indicates that either a more prolonged intervention is needed to promote longer-lasting effects, or that in terms of improving child mental health, post-partum depression may not be an efficient target (McLennan & Offord, 2002).

A similar study assessing the value of supportive psychotherapy with an interpersonal, relational focus, was offered to substance-abusing mothers (Luthar & Suchman, 2000). Children of mothers in the Relational Psychotherapy Group had fewer problems in multiple areas. At six months post-treatment they continued to be at a relative advantage, although the magnitude of differences between groups was often attenuated.

## Parent Training

This preventive intervention has grown out of treatment work with families with oppositionally-defiant children. Some parents appear to regulate the child's behaviour through coercion and criticism, fail to praise, and are inconsistent with reinforcements (Patterson, Reid & Dishion, 1992). Webster-Stratton extended her video-based parent training programme to explore the value of parent training as part of a Head Start curriculum. A large, disadvantaged sample was exposed to 8–9 sessions of group videotape parent training (Webster-Stratton, 1996, 1998; Webster-Stratton, Reid & Hammond, 2001). A total of 69% of mothers in the intervention group and 52% in the control group showed marked changes in behaviour, and 73% versus 55% of the children in the treated and control groups, respectively, showed a reduction in externalizing behaviour. The differences were no longer significant at one year. A similar large-scale implementation also failed in the Worcester public school system (Barkley et al., 2000). More successful implementation was reported from Australia (Sanders, Markie-Dadds, Tully & Bor, 2000). Toddlers were recruited by advertisement, stressing maternal concern about child behaviour. Clinician-observed ratings confirmed that the parent training programme was successful in improving the child's behaviour, particularly when supplemented with training in coping skills. In general, parent training programmes have been of limited effectiveness in the prevention context because of substantial problems of client engagement. This problem is less evident when atypical parents who are concerned about their child are recruited by advertisement.

## Emotion Education Programmes

A number of programmes have offered affective education to very young children with the aim of increasing their awareness and expression of feelings, and their ability to better understand the complex mentalistic causes of interpersonal behaviour (Fonagy & Target, 1997). Dysfunctions of processing emotion information have been implicated in both internalizing and externalizing psychological problems (Izard, 2002). A number of widely-used prevention programmes have substantial components focused on emotion (Beland, 1997; Greenberg, Kusche, Cook & Quamma, 1995; Twemlow et al., 2001b; Twemlow, Fonagy & Sacco, 2001a). The Promoting Alternative Thinking Skills curriculum (PATHS) implementation was shown to vary in terms of the level of support from school principals and classroom implementation by teachers (Kam, Greenberg & Walls, 2003). A significant number of trials ($n = 46$) have demonstrated that affective education that attempts to increase children's awareness and expression of feelings, and their ability to understand the possible causes of behaviour, is quite effective in the reduction of behavioural problems, as well as in the enhancement of competencies (Durlak & Wells, 1997). Overall, 76% of children who participated in the programme were found to be at an advantage to untreated controls. The programme was most successful in reducing problems (ES = 0.85), and slightly less successful in enhancing competencies (ES = 0.69).

Carol Izard and colleagues (Izard, Fine, Mostow, Trentacosta & Campbell, 2002) suggest a prevention strategy for the first years of life, practising free play involving positive emotional expression with the infant, which will help the infant acquire the ability to participate in synchronized, dyadic interactions (Tronick & Gianino, 1986; Weinberg & Tronick, 1994). There is evidence to suggest that increasing the frequency of positive emotion experiences has beneficial effects on mental and physical health (Fredrickson, 2001). Izzard suggests a targeted emotion-centred intervention to facilitate the induction of positive emotion and the modulation of negative emotions. The third to fifth year of life may be a particularly sensitive period for developing a dependable foundation for accurate perception and labelling of emotions in self and others (Fonagy, Gergely, Jurist & Target, 2002a; Gergely, 2002). Maladaptive emotion–cognition connections in this period probably contribute to and sustain misperceptions and misattributions that generate poor child–parent and child–peer relations in subsequent years (Arsenio, Cooperman & Lover, 2000; Schultz, Izard, Ackerman & Youngstrom, 2001). Emotion labelling, for example, represents a simple emotion–cognitive structure that may be facilitated by emotion recognition and labelling tasks (Greenberg et al., 1995), or the interactive reading of emotion-linked stories to encourage labelling and articulation, and to increase the child's ability to understand the causes and functions of emotions (Gottman, Katz & Hooven, 1997). Emotion education also facilitates the development of empathy and socio-moral behaviour in the latter half of preschool years (Hoffman, 2000).

## THE DANGERS OF PREVENTION

Finally, we should not assume that prevention initiatives are without risk. Any intervention that purports itself to be effective must carry a side effect. This is undoubtedly the case for prevention initiatives too. First, it must be acknowledged that the effectiveness of most popular and well-disseminated programmes has not yet been demonstrated (e.g. parenting books). Second, if ineffective programmes are implemented, then finding support for more effective interventions at a later stage could become more difficult. There is a real risk of building up immunity to prevention initiatives by implementing prevention programmes in 'sub-clinical doses' that have little impact on the levels of disorder within a population. Third, the easiest interventions are usually the least effective. For example, educational approaches tend to have no discernable impact. Parent education and parent support programmes in general are far less effective than structured, skill-based approaches that are a great deal harder to implement. Fourth, there are a number of counter-productive approaches that are likely to create more problems than they solve. For example, information-only models tend to create demand for assistance without providing services to meet this demand. Involving youths with adults that display antisocial norms, or aggregating high risk youths without any experienced adult leadership, are known to generate adverse outcomes. Less well-known is the fact that child-focused work carried out without addressing family problems may lead to an improvement in the child at the cost of deterioration in family function. There are many other similar examples.

## CONCLUSIONS

The promise of primary preventive intervention is considerable. From the studies referred to and others, we may conclude that early preventive interventions have the potential to improve the child's health and welfare in the short-term (including better nutrition and physical health, and fewer feeding problems, low birth weight babies, and Accident and Emergency visits, as well as a reduced potential for maltreatment).

In the short-term, the parents can also expect to benefit in significant ways (including educational and work opportunities, better use of services, improved social support, enhanced self-efficacy as a parent, and an improved relationship with both their child and partner).

In the long-term, children may further benefit behaviourally in critical ways both behaviourally (less aggression, distractibility, delinquency) and educationally (better attitudes to school, higher achievement), and in terms of social functioning and attitudes (increased pro-social attitudes), while the parents can benefit in terms of employment, education, and mental well-being.

In general, caring and protective relationships are potent protective factors against adverse outcomes. 'To hug is to buffer'—this conclusion applies as much at the level of society and community intervention as it does at the level of families and individuals.

There are a large number of prevention programmes identified as efficacious. There were perhaps only 14 in 1988, but currently more than 100 are listed (Rotheram-Borus & Duan, 2003).

These conclusions should be qualified substantially in the following ways:

- The outcomes are selective—no study achieved all of these effects together.
- Most demonstrations employed small samples, and attempts to expand small-scale efficacy studies to multiple sites have yielded disappointing results.
- Many of the studies reported unacceptable rates of refusal, which threatens generalizability. Unfortunately, it is most likely to be those in greatest need that decline the invitation to take part.
- Attrition is high in most studies, making conclusions from long-term follow-ups doubtful.
- Results are generally poorer with, what appear to be, higher-risk samples.
- The costs of implementing prevention programmes are seldom reported.
- Theoretical models of prevention lag behind those underpinning treatment interventions.
- The rationale for early intervention is often framed in terms of neuroscientific research on critical periods and irreversible effects of early experience, such as exposure to high levels of cortisol. Not only are these largely based on animal studies rather than on humans, but the biological pathways implied by these studies are rarely looked at in the context of evaluated prevention studies.
- The heterogeneity of the studies does not permit clear recommendations about 'the' effective preventive intervention programme.
- There is a dearth of integration between evaluated prevention programmes and services provided routinely, as well as genuine neighbourhood activities.
- Few evaluated programmes involve users in planning and implementing their activities.
- Many of the studies were carried out at a time when social problems (violence, substance abuse, economic split, fear, despair) were relatively mild compared to the difficulties we are facing currently.
- Even where programmes are demonstrated to be efficacious, they are rarely disseminated nationally or internationally.

In conclusion, we have much to learn about how we can get prevention to work.

# CHAPTER 3

# Overview of Child and Adolescent Mental Health Policy and Service Provision in England: Attempts to Reach the Hard to Reach

Miranda Wolpert, Paula Lavis, Richard Wistow and Bob Foster

## INTRODUCTION

The last decade has seen unprecedented interest in, and information about, child and adolescent mental health services (CAMHS) across England, accompanied by substantial increases in the level of central government investment (albeit from an extremely low baseline). A new and complex model of multi-agency provision is emerging. The model relies on the organization of well-integrated partnerships, both locally and nationally. These involve collaborations across the health, social care, education and voluntary sectors. These partnerships are guided by central government directives and clinical practice guidelines, and are assessed by a complex network of independent performance management inspectorates and regulatory bodies.

Policy documents have repeatedly emphasized the importance of creating 'comprehensive' provision that is accessible to all, including those groups seen as most vulnerable (such as children 'looked after' by the state, and children and young people experiencing multiple social disadvantages), and those for whom it was felt services had been less accessible (such as children and young people from some black and ethnic minority groups). CAMHS provision is increasingly seen as playing a key role in a range of government initiatives that seek to promote social inclusion and parity of access.

This chapter offers a brief summary of the current policy vision for CAMHS in the context of the historical development of the services in England, and current

*Reaching the Hard to Reach: Evidence-based Funding Priorities for Intervention and Research.* Edited by G. Baruch, P. Fonagy and D. Robins. © 2007 John Wiley & Sons Ltd.

levels of service provision. It goes on to provide some examples of emerging positive practice in relation to the attempts of services to access the hard to reach.

## THE CURRENT POLICY VISION FOR CAMHS

Current policy emphasizes the importance of links at a strategic level with the development of children's services generally. These are to be overseen across local authorities by a director of children's services who will be responsible for improving the outcomes for their under-19 population according to the following five headings: staying safe; keeping healthy; enjoying and achieving; achieving economic well-being; and making a positive contribution (see summary below). 'Joined-up working' is to be achieved by means of 'CAMHS partnerships'. These involve regular meetings of 'key stakeholders' within an area to agree a shared strategy. Key 'stakeholders' are likely to include primary care trusts, social care, education and mental health providers, along with other important groups, such as youth offending services, children's centres and service users. These partnerships are meant to ensure that the agreed CAMHS strategy is also joined up with other child-focused strategies and partnerships, such as in relation to child protection, and early years provision.

   The vision for CAMHS is that they should no longer be based uniquely in health service clinics, to which children and young people are referred and brought for 'treatment' by specialist staff. Increasingly the delivery of services should combine this approach with more multi-agency and community approaches, for example via common delivery sites in health centres, schools, children's homes, or youth centres. Increased support and supervision of non-specialist staff should enable a more sensitive approach to the mental health issues encountered in the course of providing general services to children and families. The aim is to work more closely with voluntary and non-statutory services in the hope that these will all offer greater use of different types of input to the benefit of children and families, providing earlier and more timely interventions. Many local discussions taking place currently reflect the tension of choosing between resource allocation of this nature and more traditional teams. Though clearly both are vital parts of the continuum of CAMHS provision, it is the balance and ways they relate to one another that remain open for discussion.

   There is a clear policy emphasis on making services not just more extensive but also more accessible to groups currently excluded, many of which might be categorized as 'hard to reach'. As discussed earlier in this volume, a range of factors (often interacting) may make services less accessible to certain groups for a variety of reasons. Poverty, homelessness, being 'looked after', being in secure accommodation, belonging to an ethnic minority, experiencing multiple adversities, having complex needs, having learning disabilities or physical disabilities, may all contribute to young people and their families being hard to reach. Many of these groups are also at increased risk of mental health problems. Much of the emphasis and policy drive in recent years has been explicitly focused on reaching those most in need, many of whom have traditionally been 'hard to reach'.

## HISTORICAL CONTEXT

### Child Guidance and Child Psychiatry

In some ways the current policy drive towards multi-agency services reflects a return to the ethos of the original child guidance clinics, which were first developed in the UK in the late 1920s. These clinics were largely funded by the local authorities but with input from medical officers and others. In parallel to the development of these clinics, psychiatry departments aimed at children and young people developed, often as sub-specialities within adult psychiatry departments of hospitals. The first academic department of child psychiatry was established in 1972.

People who worked in children's mental health services in England in the 1960s and 1970s sometimes talk wistfully of genuine multi-agency collaboration. However, provision was limited and there was no coherent, overarching, or widely-accepted model. Services during these early years grew around passionate practitioners. There was no coherent national policy and very little formal management in these services.

### Service Reorganization

With the reorganization of local government and the NHS in 1974, the health service took over responsibility for many areas that had previously been the responsibility of the local authorities. Medical staff in child guidance clinics largely became NHS employees, whilst social workers were regrouped in local authority social service departments. The dominant model of provision, whether as part of a child guidance clinic or a department of psychiatry, was that of small multi-disciplinary teams. These teams often had a strong allegiance to one particular theoretical model, operated primarily from one location, used a paper-based central referral system, and specialized in an area of work for a discrete group of children.

In the 1980s and 1990s this model came under pressure. Dramatic increase in demand (annual referrals tripled in many services between the late 80s and 90s) reflected an ever-widening conceptualization of what was meant by 'mental health needs', possibly combined with actual increases in the rates of occurrence of mental health difficulties (Hagel, 2004) and an increased identification of conditions such as attention deficit hyperactivity disorder and autism.

Pressure on public services to cut costs led to the withdrawal of key education and social care staff from many teams. The concentration of the resources from local authority education departments into the 'statementing' process (where children with special educational needs were assessed and plans to meet those needs were put in place), and the focus of the social services on child protection, meant that children with mental health problems who had previously been managed by these services were now signposted to mental health services via GPs. This resulted in disagreement between over-burdened and under-resourced service providers across health, social care and education about who was responsible for complex and challenging young people.

There was still little policy direction or interest in CAMHS before the 1990s. As Williams and Kerfoot note: 'services have grown in the UK as a result of the advocacy of strong-minded, committed and determined individuals, who were often senior practitioners or took their origin from the sapiential authority of academic development' (p. 17). (Williams & Kerfoot, 2005). This could lead to skewed and unplanned service provision that owed as much to individuals' academic interests, personal passions and therapeutic beliefs, as to any formal assessment of the needs of a given community. Links between agencies were often weak and depended on personalities.

## Early Attempts to Model CAMHS

However, at the same time crusading groups, in particular YoungMinds (founded 1989), campaigned for a more coherent and integrated, comprehensive vision.

There were some early attempts to define how rational services should be developed. Robert Goodman's Maudsley Discussion Paper no. 4 (1994), which laid out an evidence-based approach to mental health service planning, did not find widespread agreement with its radical proposals (including that psychiatrists should focus on prescription, and that the lack of an evidence base for child psychotherapy suggested this should not be promoted), but did stimulate much debate about what models should be proposed (Goodman, 1997a).

The key turning point, and arguably the point at which CAMHS as a concept was born in the UK, was the publication in 1995 of the NHS Health Advisory Service's (HAS) *Together we Stand* (Williams & Richardson, 1995). The government had commissioned the HAS (an independent, non-departmental public body) to write a report on the current state of services and to present a way forward. This also had major influence on the Department of Health's *Health of the Nation Handbook* (Department of Health, 1995), which set out a policy vision for CAMHS for the first time and linked in with the HAS document.

*Together we Stand* painted a picture of CAMHS as lacking strategy and coherent provision, with problems of inter-agency co-operation and accessibility, and limited consistency of good practice (for a good summary see Williams & Kerfoot, 2005). The HAS recommended a common language built around a four-tier 'strategic framework' to cut across sectors of care. This conceptualized CAMHS across the four tiers, often represented as an inverted cone with tier one being the large base through to tier four as the apex of the cone. The tiers and the type of professional, organization or team found at each level are as follows:

1. **Tier one**, the primary level of care—GPs, social workers, teachers etc;
2. **Tier two**, the services provided by professionals relating to workers in primary care—clinical child psychologists, educational psychologists, family therapists etc;
3. **Tier three**, the specialist services for more severe, complex, or persistent disorders—multi-disciplinary teams consisting of child and adolescent psychiatrists, nurses, occupational therapists etc; and
4. **Tier four**, the essential tertiary level services such as inpatient units—child and adolescent psychiatrists, nurses, occupational therapists etc.

Although in some ways this model has been increasingly misrepresented, its attempt to make sense of mental health provision gave the professional CAMHS community a common language, a sense of identity, and a way forward. It also offered clarity as to the potential role of CAMHS in the more holistic approach to planning for children's services generally that was about to begin.

## Evidence-based and Needs-based Practice

The advancement of service provision was also influenced by other key academic and voluntary sector developments. The push for services to undertake population-based needs assessments led to increased guidance about how this might be achieved (Kurtz, Thornes & Wolkind, 1995). A number of consultancies developed, including CAMHS, HASCAS (Health and Social Care Advisory Service) and YoungMinds. Around this time, books about CAMHS (as opposed to text books on professional psychiatry, psychology or psychotherapy etc.) started to appear (e.g. Richardson & Partridge, 2003).

The evidence-based practice movement in health led to an increase in publications attempting to summarize what little hard evidence there was in relation to CAMHS, to make it accessible to clinicians (Fonagy et al., 2002b). The encouragement of practitioners to move away from the traditional model, where they were free to offer whatever intervention they felt made most intuitive sense, towards adopting approaches that had been researched and found to be effective, sometimes in very prescribed ways, was not without controversy.

The ongoing debate about how best to apply findings from research (most of which was undertaken in the USA on very selected groups of children), and how to retain the creativity and autonomy of practitioners (without jeopardizing the effectiveness of those interventions that have been developed by constantly seeking to adapt them), is a major source of tension in services, and is likely to remain so for some time.

The formation of 'FOCUS' in 1997 (based at the Royal College of Psychiatry and funded by Department of Health and charitable foundation monies), which provided an email discussion forum free to all service providers, and whose explicit aim was to promote evidence-based practice in CAMHS, acted as a powerful and effective forum for the CAMHS community to share ideas and good practice.

## Modernization Agenda

Very soon after the Labour government came to power in 1997 a number of initiatives were taken in England in relation to CAMHS. In 1998, the Department of Health announced new monies for CAMHS, which hence became part of the 'modernization agenda' incorporating the development of a joint health and social care policy team, £80M of targeted funding added to the local authorities mental health grant and heath authorities modernization fund, a requirement for a 'joint CAMHS development strategy,' and the first guidance on developing services. This had a mixed impact on service development, but it increased awareness of, and discussion about, the role of CAMHS within the developing children's strategic partnership.

## Social Inclusion Agenda

The Social Exclusion Unit, which was set up in 1997, had a brief to lead innovative thinking in addressing some of society's most difficult problems. It was originally part of the Cabinet Office, but has subsequently been moved to the Deputy Prime Minister's Office. David Howarth MP defined social exclusion quite eloquently as a situation 'where people are unable to function as citizens because of poverty, ill health, lack of education or skills, fear of crime or discrimination' (Wahab, 2005). 2000 saw the publication of their Policy Action Team (PAT) report on young people, which looked at how government can improve policies and services for young people (Society Exclusion Unit, 2000). This report highlighted concerns about access to and quality of mental health services, and fed into other policy initiatives and government reports of that time. Their 2004 report on mental health mainly covered adults, but they did acknowledge the fact that many people experience their first episode of mental health problems during their teenage years. In addition, they looked at how parental mental health problems can impact on their children, and the importance of raising awareness of mental health issues in schools via the personal and social health education (PSHE) curriculum (Social Exclusion Unit, 2004).

## National Audits

Research and audit initiatives were undertaken to achieve a better understanding of the current situation and levels of need. The Office of National Statistics (ONS) was commissioned to carry out a survey of child mental health. Further developments followed: *Saving Lives: Our healthier nation* (Department of Health, 1999) stressed the importance of mental health and provided the impetus for recognizing that children's mental health 'is everybody's business'. The limitations of the existing systems were highlighted in reports such as the Audit Commission report, *Children in Mind* (Audit Commission, 1999). This report provided the first audit of services in England, and found that while approximately 1 in 5 (20%) of children and adolescents will have a mental health problem at some time, only a small minority accessed services. Publications such as *Bright Futures* (Mental Health Foundation, 1999) and *Standards for CAMHS* (2000) (HAS 2000, 2000) provided a vision of what might be possible.

## Child Protection

The death of Victoria Climbié, and the subsequent inquiry served as a 'wake-up call' and highlighted the need for greater inter-agency collaboration and information sharing (Lord Laming, 2003). This inquiry has been a key driver to government policy covering child protection and children's services (Department for Education & Skills, 2003). Reports into child protection arrangements highlighted the fact that there are a number of problems with the current child protection system (Department of Health, 2002b; Department of Health, Home Office & Department for Education & Skills, 2003).

## Support Services

During this time of change and of increased investment, supporting institutions were created to try to help and guide services. An annual CAMHS mapping exercise began in 2002, offering an overview of investment, service structure, capacity, and caseload. The National CAMHS Support Service (see www.camhs.org.uk) was set up in 2003 to assist local service improvement, and the National Institute of Mental Health England (NIMHE) began to take a lifespan approach to mental health issues. With support from the National CAMHS Support Service, the CAMHS Outcome Research Consortium (CORC) extended its membership nationally to allow member services to collaborate in developing models of outcome evaluation in their services (CAMHS Outcome Research Consortium (CORC), 2002).

## Child Poverty Review 2004

A raft of policy initiatives for vulnerable groups contributed to provide services with new frameworks for development. The Child Poverty Review (H M Treasury, 2004), for example, called for improvements in access to CAMHS. In particular these improvements in access were in relation to children and young people with learning disabilities and mental health issues, 16–17 year olds, and those with complex and persistent problems. The review also stressed that those who needed inpatient care should have access to a developmentally-appropriate environment.

## CAMHS AS PART OF CHILDREN'S SERVICES

Throughout CAMHS history there has always been a tension as to where the service best sits—as a part of wider mental health services or as part of children's services. CAMHS has looked to both adult mental health and to child health, or indeed child social care, as its 'parent' body. Clearly it is part of both and links to both, but one of the problems for CAMHS was that it was often overlooked by both, because each body perceived it as the other's responsibility.

In 2003 some government departmental reorganization occurred as the Department for Education and Skills took the lead for children's policy, and responsibility for children's social care moved to them from the Department of Health. However, the joint policy team was retained. This marked a decisive shift to a focus on CAMHS as part of children's services. CAMHS centrality in two key policy documents, the Children's National Service Framework (NSF) and *Every Child Matters*, has strengthened the movement towards services for children (Department for Education & Skills, 2003; Department of Health & Department for Education & Skills, 2004). The Children's National Service Framework (NSF) (Department of Health et al., 2004) laid out a vision of how services for children needed to develop to meet the needs of all children, young people, and their families. *Every Child Matters—Next Steps* lays out a vision for the future development of CAMHS. Currently these policy documents are the main drivers for CAMHS development in England. Both place CAMHS firmly as part of a wider vision for children (Department for Education & Skills, 2004).

## The Children's National Service Framework (2004)

The Children's NSF (Department of Health & Department for Education & Skills, 2004) puts forward 11 key standards:

1. Promoting health and well-being, identifying needs and intervening early.
2. Supporting parenting.
3. Child, young person and family centred services.
4. Growing up and into adulthood.
5. Safeguarding children and young people.
6. Children and young people who are ill.
7. Hospital standards.
8. Disabled children and young people and those with complex needs.
9. Mental health and psychological well-being of children and young people.
10. Medicines for children and young people.
11. Maternity services.

Each of these standards has implications for the development of provision to support the mental health and emotional well-being of children and young people. Standard nine is the NSF standard dealing specifically with mental health and emotional well-being (Department of Health, 2004) and states that: 'all children and young people, from birth to their eighteenth birthday, who have mental health problems and disorders have access to timely, integrated, high quality, multidisciplinary mental health services to ensure effective assessment, treatment and support, for them, their parents or carers'. Incorporated into standard nine are the following 10 markers of good practice:

1. Skilled staff;
2. Clear protocols;
3. Flexibility and range of provision (location and type, direct and indirect, prevention, promotion and intervention);
4. Urgent response available (within 24 h);
5. Support up to age 17;
6. Include children with learning difficulties;
7. Multi-agency approach for complex needs;

8. Sufficient size and mix of team;
9. Hospital environment appropriate developmentally; and
10. A care programme approach after inpatient admittance.

The chapter outlining this standard also suggests the following underpinnings of good practice:

- a focus on early prevention and promotion;
- partnerships with children, young people, and families;
- easy access and location of services;
- a maximizing of service equity;
- working in partnership with other agencies and groups;
- high quality inputs (evidence-based practice and evaluation);
- good planning and commissioning; and
- appropriate training and development of the workforce.

## Every Child Matters (ECM)—Next Steps (2004)

*Every Child Matters (ECM)—Next Steps* (2004) complements the NSF by outlining a framework for exploring the outcomes for all services relevant for children (Department for Education & Skills, 2004). It proposes five fundamental aims, applicable to all children. These are that they:

1. Be healthy.
2. Stay safe.
3. Enjoy and achieve.
4. Make a positive contribution.
5. Achieve economic well-being.

*Every Child Matters* also lays out some recommendations for achieving more integrated services to meet children's needs, via children's trusts (though their form are not specified), via greater information sharing, and by means of the common assessment framework.

## Proxy Indicators

Every year the various government departments make agreements with the Treasury about what targets they will commit to meeting in return for funding. These are called public service agreements (PSA). In order to measure progress in CAMHS, which had no agreed outcome measures, in 2002 a PSA was agreed specifically for CAMHS. This stated that there should be 'comprehensive provision by 2006' (Department of Health, 2002a). As a result, nearly £300 M was made available to support service expansion. The initial proxy measure for CAMHS was an annual '10% growth in staff, investment and/or provision'. In March 2005, three additional proxy measures were added as a measure of how comprehensive services were becoming, by focusing on areas seen to be particularly challenging for CAMHS: provision of services for those with a learning disability; availability of services for young people up to and including the age of 17; and availability of some form of rapid response (within 24 h) for families in crisis (Department of Health, 2005).

## The Multi-agency Vision

The vision is that the local authorities will play a major role in CAMHS decision-making as they have a lead role on all children's issues and are best placed to access groups with the greatest needs. Multi-agency delivery is emphasized here. Youth offending teams (YOTs), Sure Start/children's centres, and extended schools, are all current examples of multi-agency delivery, and it is suggested that CAMHS will develop an ever more integrated multi-agency approach.

The current children's agenda also offers a language of universal, targeted and specialist provision (Department for Education & Skills, 2004; Department of Health & Department for Education & Skills, 2004) that, whilst still allowing for a tiers model of structures, allows a new understanding of how CAMHS contributes to the wider children's agenda that Goodman foresaw (Goodman, 1997a) by contributing to universal provision (e.g. input into healthy schools etc.), targeted provision (e.g. looked after etc.), and specialist provision (e.g. specified mental health provision).

Current policy is for the development of a shared database between CAMHS and other children's services, though complex issues of confidentiality and data management are still being debated. The vision is that multi-agency commissioning and pooled budgets will allow for joined-up working across the full spectrum of child mental health needs. It is recognized, however, that the risk of rivalry, suspicion and 'turf wars' is ever present at all levels of the system. Inter-agency difficulties between service providers have been much commented upon, but there are also real difficulties in developing genuine collaboration between commissioners from different agencies, between the range of organizations charged with helping services to develop, and even between the different monitoring bodies.

Developing effective inter-agency collaboration remains a challenge. Efforts need to continue to ensure CAMHS is properly integrated into a wide range of multi-agency responses to the identified needs of vulnerable groups and communities, such as youth offending teams, looked after children's services, disabled children's services, behaviour and education support teams (BESTs), Sure Start initiatives, professional fostering projects, children's centers and complex care teams.

## CURRENT PROVISION

How does current provision link with the aspirations outlined above? Until very recently there were no reliable figures on levels of types of provision. However, since 2002 information about workforce and activity undertaken by specialist

CAMHS in England has been collated annually by the Durham University Mapping Team (Durham University Mapping Team, 2002), based on returns sent largely relating to one month's work. The process is still evolving, and the figures need to be treated with some caution, but they do provide an emerging picture of the extent of current provision.

The reported number of people working in specialist CAMHS in England in 2004, as captured by mapping, was 8894 (an increase of just under 15% from 7761 in 2003). It has been estimated that the extent of the current workforce is likely to be significantly below what is needed to provide an adequate service (York & Lamb, 2005). It has been argued that at a minimum, a threefold increase in resources is necessary to create adequate service provision based on a detailed analysis of the resources required for evidence-based practice, and estimation of the levels of need in the community currently not being met (Kelvin, 2005).

Repeated studies suggest that current provision is only reaching a fraction of those in need. Since Rutter's seminal work in this area suggested only a minority of children identified with clinical problems actually accessed services, further studies have suggested that it has remained the case that the majority of children and young people with significant mental health needs do not reach services (Meltzer, Gatward, Goodman & Ford, 2000b). Most recently, Tamsin Ford and colleagues followed up a third of the children from the 1999 British Child and Adolescent Mental Health Survey and found that three quarters of the children with psychiatric disorders had not accessed mental health services during the three-year follow-up (Ford, Hamilton, Goodman & Meltzer, 2005).

In terms of the type of service provision currently available, the Durham Mapping Team divide specialist CAMHS provision into four types:

1. Generic CAMH teams that provide a broad range of services to their local communities;
2. Targeted CAMH teams that provide services specifically for identified vulnerable groups including: looked after children; children and young people with learning disabilities; and children with common problems such as ADHD or eating disorders;
3. Specialist CAMH staff out-posted to other settings in order to target specific groups within a multi-agency perspective, including YOTs; paediatric services; Sure Start centres and BESTs; and
4. Tier-four teams that provide intensive provision, including inpatient and daycare, or community alternatives to inpatient care.

Table 3.1 shows the whole time equivalent (WTE) number of staff in post by staff type across England. Table 3.2 shows the number of staff working in different types of service provision, and Table 3.3 shows the main groups of staff working in each type of provision.

As the data in these tables demonstrates, nurses are currently the largest staff group within specialist CAMHS. However, the large number of nurses is in part linked to their high numbers in tier four (inpatient provision) (see Table 3.3). Although they are the second largest staff group in generic teams, it should be noted that 40% of such teams reported no nurses in post (Barnes et al., 2004). The second

**Table 3.1**   Main staff groups in 2003 and 2004

| Staff type | Whole time equivalent staff (2004) | Whole time equivalent staff (2003) | % Change |
|---|---|---|---|
| Nurses | 2517.3 | 2037.8 | 23.50% |
| Doctors | 1008.3 | 865.6 | 16.50% |
| Primary mental health workers | 381.7 | N/A | N/A |
| Psychologists | 1319.8 | 997 | 32.40% |
| Social workers | 639.9 | 638.2 | 0.30% |
| Child psychotherapists | 312.9 | 269.6 | 16.10% |
| Occupational therapists | 165.1 | 159.5 | 3.50% |
| Other qualified therapists | 522 | 506.9 | 3.00% |
| Other qualified | 253.9 | 426.1 | −40.40% |
| Other unqualified | 219 | 511.1 | −57.20% |
| Managers | 160.9 | 119.9 | 34.20% |
| Administrative staff | 1393.5 | 1229.7 | 13.30% |
| Total staff | 8894.4 | 7761.3 | 14.60% |

**Table 3.2**   Clinical staff by team type. wte, whole time equivalent

| | Number of teams | Number of wte clinical staff | Mean number of wte clinical staff per team |
|---|---|---|---|
| Generic teams | 492 | 4231 | 9 |
| Targeted teams | 240 | 868 | 4 |
| Dedicated workers | 143 | 246 | 2 |
| Tier 4 teams | 114 | 1996 | 18 |

**Table 3.3**   Main staff groups in different types of CAMHS provision. PCMHW, primary care mental health workers; wte, whole time equivalent

| Type of CAMHS provision | Largest staff group (wte) | 2nd largest staff group (wte) | 3rd largest staff group (wte) |
|---|---|---|---|
| Generic teams | Administrative (1075) | Psychologists (943) | Nurses (882) |
| Targeted teams | Psychologists (200) | Nurses (168) | Social Workers (150) |
| Dedicated teams | Psychologists (70) | Nurses (60) | PCMHWs (51) |
| Tier 4 teams | Nurses (1407) | Doctors (190) | Administrative (161) |

largest staff group nationally is made up of psychologists. Mapping does not differentiate between different types of psychologists (e.g. educational, clinical, and health psychologists), but it is believed that the majority of those employed in CAMHS are clinical psychologists. However, again this staff group is spread unevenly with 37% of generic teams reporting no psychologists in post, and with psychologists being particularly under-represented in tier four provision (Barnes et al., 2004). Doctors are the third largest group. Mapping does not distinguish between psychiatrists and other doctors such as paediatricians, but it is believed that child and adolescent psychiatrists account for the majority of provision. Once again provision is patchy, with 47% of generic teams reporting no doctors in post. Social workers accounted for 639.9 WTEs—7% of the total workforce, although 60% of the teams mapped had no social work input.

Overall the numbers of such key staff groups are still not large enough to meet demand, and many teams are struggling without having access to the full range of professional skills. Although a need for increased funding for training of some of these key groups has been stressed, it seems unlikely that this will be able to happen at sufficient speed and extent to meet the levels of demand.

Efforts are therefore being made to determine how best to bring new people into the workforce, and new staff groups are being developed. A key example of this is the development of primary mental health workers (Gale, Dover, Edwards & Flemming, 2004).

The biggest increase over the years of mapping has been in managers (34% increase). This is likely to reflect the move to more general management in the NHS, and the fact that CAMHS has traditionally been viewed as an 'undermanaged' service. The rise in the culture of general management in the NHS has been a source of tension in some services, and anecdotal evidence suggests a real risk of much energy and time being expended in power battles between managers and professionals (in various combinations).

Harder to interpret is the high number of administrative staff in generic teams—representing a ratio of 1 administrative staff to 4.5 clinical staff (not including managers). The children's NSF acknowledges the need for adequate administrative support, but it may be that that administrative support is being counted in the generic teams only (77% of all administrative workers are reported in generic teams), when in reality it is also supporting targeted and dedicated teams.

## Types of Service Provision

As can be seen from Table 3.2, generic teams contain by far the largest number of staff. There is currently a lack of specialist input in key multi-agency groups and targeted teams. With the move to a greater emphasis on multi-agency working as part of the wider children's agenda it is likely that input into dedicated and targeted teams will increase in future years; it can only be hoped that this will not be at the expense of generic teams. The next largest group currently is inpatient provision, but there is already an indication of a reduction in inpatient provision in recent years, and some indication that independent provision is increasing in this area (O'Herlihy et al., 2002) Thus the shape of CAMHS provision in coming years is likely to shift dramatically if the current vision for reaching the hard to reach as part of an integrated 'children's' agenda continues. It is to be hoped that in this move some of the hardest to reach, in terms of the extremes of their difficulties, are not left out, and that the move to a child-centred vision does not mean that crucial provision for the more severe mentally ill patients and older adolescents is forgotten.

## Progress in Relation to key National Service Framework-related Objectives

The children's NSF highlighted a range of priorities for CAMHS that were recognized as needing development over the ten-year life of the NSF. Key among them were the need to establish teams of sufficient size and mix, to improve access for learning disabled children and young people, to ensure the availability of 24-hour emergency provision, and to ensure that specialist CAMHS were available, where necessary, up to the age of 18.

## TEAM SIZE

The NSF stated that specialist services needed to look to develop local non-teaching generic teams with 15 WTE clinical staff for every 100000 people in the population they served. Current figures from mapping suggest that only a handful of generic teams across the country have the requisite staff numbers to meet these recommended levels (Barnes et al., 2004).

### Emergency Provision

The children's NSF calls for all services to provide on-call 24/7. There were 65 services with on-call provision in 2002, 74 in 2003, and 78 in 2004. However, the proportion of services with on-call provision has remained static over the last 12 months at 56% of all services. The overall number of services has risen, largely due to changes in how services are described, but two new small services were added to the exercise. Of the 78 services that provided on-call, 62 offered a specialist CAMHS response. This was seven more services than the previous year but the proportion remained at 78%. Overall, 60 services had no on-call provision, but 44 (73%) of these could provide an emergency appointment with specialist CAMHS the next working day, as compared with 79% in the previous year.

### Inclusion of Those with Learning Disability

The children's NSF emphasizes the need for services to develop to include children with learning disability. In 2004, 62 services (45%) reported having specialist provision for children and young people with learning disabilities in need of psychiatric care. Only 48 services in 2003, and 42 services in 2002, reported having this specialist provision. 23 of the targeted teams recorded having a focus on supporting children with mild to moderate learning disabilities. These teams reported 918 cases with the 'special characteristics' of learning disability but a total caseload of 1204, suggesting that some of the teams may have had multiple functions. Similarly, many of the 8764 children and young people with learning disabilities included in the mapping were supported by non-specialist learning disability teams.

## Access for 16–18 Year Olds

The children's NSF calls for service reconfiguration so that provision can be made up to the 18th birthday. In 2004, 677 out of 989 (68.5%) teams had an upper age limit of 17 or above, an increase from the figure of 67.8% (616 out of 909) in 2003. In total, 12% of the 2004 CAMHS caseload was recorded as being aged 16–18.

## Services for Vulnerable Groups

One of the criticisms levelled at CAMHS in the past has been that it has failed to be accessible to groups of children who are in more vulnerable situations where there is evidence that the rate of mental health problems is significantly higher. However, since 1998 there have been significant attempts to align CAMHS policy and practice with the inclusion agenda, and in particular with initiatives aimed at improving support for children in public care and the reduction in the numbers of youth offending. The latest mapping figures show that access has improved considerably with each area taking up approximately 8% of the caseload. Access for children from minority ethnic groups is clearly a problem, although the fact that almost all services are able to provide figures is a significant step forward. The swift increase in specialized staff and teams who look at children's needs in the context of vulnerability factors indicates that CAMHS were able to develop a more proactive approach.

## Conclusions from Mapping

Thanks to the mapping data we now have, for the first time, an emerging picture of specialist CAMHS provision in England at the start of the 21st century. Caution should be used in interpreting these figures, but they do suggest increased funding for services resulting in increased numbers working in CAMHS and in continuing expansion of the number of children, young people, and their families seen by services; although waiting lists have remained constant. The trend between 2002 and 2003 was for significantly more people to be seen, and for each young person and their family to be seen more quickly and for less time. In 2004 this trend has largely continued. Although the duration of treatment for cases has increased slightly over 2003, young people and families are still on average remaining in contact with services for less time than in 2002.

There appears to be some progress towards the standards set out in the children's NSF and highlighted by the Department of Health for particular scrutiny. Increased numbers of services are now indicating that they are accessible to those with a learning disability, those in crisis who need a rapid response, and those aged 17–18.

## EMERGING POSITIVE PRACTICE IN RELATION TO REACHING THE HARD TO REACH?

It is within the context of increased policy attention, focused particularly on vulnerable groups but with the reality of continued under-resourcing and the fragile development of multi-agency working, that emerging positive practice must be explored.

The NIMHE has held positive practice awards since its inception in 2003, but 2005 was the first time that the CAMHS category of the NIMHE positive practice awards included sub-categories. These focussed on key areas of service development considered as national priorities, including:

- the positive use of service user input;
- provision for black and minority ethnic communities;
- provision for 16–17 year olds;
- provision for those who require co-ordinated input from a range of services;
- provision for accessible and appropriate services for young people with learning disabilities; and
- provision of services focusing on mental health promotion and prevention.

There were 117 applications over the seven categories, representing the work of 74 separate services or projects (services could apply for more than one category, but could only win in one). A panel of professionals from within the CAMHS field judged the applications and the category winners were then put forward to a panel of young service users from Barnardos UR Voice young people's advisory group, Leeds, to choose the overall winner.

In turning to examine these winning and highly commended entries we can start to get a snapshot of what emerging practice looks like in England today. All the winning and highly commended entries reflect the levels of innovation and hard work currently taking place across services. They demonstrate the diverse ways in which services are collaborating across agency boundaries, between service providers and service users, and across different age ranges and different cultural groups, in order to develop models of service provision that can best meet the needs of all children and young people and their families within a community, and to shift the culture of stigma and fear that otherwise can obscure thought and progress in this area. A booklet containing information about all of the CAMHS category winners is available from www.camhs.org.uk, as is a library of emerging practice that includes information about all of the services that entered for these awards.

The winning and highly commended entries for these categories are summarized below. Interestingly many of the winning entries included voluntary sector input.

**On the Edge** (Devon) were the overall winner of the CAMHS Positive Practice Award (and joint winner of 'Positive Use of Service User Input'). This project is a dramatized health education programme. It has helped break the taboo of silence about mental health problems in educational settings, and contributes towards building better futures for young people and their families. Service users have been involved with the programme from the start, and it has been extensively evaluated and has been shown to strengthen individuals and communities and to reduce barriers between schools and mental health services.

**Hear Our Voice** (Cornwall) was joint winner for 'Positive Use of Service User Input'. This organization works with 11–25 year olds who are experiencing, or at risk of experiencing, mental health difficulties. The young people are encouraged to get involved in the work of the project and develop a sense of ownership. The service has a variety of easy referral routes including texting and emails. They offer a range of services including peer support groups, advocacy, and one-to-one support, and they work with a range of organizations to develop their own user involvement.

**Tower Hamlets CAMHS** (London) won the award for 'Provision for Black and Minority Ethnic Communities'. Tower Hamlets is an area in which there is a high proportion of children from minority ethnic groups, but these groups are under-represented amongst their CAMHS users. They have tried a number of ways to 'reach out'—to ensure that those who need a service are receiving one, and they created a number of initiatives to reach young people from minority ethnic groups and their families. These initiatives include bilingual co-worker posts from the local Bangladeshi community to help other services connect better with service users; the multi-agency preventive (MAP) project, which aims at meeting the needs of Bangladeshi boys in secondary school; and the African families project, where white service workers work alongside workers of African origin in other organizations. The aim is to help them link up with African parents in the first instance, and then with their children. They also have a Muslim families working party, made up of representatives of the Muslim community and local professionals, dedicated to improving services for Muslim children and their families.

**Building Bridges** (Liverpool) was highly commended in this category. Some key highlights that stood out were their use of language that was accessible to children and young people, their focus on preventive work to reduce the numbers of looked after children, and their work on engaging with families—in particular with fathers—in helping to meet the emotional and well-being requirements of their black and minority ethnic communities.

**Springfield Youth Club** (London) won the category 'Provision for 16–17 Year Olds'. Springfield Youth Club was set up to help deaf and hearing-impaired young people aged 11–18 who were experiencing severe mental health difficulties and were being cared for by the South West London and St George's Mental Health Trust. They set up a youth club to make their lives easier and more 'normal', and to minimize the stigma and trauma associated with their conditions and with hospital admissions.

**The Junction–Colchester Mind** was highly commended in this category. The Junction is run out of Colchester Mind and provides a range of services to young people aged 11–18. They often see young people who find it difficult or are unwilling to go to statutory services. This is because they provide an accessible and young person-friendly service that involves users in the development and evaluation of the service. The service is a good example of how young people with complex and sometimes hard to manage problems can be offered support in a low-key environment that is sufficiently flexible to meet their needs both in terms of range of services and opening times.

**Reframe Conduct Disorder Outreach Team** (London) won the award for 'Provision for Those Who Require Co-ordinated Input from a Range of Services'. The team, which is based in the London Borough of Newham, was set up four years ago to work on an assertive outreach basis with children aged between 5–13 with a conduct disorder, and their families and networks. Their method of working has resulted in them engaging families in treatment who would otherwise not be receiving a service. This team also liaises with other agencies and streams to reduce anti-social street behaviour, truanting, and school exclusion. In addition, at a managerial level the team leader is involved with a number of other initiatives focusing on highly marginalized populations; i.e. the local YOT, local BEST, etc.

**Keepsafe Project** (Bath) was highly commended in this category. This project is an innovative partnership of children's agencies in Bath and North East Somerset. They provide a response, assessment, and intervention service to juveniles whose behaviour is sexually harmful, and to their families.

The **Dual Diagnosis Team**, based in Sheffield, works with children and young people with learning disabilities who also experience emotional and behavioural difficulties. They work across Sheffield and are the only service of their kind in Yorkshire. The team act as an additional service to what is currently offered by their local CAMHS and other local services. Their approach has been successful in reducing out-of-city placements.

The **FRIENDS Programme** (Bath) was joint winner for 'Provision of Services Focusing on Mental Health Promotion and Prevention'. This is a 10-week programme that helps children learn ways of dealing with worries, unpleasant feelings and problems before they become too big. The children were involved at all stages of the development and implementation of the project.

**CAMH Community Service to On Track** (Luton) was the other winner of this category. On Track was developed to satisfy the need to offer services for younger children, to prevent them developing more serious and long-standing social problems. In Luton this was translated to developing community services through local primary schools for a largely South Asian population, who have been traditionally suspicious and disengaged with statutory services, and who potentially have complex needs. They have developed a three-level service model that offers training/consultation liaison to tier one (school/project/On Track frontline staff), co-working, and easy access to direct interventions.

There are many other services or interventions that represent good examples of emerging practice. For instance, there is **The Headspace Toolkit** (Advocacy in Somerset, 2005). Their main aim is to help young people in inpatient units by giving them the information, power and skills that they need to express their views, wishes and feelings about their care and treatment. The Toolkit comprises a 32-page A4 booklet with four sections: 'What's What' (including a jargon buster); 'Rights, Treatment and Legal Stuff'; 'Getting Yourself Heard'; and 'How do I use the Power Tools?' It also has ten loose-leaf 'Power Tools' that young people can fill in themselves.

Children and young people may be reluctant to talk to someone face-to-face. The growth in Internet use has resulted in the development of several websites that provide information and/or advice to children and young people. For younger children there are websites such as Childline, which complements their well-known telephone helpline. In addition, there is the NSPCC's there4me website. As well as information this website provides access to an online agony aunt, and online advisors. For teenagers there is The Site. This website, which is run by YouthNet UK, provides a range of information on various issues that would be of concern to young people. Well-known adult mental health charities are also developing their services to engage with older teenagers and young adults. For instance, the Samaritans now provide an email service where anyone can email them for help and advice on mental health issues. It may well be that Internet technology will provide a major spur to developments in CAMHS provision in the future.

## CONCLUSION

The policy vision and aspirations for CAMHS are ambitious, and the models of true 'joined-up' services that might wrap around even the hardest to reach young people and their families to provide evidence-based and non-stigmatizing help and support, is very enticing. However, huge challenges remain; CAMHS in England at the start of the 21st Century is still in a fragile state. Many of the projects referred to above are financed by short-term funding that is often in danger of drying up, and services nationally are still massively under-resourced relative to need. Even where funding is available there are huge difficulties in accessing the necessary skilled people to provide the services, in agreeing an evidence-based approach to service development, and in finding ways for complex organizations to work together in meaningful ways. However, what is emerging is an increasingly-articulated vision of how services look currently and how they might look in the future if they really are to fulfil the challenge of meeting the needs of all children and families across the country.

# PART TWO

# Specific Intervention Programmes Working with the Hard to Reach

# CHAPTER 4

# A Study of Multisystemic Therapy: A New Type of Help in the UK for Young People in Trouble with the Law

Geoffrey Baruch and Jacqueline Cannon

## INTRODUCTION

The goal of multisystemic therapy (MST) is to reduce the level of reoffending among high-risk young offenders, and to decrease costs by reducing the use of custody and residential treatment and placement. MST is a short-term, community- and home-based intervention that primarily involves the young offender and her/his parent(s),[1] drawing upon their strengths to improve relations between them and with peers, and to improve school performance. Over $10 million has been invested into research in MST in the United States. Follow-up studies have documented a 25 to 70% reduction in rearrest rates among MST cases compared to controls, with subsequent significant cost savings in policing, court, and correctional budgets. American research has shown that MST can reduce the number of days in out-of-home placements by 47 to 64%. The US Office of Juvenile Justice and Delinquency Prevention asked the Center for the Study and Prevention of Violence at the University of Colorado to identify ten exemplary programmes to promote as models that communities should implement (www.colorado.edu/cspv/blueprints/); MST was one of the ten. MST is also useful in the treatment of young people engaged in substance abuse. The National Institute of Drug Abuse identified MST as one of 12 scientifically-based approaches to drug addiction treatment in a 1999

---

[1] The term 'parent' is also used to refer to a close relative carrying out the principal caring role, or contributing with a parent to a caring role.

---

*Reaching the Hard to Reach: Evidence-based Funding Priorities for Intervention and Research.* Edited by G. Baruch, P. Fonagy and D. Robins. © 2007 John Wiley & Sons Ltd.

publication called *Principles of Drug Addiction Treatment: A Research-Based Guide* (http://165.112.78.61/PODAT/PODATindex.html).

As evidence mounted that the MST approach is a cost-effective way to keep serious young offenders out of custody without putting the community at risk, the Brandon Centre[2] was keen to mount a study examining whether MST would work in the youth justice system in England. Since starting the study, recently published systematic reviews of the effectiveness of MST by Julia Littell and colleagues conclude 'that the results of 8 randomised controlled trials of MST conducted in the USA, Canada and Norway conclude that Multisystemic Therapy (MST) is not consistently more or less effective than other services in preventing restrictive out-of-home living arrangements (e.g. incarceration, psychiatric hospitalisation), reducing arrests or convictions, or improving youth and family functioning' (Littell, Popa, & Forsythe 2005). The reviews make a number of criticisms about the trials by the developers of MST and the interpretation of the results although these criticisms are strongly contested by the developers (Henggeler, 2006). Thus it would seem that further investigation would be helpful in evaluating the effectiveness of the intervention.

The Brandon Centre has obtained substantial funding from The Tudor Trust, an English Charitable Trust and The Atlantic Philanthropies, an American Charitable Foundation for a period of four years that covers the cost of implementing a clinical trial. The Youth Justice Board for England and Wales has approved the study and provided some additional financial support. The study has received ethics committee approval from Camden & Islington Community Local Research Ethics Committee.

Following recruitment of MST staff by the Centre, training, and accreditation of an MST team that includes three counselling psychologists and a supervisor of Multisystemic Therapy Services from South Carolina, the intervention was piloted for a period of six months from 1st April 2003. The clinical trial started in October 2003.

Referrals come from social workers at Haringey Youth Offending Service (YOS) and Camden YOS. Young people are considered candidates for MST if they are identified as being at high or very high risk of criminal offending in the future. All will have a prior record of at least one reprimand and a final warning and/or at least two convictions, and many have other presenting problems, such as school refusal, substance abuse, parent/child conflict, or serious behavioural problems.

The research design involves assigning half of qualifying cases to both MST and the services currently available to young offenders who are the responsibility of Haringey YOS or Camden YOS, and half only to the services currently available to young offenders from both YOSs, as controls. Pre- and post-testing of the treatment group is carried out, and both the controls and the treatment group are being followed for up to three years post-intervention to gauge their levels of subsequent offending and service utilization.[3] The parent and the young person who agree to

---

[2] The Brandon Centre is based in Kentish Town in the London borough of Camden. It is a voluntary organization that provides psychotherapeutic, contraceptive, and sexual health services for young people aged 12 to 21 years.

[3] The Brandon Centre has engaged Dr Stephen Butler, a Senior Lecturer in the Sub-Department of Clinical Health Psychology, University College London, to manage the evaluation of the trial. Dr Butler worked on the *Multi-site Evaluation of Multisystemic Therapy in Ontario, Canada.* He reports to the Director of the Department, Professor Peter Fonagy.

participate in the trial (i.e. those who receive MST in addition to the usual services, and those who receive only the usual services) are given a total of £25 for completing questionnaires prior to the intervention, and a total of £25 when the questionnaires are completed at the five month follow-up.

Over three and a half years we anticipate involving up to 220 young people. At least 100 will receive MST.

## WHAT IS MST?

It was the researchers and clinicians at the Family Services Research Center in the Medical University of South Carolina that developed MST (Henggeler et al., 1998). Prior to its introduction it was apparent that mental health services for serious young offenders were minimally effective at best, extremely expensive, and not accountable for outcomes. Initially a review of the research literature was carried out, looking for interventions with documented success in determining good outcomes for the antisocial young person, and also noting interventions—some quite popular—that have no empirical support. This process of discarding ineffective techniques and identifying and collecting those that are most effective means that MST is really more an amalgam of best practices than an entirely new method. What is unique is the analytical process that governs the course of treatment in each case (see description and case study below).

MST adopts a social-ecological approach to understanding antisocial behaviour. The underlying premise of MST is that criminal conduct is multi-causal; therefore, effective interventions would recognize this fact and address the multiple sources of offending behaviour. These sources are found not only in the young person (values and attitudes, social skills, biology, etc.) but also in the young person's social ecology: the family, school, peer group, and neighbourhood. A key premise of MST is that community-based treatment informed by an understanding of the young person's social ecology will be more effective than costlier residential treatment. This is true even when candidates selected for MST are young people who are bound for residential treatment or custodial placements because of the seriousness of their conduct or emotional problems.

Research has shown that treating the young person in isolation of the family, school, peer, and neighbourhood systems, means that any gains are quickly eroded upon return to this environment. Custodial stays could also be counter-productive because an already-troubled young person is immersed in a peer culture in which antisocial values predominate.

MST uses the family preservation model of service delivery in that it is home-based, goal-oriented, and time-limited. It focuses on current behaviour as opposed to influences from the young person's past, and seeks to identify, reduce, and if possible remove behaviours that are of concern to the referring agents and to the young person's parent or principal carer. The implementation of MST draws on family members, in contrast to many interventions that define the young person as the 'identified client.' MST involvement will typically be between three to five months in duration. Again unlike many interventions for high-risk young people, MST does not provide follow-up help once the intervention has been completed.

Collaboration with community agencies is a crucial part of MST. Establishing or in most cases re-establishing engagement between the young person, their parent, and the school, is a critical part of the treatment and the MST therapist may be in regular contact with teachers. The MST therapist also works in close partnership with the social worker from the YOS that is responsible for the young person following her/his conviction by the court. The MST team works closely with the social workers in ensuring that MST is implemented to maximum effect in the context of the requirements of the criminal justice system for young offenders. For example, there may be a need to involve the young person in treatment for substance abuse or to seek a psychiatric consultation about a parent. This may be best facilitated in partnership with the young person's social worker at the YOS.

The initial MST involvement is intensive, perhaps daily, but the ultimate goal is to empower the parent and the young person to take responsibility for making and maintaining gains. An important part of this process is to foster in the parent the ability to be a good advocate for their child and themselves with social service and other community agencies, and to seek out their own support. In other words, parents are encouraged to develop the requisite skills to solve their own problems, rather than to rely on professionals.

MST is therefore a flexible intervention, tailored to each unique situation. There is no one recipe for success. Instead, there are nine guiding principles:

1. The primary purpose of assessment is to understand the 'fit' between the identified problems and their broader context.
2. Therapeutic contacts should emphasize the positive and should use systemic strengths as levers for change.
3. Interventions should be designed to promote responsible behaviour and decrease irresponsible behaviour among family members.
4. Interventions should be present-focused and action-oriented, targeting specific and well-defined problems.
5. Interventions should target sequences of behaviour within or between multiple systems that maintain the identified problems.
6. Interventions should be developmentally appropriate and fit the developmental needs of the young person.
7. Interventions should be designed to require daily or weekly effort by family members.
8. Intervention efficacy is evaluated continuously from multiple perspectives with providers assuming accountability for overcoming barriers to successful outcomes.
9. Interventions should be designed to promote treatment generalization and long-term maintenance of therapeutic change by empowering caregivers to address family members' needs across multiple systemic contexts.

## THE WORK OF THE MST THERAPEUTIC TEAM

The average caseload for MST therapists is four families. They carry out their work in the family home and the community rather than in a clinic, and are on call 24 hours a day, seven days a week. Appointments are made to suit the members of the family involved in the treatment, so they may take place in the evening or at weekends. The therapists tailor their working week and time off accordingly and in co-ordination with the team supervisor and the other therapists. The MST team members cover each other so that during time off families can be supported and be in contact with the team; remuneration takes account of the flexibility expected. Particularly in the beginning, the therapist may be in the home three times a week and may speak to the young person's parent or principal carer on days when no visit has been arranged. They will also spend time at school and will meet with the young person's peer group and extended family, as required. A key part of the process begins with engaging with the family; a significant challenge in some cases.

MST therapists are closely supervised and monitored for adherence to the MST principles, and receive weekly guidance and feedback about their interventions with the families in their caseload. The therapist meets the MST supervisor for individual supervision on a weekly basis. In addition, the team meets together for group super-vision, also on a weekly basis. Every week there is a telephone discussion with a consultant from MST services that has been assigned to the team. The consultant is also responsible for running booster training events that take place four times a year, and that follow the initial intensive five-day training that takes place at MST Services in Charleston South Carolina. This structure is part of the license agree-ment between the organization that hosts the MST team and MST Services.

In addition to the therapeutic team there is an MST team administrator. Given that the therapeutic work takes place exclusively in the community and in the family home, and that appointments between the therapist and the family may not follow a regular pattern, the administrator is crucial. There are issues of safety involved in the MST therapist going into the home of a high-risk family, possibly in a run-down neighbourhood; therefore the administrator, along with the MST supervisor, is responsible for ensuring that there is a system in place to monitor and track the daily visits. The MST administrator also assists in collecting and disseminating information that is relevant to the treatment to the members of the therapeutic team; for instance, information about pro-social activities in the local community for young people. Considerable paperwork is produced by both the MST therapists and the supervisors involved with the analytical process, and the collection and collation of this is also the responsibility of the administrator. Finally, the adminis-trator in the Brandon Centre clinical trial works closely with the research manager in organizing, storing, and analysing the clinical data collected by the therapists for the study.

The MST process begins with the identification of the problem behaviour, a process that involves the members of the family involved in the intervention. In other words, the parent is key to enabling the identification of treatment targets. Examples of such behaviour include non-compliance with family rules, failure to attend school, failure to complete schoolwork, substance use, showing disrespect to figures in authority, and offending behaviour. While the focus is on elimination of problem behaviour, this is accomplished to a large extent by building upon strengths. The assessment process also involves identifying the strengths in the young person and his family, which can include a hobby, sports achievements, a trusting relation-ship with an extended family member or teacher, warmth and love among family members, etc. The next step is an assessment of the factors in the young person's ecology that support the continuation of the problem behaviour, and the factors that operate as obstacles to their elimination. These factors may be found in any sphere of that individual's ecology: family, peers, school, neighbourhood, or the linkages between them. Therefore, therapists are called upon to find information from all of these sources, by going to the school, spending time with the peer group, or speaking with extended family members. Examples of these factors might include poor discipline skills on the part of the parents or teachers, marital discord, parental psychiatric illness, parental substance use, poor monitoring and supervision arrangements, reinforcement of problem behaviour by peers, a neighbourhood culture that condones or encourages antisocial values and behaviour, low commitment to education, a chaotic school environment, poor parent–school communication, or financial stresses experienced by the parent or principal carer.

By identifying the 'fit' between the problems and the broader systemic context, MST workers are defining both the targets of intervention and the indicators of whether the measures undertaken have been effective. A therapeutic strategy should produce observable results in the problem behaviour; if it does not, the strategy should be revised. In other words, a positive change in the young person's behaviour, for example improved school attendance or regularly being at home by curfew, is used as an indication that the intervention is on the right track, for example the parent contacting the school daily or implementing a curfew 'contract' with the young person. Failure to achieve positive changes requires a reassessment of the 'fit' and plainly indicates the need to try a new approach. The MST team is ultimately responsible for overcoming barriers to change. Language such as 'sabotage,' 'resistance,' and 'intractable problems', which imply that the members of the family are to blame, is eschewed in favour of a perspective that focuses on challenges and strengths. Similarly diagnostic labels of any type are discouraged in favour of understanding behaviour, for instance by using sequential analysis. Violent behaviour by the young person in the home would be seen as an outcome of a particular sequence of events rather than the behaviour exemplifying a conduct disorder in the young person.

MST is designed to be an intense but short-term involvement, which is meant to result in the generalization of treatment gains over the long-term. Ideally, the frequency and duration of contacts will decrease over time, being intense in the beginning but lessening as improvements are observed. No therapeutic intervention can last forever, so the ultimate goal is to empower the parent to continue with the strategies and interventions that were successful. The clearly-articulated definition of success permits objective definition of when the case can be closed. This success occurs when there is evidence that an overarching goal for the treatment has been achieved—for instance police and youth offending records showing that the young person has not offended for a set period of time, usually three months. In the case report below, Jacqueline Cannon articulates the structure of MST treatment, as well as giving an account of the process.

## THE EVIDENCE BASE FOR MST

Several randomized and quasi-experimental studies of MST have been conducted in the United States—in Missouri, South Carolina, and Texas, and others are now underway (Henggeler et al., 1993; Borduin et al., 1995; Schaeffer & Borduin, 2005). MST has been shown to reduce the rates of criminal activity (officially recorded and self-reported) and time spent in custody. The MST approach is also successful at engaging and retaining families in treatment and encouraging completion of substance abuse programmes. It can also result in improvements in family functioning and cohesion. In addition, MST has been shown to be highly cost-effective. A study in 1998 by the Washington State Institute for Public Policy, rated MST as the most cost-effective of the 16 programmes analysed. After subtracting the cost of the MST intervention itself, there was an average saving of $7881 (US) per young person for services associated with criminal behaviour, such as incarceration. In addition, the reduction in crime was associated with $13 982 in savings to potential victims. The study, called *Watching the Bottom Line*, is available on their web site (www.wa.gov/wsipp/reports/bline.html).

These results are notable in a field where successes are few and far between, but especially remarkable because MST has been effective in inner city urban areas, among young people with serious criminal records, young people identified as at high risk of reoffending, and among economically marginal families and those with long histories of unsuccessful interventions. However, we cannot simply assume that the success in the US will automatically be replicated in England and in other places outside the US. The team from the Family Services Research Center at the Medical University of South Carolina found that initially MST transferred with poor results to other sites in the USA (Henggeler et al., 1997). This prompted them to set up a system of licensing, training, ongoing support, and monitoring of adherence, to ensure that new teams adhered to the MST model of treatment, which they identified as the strongest predictor of success.

The largest study ever carried out outside the USA, in Canada, did not replicate the results obtained in earlier randomized controlled trials carried out by the developers of MST in the USA. We therefore needed to carry out a clinical trial in the UK to determine if the use of MST with serious young offenders would produce better outcomes than the services and interventions already available in a typical YOS with inner city characteristics. Since 1997 there has been an enormous investment in community-based interventions by the Youth Justice Board. We cannot assume that MST will have superior outcomes. Hence a clinical trial of this clinically exciting intervention is appropriate and timely.

## OUR EXPERIENCE THUS FAR

The following are some preliminary observations after only two years of work.

### MST Cannot be Done 'on the Cheap'

MST is a demanding treatment. The MST therapist usually works on her/his own, sometimes works unsocial hours, with challenging families in discouraging circumstances, and usually encounters a high degree of negativity from family members at the start of an intervention. The parents in these families can feel like failures;

they can feel emotionally burned out in their efforts to bring up their child; they can also feel cynical about the promises of a new service like MST when they feel let down by so many other services that have failed them, and in some instances have made them feel that they are 'bad' parents. These are ingredients for poor engagement, MST therapist disillusionment, 'burn out', and high staff turnover. As well as a strong support structure, ensuring that the therapist is well remunerated is a key to staff retention. The Brandon Centre pays MST therapists 25% above the normal spine point they would have been on. After two years our team remained intact, although recently two of the three therapists resigned—one for personal reasons and the other for professional reasons. Both have now been replaced. The stability of the team in the first two years of the study was helpful for the conduct of the trial since it meant that therapists that became increasingly experienced and competent were delivering MST.

## MST Therapists Require a High Level of Relevant Clinical Skills and Experience

The three therapists that we originally appointed are counselling psychologists, although none have yet achieved chartered status with the British Psychological Society (BPS). Two of them worked with disaffected families of antisocial young people before being recruited to the MST team. The third had worked in a residential home for children and adolescents who were from very difficult backgrounds and whose behaviour was highly volatile. One of the team had also previously been a teacher and another had experience of working in a Youth Offending Team. In addition to their counselling psychology training, additional training courses undertaken before becoming MST therapists have given them basic clinical skills in family therapy, solution-focused, and cognitive-behaviour techniques such as behaviour contracts and reinforcement strategies. Training opportunities arranged by the MST supervisor in addition to the quarterly MST booster trainings have further augmented clinical skills. In a personal communication, Dr Alan Leshcied who was one of the directors of the Canadian MST trial, observed that therapists emerge from training in and experience of delivering MST with greatly enhanced skills in working with difficult-to-treat families. I would certainly concur with this observation.

   The project has also been particularly fortunate in being able to appoint a supervisor, Charles Wells, who is a British Psychological Society chartered counselling psychologist, and who previously worked with the director of the Brandon Centre in piloting a manualized intervention for persistent young offenders. This trial enabled a solid partnership to be built up between the Brandon Centre and Haringey and Camden YOSs, which included Charles being seconded two days per week to Haringey YOS as their psychologist—a position that he still occupies one day per week. In summary this recruitment gave the MST project someone with a high degree of experience in working therapeutically with persistent young offenders, with a sound knowledge about working in the youth justice system, and with existing strong relationships with potential partners in the study, all of which have smoothed the implementation of the trial and MST.

## MST is Not Just About Engagement; it is About Treatment

There is a vogue among some CAMHS professionals when trying out new initiatives, even when the effects of treatment are unknown or ineffective, to commend themselves for having achieved engagement with high-risk groups that under normal circumstances would rarely engage. Engagement is of course fundamental to MST case work but it is only the 'hors d'oeuvre to the main course', which is delivering evidence-based interventions that are empirically tracked for their effectiveness in achieving MST goals. It is this commitment to empirically-based treatments and the analytical processes tracking their impact that are outstanding features of the MST model, as well as its ability to facilitate engagement with difficult-to-treat families.

## Transferability

Our experience thus far, and that of Cambridgeshire YOS, which has been delivering MST over the last three years as part of the Youth Justice Board's intensive surveillance and supervision programme, suggests that, notwithstanding the outcome of the Brandon Centre clinical trial, with modification MST is transferable to the English context. MST was developed in a culture that does not offer the universal level of free services that we are used to in the UK. National standards for youth justice mean that a YOS now has a rich menu of assessments and interventions for the young offender and her/his parent at its disposal. They can include victim reparation, analysis of offending behaviour, group-based anger management, assessment and treatment for drug and alcohol abuse, assessment of education or employment needs, physical health and mental health needs and, if necessary, making appropriate arrangements for these to be met, and help with parenting on a voluntary or compulsory basis as a result of a parenting order. The gap that MST fills is in the direct work with the parent in the family home and the pursuit of therapeutic goals in the young person's ecology, which are not taken on by the YOS social worker. These goals may indeed be similar to those of the YOS, for instance establishing the young person's involvement in the education system, greater involvement in activities that are prosocial and exclude the delinquent peer group in favour of relationships with pro-social young people, or elimination of substance abuse. The difference lies in their implementation. For example, the YOS education worker may make an arrangement for the young person to re-enter school, with the expectation that the parent and the young person will make this happen; however the parent may be unable to follow through the arrangement for a variety of reasons. The MST therapist identifies the barriers and finds ways of overcoming them. The remit of the MST therapist will then be to equip the parent with whatever strategies they need to get their child to attend school; for instance a strategy that may involve improved communication by the parent with the school to cut down the scope for truancy, or a strategy for ensuring that the young person is up and ready on time to attend school in the morning, including working out an arrangement with a close relative who is willing to help if the parent has to go to work and cannot monitor their child. Thus far, our experience is that the MST intervention complements the work of the YOS social worker.

However, the disadvantage of MST dovetailing with YOS interventions is that treatment integrity may be threatened. Unfortunately, some standard youth justice interventions currently in use not only do not have an evidence-base, but can also actually promote rather than attenuate offending behaviour. For example, group programmes for young offenders tend to be favoured within the youth justice system. There is research evidence that demonstrates conclusively that such programmes promote antisocial behaviour and delinquency. Even some benign interventions such as individual-based anger management therapy may not fit the MST model. For example, anger management programmes would tend to assume that the problem lies in the young offender. MST, while not ignoring the fact that some individuals more than others are predisposed to angry and aggressive behaviour, sees such behaviour as being context-dependent. The MST therapist would perform a sequential analysis to determine interactions that lead to the angry or aggressive behaviour and would hence recommend an intervention based on the analysis. For instance, take a difference of opinion between siblings over watching a particular TV programme that escalates despite attempts by a parent to settle the dispute, and culminates in the young offender 'trashing' the sitting room and his bedroom. Following a sequential analysis the MST therapist might identify the driver for the angry and aggressive behaviour as the absence of a household rule about watching TV, and would then work with the parent and young person to draw up a rule. The MST therapist would monitor what happens when the rule is in place to see whether disputes over TV programmes decrease.

In summary, the array of provision within the youth justice system inevitably modifies the delivery of MST, as originally intended. As intended, the MST worker would be expected to tackle in each case all aspects of what is needed to meet the overarching goals of treatment. Since this does not happen in our study, we try to ensure when delivering MST that harmful treatments are avoided as much as possible. Another difference between here and the USA in the delivery of MST is that the workload of the English MST therapist appears to be lower than that of their American counterpart, probably because the YOS is mandated to supply certain interventions. Our colleagues in Cambridge and ourselves have also found that the demand on the MST therapist to work with families during unsocial hours is less than we were led to expect. Nevertheless, the expectation that the MST therapist will be on call 24 hours a day and seven days a week conditions the MST therapist to be flexible in their engagement with families.

The following case treated in the clinical trial is a good example of MST in practice. JC was responsible for delivering treatment.

## CASE EXAMPLE: BEN

Ben was 13 when he was referred to the MST trial. He had been a persistent offender from the age of 12 and was well-known to the local police. At the time of referral his convictions included criminal damage, theft, taking and driving away, and breaches of his supervision orders. Ben was also referred for his non-compliance at home: he stayed out late, only returning home in the early morning. Ben's mother, Doreen, found it difficult to set any limits around this behaviour. Ben had been out of school for over a year. He spent much of his time on the street with deviant peers, regularly using cannabis. He also had a history of solvent abuse.

When I started working with this family it was apparent that both Doreen and Ben were frustrated with their situation. They appeared very despondent, and were very apathetic about the possibility of anything changing for the better. Doreen's proposed solution was to have Ben taken into care and that would 'be the answer'.

Ben lived at home with his mother and younger brother John, who was 10. Doreen had separated from Ben's father when Ben was five and contact with the father was virtually non-existent. Also living in the area were Ben's grandmother, great-grandmother, and a great-uncle whom Ben had once had a good relationship with. This had broken down after Ben was discovered stealing from him and his family. Doreen also had a boyfriend that she had been seeing regularly for two and a half years. He did not live at the family home but stayed over on a regular basis. Doreen worked in a local school as a learning-support assistant, but intended to leave as she felt that she needed to be at home to tackle Ben's behaviour and get him back into education. Because of Ben's non-attendance at school the court had also placed Doreen on a six month parenting order, which she was attempting to adhere to.

MST treatment planning and implementation follows the analytical process defined by MST treatment principles: the first step is to consider the referral behaviour and presenting problems. As explained earlier, the problem behaviours are identified by involving all members of the family and other key participants in the young person's ecology, in Ben's case the social worker from the local YOS. The analytical process involves the MST therapist identifying the 'drivers' of the behaviour, how they are supported, and the factors that are apparent in obstructing their elimination. The therapist gathers all of this information from initial meetings with the family; additional information informs the process as and when it becomes available.

The main goal of MST assessment is to 'make sense' of the young person's behavioural problems within their systemic context, so I began by examining all of the strengths and weaknesses of Ben's systems, and identifying how they contributed to the referral behaviour and problems. Figure 4.1 shows this information. Several factors associated with Ben's delinquent and offending behaviour were identified, including low parental warmth, ineffective parenting skills, a casual attitude towards offending, Doreen's alcohol problems, negative peer influences, and unstructured days because of being out of education. However, several strengths were also identified that might help improve Ben's behaviour, including his wish to get on better with his family, his previous skills at mathematics at school that showed some ability, and good support from other agencies and from the extended family in the local area.

To understand the 'fit' between the identified problems and their broader systemic context, and to develop hypotheses and design interventions in accordance with the MST analytical process, I developed a 'fit circle' with the family (see Figure 4.2). This shows the drivers that contribute to the target behaviour.

The above 'fit circle' shows the factors that were directly driving Ben's delinquent behaviour. The factors outlined in bold were identified as significantly contributing

| Systemic strengths | Systemic weaknesses/needs |
|---|---|
| **Individual:** <br><br>• Popular with peer group <br><br>• Admits drug use <br><br>• Honest about his behaviour <br><br>• Would like to get on better with family | **Individual:** <br><br>• Appears low and apathetic <br><br>• Has a casual attitude towards offending <br><br>• Does have difficulty engageing with others <br><br>• Drug use includes regular use of cannabis and some solvent abuse <br><br>• Appears quite impulsive and does not think through consequences <br><br>• Very high risk of offending |
| **Family:** <br><br>• Mum is honest about her parenting skills and other problems <br><br>• Mum has support through several agencies <br><br>• Mum is attempting to keep to her parenting order and has volunteered herself to MST <br><br>• Half-sister in Manchester who Ben did have a relationship with, although not seen for over a year | **Family:** <br><br>• Mum has alcohol problem <br><br>• Ben has stolen from the family, including mum, Jack (boyfriend), and Nan <br><br>• Low parental warmth towards Ben; Mum has asked that he be taken into care and feels this is the answer <br><br>• Dad is not in the area and Ben has reported that he does not like him <br><br>• History of domestic violence and financial hardship <br><br>• Mum allows Ben to smoke cannabis at home |

**Figure 4.1** Initial contact sheet showing strengths and needs of each system. MST, multi-systemic therapy; SEN, special educational needs

| **School:** | **School:** |
|---|---|
| • Ben is good at Maths<br><br>• Good marks in SATS exams<br><br>• Education welfare involved with family; Ben recognized as special educational needs because of behaviour and on stage three in SEN statement procedure | • Ben has not attended school regularly for over 12 months and is now awaiting new school<br><br>• Mum on court parenting order because of Ben's non-attendance<br><br>• Ben reports that he will not attend school He could not tell me one positive thing about school and does not appear to be able to engage |
| **Peers:** | **Peers:** |
| • Ben reports that his friends do not influence him | • All of Ben's friends are offenders and well known to police<br><br>• Peers are all older than Ben<br><br>• Mum and Ben very friendly with well-known offending family<br><br>• No pro-social peers at all |
| **Community:** | **Community:** |
| • Borough has good facilities for young people<br><br>• Agency involvement with family | • Family was moved from previous address because of Ben's antisocial behaviour<br><br>• Police know Ben and his peers |

**Figure 4.1**  *Continued*

to this behaviour and were therefore given priority in developing a plan for intervention. I also collected the desired outcomes from all the key participants, i.e. the changes that Doreen, Ben, and his YOS social worker wanted MST to bring about. The desired outcomes were:

1. For Doreen:
   (a) Ben to attend school;

(b) Ben to be at home at a reasonable time and stay in; and
(c) Ben to respect the family and the family home.
2. For Ben:
   (a) to not have to attend the YOS anymore; and
   (b) to get on better with the family.
3. For the YOS social worker:
   (a) Ben to be back in education;
   (b) Ben not to re-offend;
   (c) Ben to build his self-esteem;
   (d) Ben to have some idea of family relationships; and
   (e) Ben to be able to step into others' shoes, i.e. victims of crime.

The desired outcomes are then incorporated as the overarching goals, which set the overall general treatment direction. These establish success criteria and are clearly connected to Ben's referral behaviour. The overarching goals were:

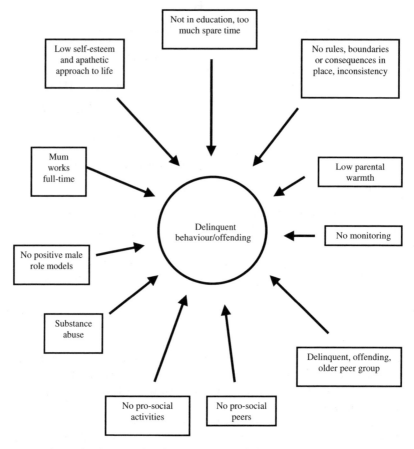

**Figure 4.2**   A fit circle showing the drivers of Ben's delinquent and offending behaviour

1. Ben to comply with his curfew time each evening, as evidenced by parent report and police report of any further arrests;
2. Ben to be attending school at least three days per week, as evidenced by school attendance reports and mum;
3. Ben to comply with household rules put in place, as evidenced by parental reports; and
4. Ben not to offend for three months, as evidenced by police and YOS reports.

Following the MST analytical process, the next step is to design interventions to address the prioritized drivers. Early interventions in this case addressed the driver of inconsistent rules and consequences through establishing the rules that Doreen would like in the house. Doreen initially decided that she would like to make a rule about not smoking cannabis at home. I explored different scenarios for enforcing the rule and what might happen and any effective rewards and consequences. This was a daunting prospect for Doreen as in the past Ben had not complied with rules she had set. She now felt that Ben was the problem and setting rules would have no effect on his behaviour. Doreen's friends agreed with her point of view that she 'didn't have to live like this', and that custody or care was the only solution for Ben's behaviour.

Doreen's cognitions were proving a barrier to establishing any rules and it became apparent that she felt so negatively about Ben and his behaviour that she could not see any point in trying. She was also very anxious about being an adequate mother to Ben. Generally she felt overwhelmed, and unable to control his behaviour. There were frequent rows at home with Ben doing increasingly more of what he wanted and Doreen being unable to set and impose limits to stop him. She was therefore left feeling unable to cope and felt little warmth towards Ben.

Barriers to interventions in MST require a reassessment of the original fit and a readjustment of the focus. In this case, I decided that the low warmth between Doreen and Ben needed to be addressed first before other interventions could be successful.

A significant factor in the deterioration of their relationship was Doreen's lack of trust. Ben and his friends had frequently stolen her, and her partner's, belongings, so she now locked Ben out of the house when she was not at home. Ben felt rejected and appeared quite depressed and apathetic.

To address this barrier I focused on one of the strengths I had noticed in the family—that Doreen was still committed to helping Ben, despite protests to the contrary and her wish that he would be taken into care. I began to look at interventions that would address low warmth and lack of trust. I started by addressing Doreen's concerns about Ben being at home on his own when she was not there. As already discussed, her main concern was Ben and his friends being in the home. I also helped her see how her current strategy of putting Ben out onto the streets had a direct causal effect of giving him the opportunity to reoffend.

At this stage I was meeting Doreen two to three times a week to keep momentum going as part of the process of helping her to engage with MST, since she was still unsure about the benefits of our work. Often these meetings included Ben, with the intention of helping them both to think about a problem and possible solutions together.

This process revealed that Doreen and Ben actually had a similar goal: that Ben should be able to spend time at home without the threat of friends stealing his mother's belongings. This was a turning point as it helped Doreen accept that Ben's motives were not malicious.

The next step towards this goal was to suggest a practical solution for keeping belongings safe in the house. Doreen agreed to put a lock on her bedroom door. I helped by providing a drill and tools and she and I fitted the lock to her door. This intervention had a positive effect on both Doreen and Ben. She felt that she did not have to lose her social life by being at home and having to constantly monitor Ben as she could now leave him in the house when she went out, knowing that any valuables were locked away. Ben felt he could lock food and other 'goodies' away so his friends would not take them when they were in the house. The successful implementation of this intervention meant that Doreen could begin to trust Ben again, and she felt warmer towards him. They increased the time spent in each other's company—something Ben had been wanting for a long time.

As part of the MST process I was also working on other drivers that were contributing to his delinquency, in particular his long-standing absence from school. There was an offer of a place at a local school, so Doreen and I considered how to support Ben in attending. Doreen was accountable for ensuring that Ben attended school, but she needed support for this to happen. After brainstorming ideas, Doreen agreed to a behavioural contract that would reward Ben for attending school. Figure 4.3 shows the behavioural contract that was constructed. Doreen suggested that Ben's Nan could get involved by rewarding Ben with pocket money for each day he attended the unit, therefore involving other people in Ben's ecology and family network.

Doreen spoke to her mother, who agreed to her role as part of the contract, and I too then met up with her to go through the written contract and to get her permission to monitor its success and to give encouragement. Ben was also involved in drafting the contract and his rewards. Although he seemed indifferent when he was shown a copy of the contract, it became apparent later that he was pleased to be rewarded and he had informed his teacher of the money he could earn if he attended school daily.

Ben began to attend a school re-integration unit on his own and was complying with the contract. I supported Doreen and his grandmother in maintaining the rewards and encouraging Ben each day to attend the unit. To increase the link between home and school I met with the teachers who agreed to telephone Doreen on a daily basis to inform her of Ben's attendance, thus keeping the contract up to date on a regular basis. Once this link was established, after two weeks Doreen was encouraged to take on the task of telephoning the teachers to check Ben's attendance, thus increasing her sense of responsibility and confidence.

With these strategies working successfully, my task was now to help Doreen to maintain these changes and to identify with her possible future drivers of Ben re-engaging in offending behaviour. Without anticipating future pitfalls the work that had been done could be easily sabotaged. One area of risk was the forthcoming summer holiday period. Unless activities could be found for Ben he would be likely to spend his time aimlessly on the streets and gravitate back to the delinquent peers

**Rule:**

Starting on the 21st May 2004, Ben will attend the Oak Unit. Ben will attend

Monday, Tuesday and Wednesday from 9.30 AM until 3.30 PM. Mum will

accompany Ben on the bus to ensure he gets into class until she decides otherwise.

Ben will attend everyday he is required to; he will attend each class unless there is a

medical emergency. Mum will determine this and will contact the unit each week to

monitor Ben's attendance.

**Reward:**

If Ben attends Oak all day for the three days he is required to attend, Nan will put

£2.00 into a holiday savings account each week. Nan will then tell Ben at the end of

the week how much his holiday money is adding up.

If Ben attends Oak everyday for two weeks without missing a class or a day, mum

will put £2.00 away as a bonus towards an item Ben wants, e.g. a baseball cap.

**Consequence:**

If Ben misses any class or day without good reason e.g. medical emergency that is

determined by mum, then Nan will not pay any money into his savings that week.

**Signed ............................ Mum**

**Signed ............................ Ben**

**Figure 4.3**   School attendance contract

he had been spending most of his time with until MST came on the scene. Doreen
gathered information on possible summer activities for Ben to enable his time to
be more structured. Doreen was also thinking about how she could make her life
more worthwhile and interesting and looked into college courses.

These were significant and positive changes in this family. Doreen felt more
capable of parenting Ben and could see success in her efforts; Ben attended school
99% of the required time in his first term. Doreen reduced her time away from her
children and the family was spending more time together. A curfew contract was
set up that demonstrated to Doreen that she could set limits and stick to them.
Reports on Ben from various sources were that Ben was recognizing the changes
around him and responding positively to his mother's warmth, and to the boundaries and limits being put in place.

The outcome of this MST intervention was that all of the overarching goals that had been set to provide the direction for treatment had been met. Ben was complying with his curfew times, he was attending the education unit, and his attendance was increasing to five days per week. His grandmother also agreed to increase his rewards as his attendance improved. This was maintaining the family network support that is so crucial to the success of a MST intervention. Doreen allowed Ben to have a key to the house, the use of which was guided by rules, and Ben was complying with them. Most importantly police and YOS reports confirmed that Ben had not offended in the last three months, thus meeting a major goal of treatment.

I have followed up the family six months after the termination of treatment and the success of the intervention is being maintained. Although Ben did not re-integrate back into full-time mainstream education, Doreen sought out courses that he could attend to continue his education on a vocational basis. Doreen is attending a college course to improve her qualifications and improve future work prospects, and she appears more confident and happy. Doreen and Ben's relationship continues to be positive and Ben has not reoffended. The ultimate goal of MST's involvement has been reached—Doreen has gained the skills and confidence that enable her to parent effectively and to continue with the strategies and interventions that she learned during this involvement.


## MST FURTHER READING

### American Publications

Borduin, C. M. (1994). Innovative models of treatment and service delivery in the juvenile justice system. *Journal of Clinical Child Psychology, 23*, 19–25.

Borduin, C. M., et al. (1995). Multisystemic treatment of serious juvenile offenders: Long-term prevention of criminality and violence. *Journal of Consulting & Clinical Psychology, 63*, 569–578.

Borduin, C. M., Henggeler, S. W., Blaske, D. M., & Stein, R. (1990). Multisystemic treatment of adolescent sexual offenders. *International Journal of Offender Therapy & Comparative Criminology, 34*, 105–113.

Brondino, M. J., et al. (1997). Multisystemic therapy and the ethnic minority client: Culturally responsive and clinically effective. In D. K. Wilson, J. R. Rodrigue, & W. C. Taylor (Eds.), *Health-promoting and Health-compromising Behaviors Among Minority Adolescents: Application and Practice in Health Psychology* (pp. 229–250). Washington, DC: American Psychological Association.

Brunk, M., Henggeler, S. W., & Whelan, J. P. (1987). A comparison of multisystemic therapy and parent training in the brief treatment of child abuse and neglect. *Journal of Consulting and Clinical Psychology, 55*, 311–318.

Henggeler, S. W. (1989). *Delinquency in Adolescence*. Newbury Park, CA: Sage.

Henggeler, S. W. (1997). Treating serious antisocial behavior in young person: The MST approach. *OJJDP Juvenile Justice Bulletin*.

Henggeler, S. W., & Borduin, C. M. (1990). *Family Therapy and Beyond: A Multisystemic Approach to Treating the Behavior Problems of Children and Adolescents*. Pacific Grove, CA: Brooks/Cole.

Henggeler, S. W., & Borduin, C. M. (1995). Multi-systemic treatment of serious juvenile offenders and their families. In I. M. Schwartz, & P. AuClaire (Eds.), *Home-Based Services for Troubled Children*. Lincoln, NB: University of Nebraska Press.

Henggeler, S. W., Borduin, C. M., Melton, G. B., Mann, B. J., Smith, L., Hall, J. A., Cone, L., & Fucci, B. R. (1991). Effects of multisystemic therapy on drug use and abuse in serious juvenile offenders: A progress report from two outcome studies. *Family Dynamics of Addiction Quarterly, 1,* 40–51.

Henggeler, S. W., Borduin, C. M., & Mann, B. J. (1993). Advances in family therapy: Empirical foundations. *Advances in Clinical Child Psychology, 15,* 207–241.

Henggeler, S. W., Melton, G. B., Brondino, M. J., Scherer, D. G., & Hanley, J. H. (1997). Multisystemic therapy with violent and chronic juvenile offenders and their families: The role of treatment fidelity in successful dissemination. *Journal of Consulting and Clinical Psychology, 65,* 821–833.

Henggeler, S. W., Melton, G. B., & Smith, L. A. (1992). Family preservation using multisystemic therapy: An effective alternative to incarcerating serious juvenile offenders. *Journal of Consulting and Clinical Psychology, 60,* 953–961.

Henggeler, S. W., Melton, G. B., Smith, L. A., Schoenwald, S. K., & Hanley, J. H. (1993). Family preservation using multisystemic treatment: Long-term Follow-up to a clinical trial with serious juvenile offenders. *Journal of Child & Family Studies, 2,* 283–293.

Henggeler, S. W., Pickrel, S. G., Brondino, M. J., & Crouch, J. L. (1996). Eliminating (almost) treatment dropout of substance abuse or dependent delinquents through home-based multisystemic therapy. *American Journal of Psychiatry, 153,* 427–428.

Henggeler, S. W., Rodick, J. D., Borduin, C. M., Hanson, C. L., Watson, S. M., & Urey, J. R. (1986). Multisystemic treatment of juvenile offenders: Effects on adolescent behavior and family interactions. *Developmental Psychology, 22,* 132–141.

Henggeler, S. W., Schoenwald, S. K, Borduin, C. M., Rowland, M. D. & Cunningham, P. B. (1998). *Multisystemic Treatment of Antisocial Behavior in Children and Adolescents.* New York, NY: Guilford.

Henggeler, S. W., Schoenwald, S. K., & Pickrel, S. G. (1995). Multisystemic therapy: Bridging the gap between university—and community-based treatment. *Journal of Consulting and Clinical Psychology, 63,* 709–717.

Henggeler, S. W., Schoenwald, S. K., Pickrel, S. G., Brondino, M. J., Borduin, C. M., & Hall, J. A. (1994). *Treatment Manual for Family Preservation Using Multisystemic Therapy.* Columbia, SC: South Carolina Health and Human Services Finance Commission.

Henggeler, S. W., et al. (1994). The contribution of treatment outcome research to the reform of children's mental health services: Multisystemic therapy as an example. *Journal of Mental Health Administration, 21,* 229–239.

Henggeler, S. W., et al. (1996). Multisystemic therapy: An effective violence prevention approach for serious juvenile offenders. *Journal of Adolescence, 19,* 47–61.

Huey, S. J., et al. (2000). Mechanisms of change in Multisystemic Therapy; Reducing delinquent behaviour through therapist adherence and improved family and peer functioning. *Journal of Consulting and Clinical Psychology, 68,* 451–467.

Kazdin, A. E. (1997). Practitioner review: Psychosocial treatments for conduct disorder in children. *Journal of Child Psychology and Psychiatry, 38,* 161–178.

Mann, B. J., et al. (1990). An investigation of systemic conceptualizations of parent-child coalitions and symptom change. *Journal of Consulting and Clinical Psychology, 58,* 336–344.

Santos, A. B., et al. (1995). Research on field-based services. Models for reform in the delivery of mental health care to populations with complex clinical problems. *American Journal of Psychiatry, 152,* 1111–1123.

Scherer, D. G., et al. (1994). Multisystemic family preservation therapy: Preliminary findings from a study of rural and minority serious adolescent offenders. *Journal of Emotional & Behavioral Disorders, 2,* 198–206.

Schaeffer, C. M., & Borduin, C. M. (2005). Long-term follow-up to a randomized clinical trial of multisystemic therapy with serious and violent juvenile offenders. *Journal of Consulting and Clinical Psychology, 73,* 445–453.

Schoenwald, S. K., Ward, D. M., Henggeler, S. W., Pickrel, S. G., & Patel, H. (1996). MST treatment of substance abusing or dependent adolescent offenders: Costs of reducing incarceration, inpatient, and residential placement. *Journal of Child and Family Studies*, *4*, 431–444.

Sondheimer, D. L., Schoenwald, S. K., & Rowland, M. D. (1994). Alternatives to the hospitalization of young person with a serious emotional disturbance. *Journal of Clinical Child Psychiatry*, *23*, 7–12.

Tolan, P. H., Guerra, N. G., & Kendall, P. C. (1995). A developmental-ecological perspective on antisocial behavior in children and adolescents: Toward a unified risk and intervention framework. *Journal of Consulting and Clinical Psychology*, *63*, 579–584.

## Canadian Publications

Leschied, A. W., & Cunningham, A. (1998). Alternatives to custody for high-risk young offenders: Application of the multisystemic approach in Canada. *European Journal on Criminal Policy and Research*, *6*, 545–560.

Leschied, A. W., & Cunningham, A. (1999). Clinical trials of multisystemic therapy in Ontario: Rationale and current status of a community-based alternative for high-risk young offenders. *Forum on Corrections Research*, *11*(2), 25–29.

## Meta-analytic and Systematic Reviews

Curtis, N. M., Ronan, K. R., & Borduin, C. M. (2004). Multisystemic Treatment: A Meta-analysis of Outcome Studies, *Journal of Family Psychology*, *18*(3), 411–419.

Hengeller, S. W. (2004). Decreasing Effect Sizes for Effectiveness Studies-Implications for the Transport of Evidence-Based Treatments: Comment on Curtis, Ronin & Borduin. *Journal of Family Psychology*, *18*(3), 420–423.

Hengeller, S. W. (2006). Methodological critique and meta-analysis as Trojan horse. Children and Youth Services, *28*, 447–457.

Littell, J. H. (2005). Lessons from a systematic review of the effects of multisystemic therapy. *Children and Youth Services Review*, *27*, 445–463.

Littell, J. H., Popa, M., & Forsythe, B. (2005). Multisystemic Therapy for social, emotional, and behavioural problems in youth aged 10–17 (Review). The *Cochrane Library*, *Issue 3*.

Littell, J. H. (2006). The case for Multisystemic Therapy: Evidence or orthodoxy. *Children and Youth Services Review*, *28*, 458–472.

# CHAPTER 5

# Barefoot Practitioners: A Proposal for a Manualized, Home-based, Adolescent Crisis Intervention Project

Eia Asen and Dickon Bevington

## INTRODUCTION

Adolescence is a transitional area of experience, and there are many different and often opposing definitions of this developmental stage. Cultures, neurosciences, psychiatry, psychology, and social sciences, offer a wide range of definitions for adolescence, ranging from a biologically-determined process, through to a social-constructionist denial of its existence per se. In keeping with anthropological theories about transitional or liminal states of being, adolescence across all societies is hedged with exclusionary rules and rituals (Schlegel & Barry, 1991). Thus, society's stance towards adolescence is, at best, ambivalent, and it is reasonable to view adolescents in psychiatric crisis as a marginalized, excluded, and hard-to-reach group.

Any clinician involved in managing adolescents in crisis will be familiar with the enormous difficulties of finding appropriate services to contain the young person. Hospital admission is frequently considered because no other realistic alternatives exist. However, it is generally very difficult to find a hospital bed for an acute admission. Many adolescent units will not admit a teenager in crisis and this results in them either being inappropriately placed in adult wards or being admitted to private hospitals, which are often far away from where the young person lives and with few, if any, links to local services. NHS adolescent units are also often geographically distant from the young person's home, making it difficult to maintain regular contact between the young person and their family, and between family/local networks and the inpatient therapeutic team.

Hospitalization may help to contain the immediate crisis, but after discharge relapses are not infrequent, particularly when the teams treating the young persons

*Reaching the Hard to Reach: Evidence-based Funding Priorities for Intervention and Research.* Edited by G. Baruch, P. Fonagy and D. Robins. © 2007 John Wiley & Sons Ltd.

in crisis are disconnected from the teams into whose care they are discharged. Families often experience the admission of their child as a profound blow to their perceived self-efficacy in managing their own child, and this can make discharge problematic. Changes achieved within the individual during admission may not be supported by complementary changes in the local systemic context. Furthermore, there are often arguments between adult and adolescent services as to who should take responsibility. The arrangement of mental health services into CAMH and adult services has created a huge potential gap between the two for the mentally ill adolescent to fall into. It is perhaps reasonable to hypothesize that this arrangement of services speaks of society's ambivalence towards adolescence, resulting in our target population becoming ever harder to reach.

Young persons in crisis and their families—particularly in the inpatient setting— are attended to by numerous different mental health professionals who may have fragmented clinical skills and competencies. Families and young people are often therefore involved with multiple conversations with different professionals who, in keeping with their own professional discipline, may frame the problem(s) and their proposed solutions using very different languages. This 'Tower of Babel' experience places the responsibility of integrating multiple models and modalities of treatment upon the young person and the family; something that research and academic developments over the past hundred years have as yet failed to achieve.

In this chapter we propose an innovative model that includes the recommendation for an entirely new form of mental health professional. Our model offers a seamless, home-based, community outreach service for acutely mentally ill adolescents and young adults, aged 14–21. Such individuals will be presenting in acute crisis with psychosis, suicidal depression, serious eating disorder, severe obsessive– compulsive disorder, and acute symptoms related to emergent (borderline) personality disorder. We envisage referrals to the team as representing a potential alternative to acute hospitalization—although we acknowledge the occasional need for such a response—and the overarching aim is to strengthen the existing networks, rather than to replace them.

We also recognize that we work in a world with (very) limited resources, and it is unreasonable to expect this to change in the foreseeable future. Whatever the merits or otherwise of having a range of highly-trained (and expensive) specialists available to the young person and family, pursuing this as a goal in the current climate of staffing shortages unwittingly serves an exclusionary agenda.

We emphasize that the model we propose is based on established evidence-based treatments in a variety of modalities. What is innovative is the manner in which these are integrated, and the manner in which they are delivered. The intervention and the training for the workers have both been manualized but await a pilot project to put them into practice.

The work of manualizing the intervention and the training has been part of a project that we have shared with Professor Peter Fonagy and Dr Mary Target (University College London and the Anna Freud Centre), and Rabia Malik and Neil Dawson (Marlborough Family Service), and we acknowledge their contribution to the thoughts presented herein.

# FROM MULTIPLE MODELS TO A MULTI-MODAL APPROACH

The interventions we outline below are carried out by mental health professionals who have received special training in delivering 'multi-modal' rather than fragmented 'discipline-oriented' interventions. These 'barefoot practitioners' are able to respond rapidly, providing intensive and time-limited (three months) work 'on the ground', which is integrated with local services and facilities. A major aim is to empower the family to contain the adolescent and carers. Ex-service users are centrally involved in the work. In order to maintain the young person's educational and social network, a day setting—the education centre—allows the adolescent to have an educational (school, higher education) focus, as well as providing a context where other service users and families can exchange ideas and learn from each other.

The interventions are mainly delivered, in any one case, by two specially-trained mental health workers, recruited primarily from nursing, occupational therapy, social work, and psychology backgrounds. Reducing the number of professionals interfacing with the young person and their family is an explicit aim within the proposed model. The rationale for this is to reduce the potential for inter-professional splits and to offer greater opportunities for developing security in the therapeutic relationship, which in turn facilitates the activation of secure internal working models of attachment. Implicit in the proposed model is a significant increase in the emphasis on supervisory structures to support the 'barefoot practitioners' in what are, predictably, stressful situations. These mental health professionals are formally trained prior to participating in the service, as well as participating in a 'top-up' programme in the form of ongoing supervision and in-service training.

Whatever the intra-personal predisposing or precipitating factors (genetic, constitutional, biochemical, early traumatic), adolescent psychiatric crises are assumed to occur in relation to developmental/transitional processes specific to adolescence. These developmental processes can be characterized as a set of tasks in the following domains:

1. **Physical:** The main changes associated with puberty are driven by increased levels of gonadal hormones, which trigger associated brain/behaviour changes and the development of secondary sexual characteristics. The changes occurring to brain function are as follows:
   (a) An acceleration of synaptic pruning, facilitating and accelerating use-dependent iterative changes in brain connectivity.
   (b) Changes within the social information processing network, specifically the relative lag (early puberty) of the cognitive-regulatory node compared to the detection and affective nodes (Monk et al., 2003; Nelson, Leibenluft, McClure & Pine, 2005).
   (c) These are followed (late puberty) by increasing frontal lobe activity and corresponding decreases in impulsivity and increasing capacity for advanced functions, such as mentalization.
2. **Cognitive:** Adolescence sees the growing capacity for increasingly complex and abstract modes of thinking (from Piagetian 'concrete operational thought'

towards 'formal operational thought') in a systemic context, wherein the application of these capacities (academic attainment) is assessed ever more intensively. In combination with developing emotional capacities (see 3 below), these new cognitive capacities are also increasingly deployed in self-conscious theory-of-mind/mentalizing tasks to cope with an exponential increase in the social complexity of the adolescent environment.

3. **Emotional:** In step with the neurocognitive developments mentioned above, this task is the refinement of the young person's capacity for affect-regulation, and this is facilitated in a context of contingent caregiving and adequate security and containment. This in turn facilitates shifts towards a capacity for tolerating deferred gratification, and increasing capacity to tolerate the 'depressive position' (Klein, 1945), thus permitting a more integrated view of the parent as a whole object. In addition, using mentalizing function helps to negotiate a path through an increasingly complex psychosocial milieu.

4. **Identity Formation:** This task is ultimately to allow appropriate separation from the family of origin, in order to facilitate integration into the new social systems that become available in adolescence. It is highly contingent upon cultural variations, but includes the requirement to form mature ethnocultural, gender, and sexual identities.

5. **Social:** This task is to adopt adult roles in relation to work, social relationships, and leisure activities. This requires a shift from narcissistic 'gang' organizations of relationships, towards more 'adult' task-based, collaborative, group organizations. Included in this is the growing capacity to distinguish and choose between pro-social and antisocial peer groups.

It is assumed that, regardless of the internal processes that have contributed to the crisis, the call for hospitalization occurs when the family has temporarily lost its capacity to contain and/or tolerate the young person in crisis. Whilst the young person needs treatment in their own right, their emotional states can also be modulated and stabilized by enhancing the security of the various systems affecting them. It follows that interventions need not only to address the young person's condition, but that they must simultaneously effectively reinforce the family's function to face the complex challenges both from within and without the family.

A basic aim of our approach is to stop the family from being placed in the position of handing over responsibility for the young person in crisis to psychiatric teams and inpatient units. Thus the aim is to prevent hospitalization, even if the family's structure appears fairly disorganized. To contain an acutely disturbed adolescent within the family can be a difficult task and requires significant home-based input from a team of committed clinicians, well-trained in a variety of treatment modalities, who are able to provide intensive and ongoing support for the family throughout the crisis.

We have called these clinicians '**barefoot practitioners**', as they are quick and flexible, 'down-to-earth' with common-sense and natural engagement skills, as well as being trained to use a multi-modal 'tool kit' on site. In any one case interventions are mainly delivered by two of these practitioners, supported by a strong supervisory structure and working according to a manualized treatment programme. The idea of a multi-modal worker, trained specifically in a number of different approaches found to be useful for adolescents in crisis, is based on the common experience that no single approach is effective in isolation. Instead, different models and approaches, each with valuable techniques and practices, need to be integrated into a coherent multi-modal approach. It would seem that the main approaches employed in the work with adolescents in crisis are:

- individual neurobiological/pharmacological
- individual psychodynamic
- individual cognitive behavioural
- family systemic
- peer group work
- social-/community-based
- educational.

The following sections provide further information on the main ingredients of the interventions within different domains.

## Individual Neurobiological Approaches

Keyworkers require a sound understanding of the main physiological and neuro-developmental processes that underpin the changes that take place in adolescence, as well as the developmental trajectories that mental disorder in adolescence can disrupt. Physical illnesses such as epilepsy, endocrine disorders, multiple sclerosis, tumours, early dementias, or lupus, can mimic the symptoms of adolescent-onset mental illnesses. The assessment phase of the intervention ensures that appropriate history-taking, examination and investigations have been carried out to exclude such diagnoses, directed, as expected, by the psychiatrist. Barefoot practitioners are trained in the recognition of a range of sinister signs and symptoms as a further safeguard against missing significant changes in presentation that might herald such eventualities. Evidence-based pharmacological treatments, either as an adjunct or as a central plank of treatment plans, are included among the treatment options. Family systemic (enlisting the family's support of the adolescent's compliance with prescribed medication), psychoeducational and cognitive interventions to maximize treatment adherence, form an important part of the keyworker's input to interventions within this domain. Keyworker monitoring of side effects, and the facilitation of a prompt response to unwanted effects, further increases the likelihood of adherence to treatment. Keyworkers will be trained to recognize the common side effects of medications, as well as the rare, but potentially serious untoward effects, such as neuroleptic malignant syndrome.

The keyworkers are trained in adolescent aspects of substance misuse work, including an understanding of the impact of substances on pre-existing vulnerabilities and their role in the genesis, maintenance, and relapse of mental health disorders, as well as the range of physical illnesses (blood-borne viruses, local infections, etc.) associated with their use. They will have a basic understanding of the assessment for substance misuse, and of motivational, psychoeducational, and harm-minimization approaches to treatment, as well as the place of prescribing in their treatment.

## Individual Psychodynamic Approaches

The capacity to observe and think about one's own as well as other people's mental processes has been termed 'mentalization' (Fonagy, 1991; Fonagy & Target, 1997). Mentalization is the ability to think about mental states as separate from, yet potentially causing actions, and to perceive and interpret human behaviour as meaningful on the basis of intentional mental states, such as personal desires, needs, feelings, beliefs, goals, purposes, and reasons (Bateman & Fonagy, 2004). There are demonstrable and significant associations between security of attachment in the child and the levels of mentalizing function in the parent. The resulting approach—mentalization-based treatments (MBT) (Bateman & Fonagy, 2004)—focuses on the clinician establishing an attachment relationship with the patient, using the interpersonal context to help the patient to understand his mental states as intentional and real, without being overwhelmed by them. The mentalization-based approach is particularly suited to adolescents whose cognitive apparatus may not yet be mature enough, or may be too disturbed, to make use of transference-based psychodynamic approaches.

Mentalization-based treatments would be available to keyworkers, using the strong supervisory structures in place to maintain best practice. They aim to help the young person in crisis to examine the sources and causes of their distress and to promote adaptive strategies, with emphasis on mental states in the here-and-now rather than the past. A major endeavour is to help the young person to develop the capacity to take a perspective on themselves and others, and to encourage self-reflection as well as encouraging reflection about relationships.

## Individual Cognitive Behavioural Approaches

Cognitive behavioural therapies (CBT) are well-evidenced in the treatment of a range of adolescent-onset mental health disorders, such as depression, obsessional–compulsive symptoms, or phobias. Keyworkers will be trained in establishing simple CBT interventions for a range of disorders, including the use of relaxation techniques, graded exposure, and challenging distorted cognitions, using the strong supervisory structures in place to maintain best practice.

## Systemic Family Approaches

These tend to contextualize the presenting symptoms, placing them in perspective with the individual's current and past relationships with family members and significant others, as well as viewing them within specific socio-cultural settings. Systemic interventions aim to help the young person and the various family members to gain new perspectives on the crisis and acute ill health and to attach different meanings to these. They also help them to experiment with new ways of relating to one another and to jointly find pragmatic solutions to presenting problems and dilemmas. Systemic interventions target seemingly dysfunctional family interactions and communications, questioning and blocking these so as to help new and more functional transactions to emerge. A whole range of different systemic interventions have been found to be helpful, from psychoeducation-based approaches for psychotic presentations (for example, Anderson, Reiss & Hogarty, 1986; Kuipers, Leff & Lam, 1992), to depression (Jones & Asen, 2000; Klerman, Weissman, Rounsaville & Chevron, 1984) and parasuicide (Asen, 1998), anorexia nervosa (Russell, Szmukler, Dare & Eisler, 1987) and substance misuse (Stanton & Shadish, 1997).

## Evolving a Multi-systemic, Multi-family and Multi-cultural Framework, Including Educational/Vocational Input

Intensive home-based interventions are not a novelty; they have been around in different guises and under different names for many years. Multisystemic therapy (MST), for example, has focused on a specific group of adolescents, presenting with conduct disorder and delinquency, and has devised interventions to promote 'responsible behaviour' among family members, targeting sequences of behaviour within or between multiple systems, and evaluating the interventions continuously from multiple perspectives (Henggeler & Borduin, 1990, Chapter 4, this volume). It is a home-based, intensive, goal-oriented, and time-limited treatment, 'saving' young persons by 'saving' families (Nelson & Landsman, 1992). The treatment offered in this model includes individual psychotherapy and family therapy, peer-group interventions, as well as work to enhance the relationship between families and institutions or agencies. The therapists are 'generalists' rather than 'specialists', trained to meet the unique needs of each client and their families. The team is available each day for 24 hours and there is daily contact in most cases. Interestingly, the treatment outcome is regarded as being the responsibility of staff, who make maximum effort, with the family's help, to attain specific and concrete goals. MST has some impressive outcome results for adolescents that are delinquent and display conduct disorder (Henggeler, Melton, Smith, Schoenwald & Hanley, 1993), but this form of therapy has not been systematically applied to other psychological and psychiatric presentations. It is also very expensive.

Another influence informing the model of work presented in this chapter has been psychoeducational group work for relatives and carers of persons with schizophrenia (Anderson et al., 1986; Falloon et al., 1985; Goldstein et al., 1978; Kuipers et al., 1992; Leff & Vaughn, 1982; Petersen, Jeppesen, Thorup et al., 2005). Its major aim is to reduce the key relatives' levels of expressed emotion (EE), in particular, critical comments and over-involvement (Leff & Vaughn, 1985), in line with the well-documented research findings of significantly reduced relapse rates if EE levels are lowered (Leff & Vaughn, 1982). Other clinicians have also directly involved the patient in large family group meetings (Bishop, Clilverd, Cooklin & Hunt, 2002; Laqueur, Burt & Morong, 1964; McFarlane, 2002).

The major rationale for multiple family group therapy (MFGT) is the recognition that individuals and families who face similar problems can share their experiences and advise and support one another. Over recent years, MFGT has become an increasingly popular approach for the treatment and management of a whole variety of presentations and conditions, including alcohol and substance misuse, eating disorders, chronic physical illness, child abuse, and social and educational exclusion (Asen, 2002). A team based at the Marlborough Family Service first created a day unit for 'multi-problem' families (Asen et al., 1982; Cooklin, Miller & McHugh,

1983), with between six and eight families attending simultaneously for prolonged periods of time, in a 'therapeutic community' of dysfunctional families. This permitted detailed '*in vivo*' observation of family interactions and communication and of how families and their individual members addressed daily problems and managed their conflicts.

In such a day setting there is much room for cross-fertilization between families. They generally become interested in observing one another, commenting on what they see, supporting and questioning one another. With 10–20 different persons being present in MFGT, multiple ideas and perspectives get generated by all the participants and not only by clinicians. Families do indeed inspire each other and can even provide home-grown 'psychoeducation' from family to family. The group work helps them to experiment with enlarging their social networks, building mini-communities over time, with experienced 'graduate' families later joining the team to reach out to 'hard to reach' individuals and their families.

A further application of the MFGT model of 'connecting families with families' in day settings (Asen, Dawson & McHugh, 2001) is the Marlborough Family Service's unique 'Education Centre', for children age 5–16. Here not only problem pupils, excluded from mainstream schools because of severe conduct and emotional disorders, but also one of their parents (or other carers) have to attend a 'family school'. This allows parents to experience their children's educational problems first hand, whilst at the same time staff can witness how family issues are often re-enacted in an educational setting (Dawson & McHugh, 2000). The focus is not merely on the individual pupil, but on the interactions within the family, as well as between family and school and the wider system. With pupils and parents attending up to four half-days per week, this becomes a context for mutual support and reflection, and for experimentation with new ways of relating and communicating. Issues raised in multiple family groups not only relate to one family, but tend to have significant meanings for other families in the group. At times work goes on in parallel, with the pupils following their specific curricula, whilst their parents are involved in a parallel literacy programme. This creates strong bonds between the carers, which often persist long after they have been discharged from the education centre. A considerable number of service ex-user 'graduate parents', are involved as co-leaders in running mainstream school-based, multi-family groups. Here, as 'experts by experience' they help other struggling families to avoid one of their children being excluded from school. Quite a number of children take part in school-based 'buddy' projects whereby they support individual children who are encountering similar problems to those that they had once experienced themselves.

To fully understand the young person, the family, and their social ecology, their multiple cultural contexts need to be taken into account. We assume that 'culture' is a system of shared meaning and that it is not static, but always emerging and changing. In multicultural societies, cultures exist within cultures, and in hierarchical power relationships. Professional practices are rooted in culturally-constructed normative ideas about health and illness, which minority cultural groups may experience as conflicting with their values and beliefs. Practitioners, 'barefoot' or not, must hold multiple views of the 'problem' and the 'solutions' and aim to improve the ecological 'fit' between the cultural contexts in which the adolescent and family move.

Multisystemic, multi-family and multicultural practices are major ingredients of our 'barefoot practitioners' model. It is not only the clinicians who adopt a community-based 'barefoot' approach, but it is also the involvement of the young person's family and other 'experts by experience', namely individuals and their families who have had similar experiences, which distinguishes this approach from others— whatever their official names, be that 'assertive out-reach', 'crisis resolution' or 'early psychosis intervention'. However, a young person presenting with a major psychiatric crisis is a demanding and exhausting proposition for any carer(s). It is difficult to be in the presence of an acutely disturbed adolescent for 24 hours a day, over a period of weeks or longer. It is often the burden and stress of the carer that leads eventually to the young person's hospital admission. Attendance at the education/vocational centre, a day setting but not a traditional 'day hospital', provides an opportunity not only for 'time out' from the family home, but also a focus for connecting with other young persons and families. Half-day attendances in the afternoon for the young person, up to five days per week, with multi-family group work during the second part of some of these afternoons, achieves an appropriate mix of attending to the individual needs of the young person, as well as involving their families with other families and with ex-users of the service.

## Social-ecological Approaches

The social ecology of the young person (his or her peer group, the range of available opportunities for educational/vocational, leisure, employment, cultural and religious activities) is assumed to have a significant impact on the genesis, maintenance, and relapse-rate of adolescent disorders. Included in this is the young person's capacity to access such resources, which may be limited by factors such as avoidance of public transport, or fear of crowded spaces. Drawing up a needs-assessment, alongside a local database of opportunities for young people, including links with organizations such as Connexions, local sports and leisure facilities, local ethnic, cultural and religious groups, and youth groups, allows for the matching of needs with available resources in the local community. The emphasis is on restoring normative (pro-)social contact and meaningful activities, in keeping with the young person's developmental stage and capacities. These activities provide opportunities for *in vivo* monitoring of functional abilities, as well as a testing ground for newly-developed skills in self-management. In so far as they accord with the stated needs and wishes of the young person, they also provide a 'value-added' component to the intervention as a whole, which increases the likelihood of meaningful engagement.

## STRUCTURE OF THE MULTI-MODAL INTERVENTION

### Stage 1 (Intensive Phase): Multilevel Assessment

The preliminary stage of a multimodal intervention consists of a sequence of formal procedures, as follows:

1. Initial referral (telephone liaison);
2. Emergency (see within three hours), urgent (one day), or routine (one week);
3. Team discussion;
4. Consideration of safety issues, allocation of keyworkers, and urgency of response;
5. Telephone contact;
6. Introductions, clarification of what the team do, arranging contact;
7. The first meeting with family;
8. Engagement with the family, setting up contingency plans;
9. Subsequent assessment/intervention meetings;
10. Completion of assessment, initial interventions;
11. Elaborating and reviewing contingency plans;
12. Mobilizing the family network, medication; and
13. Liaison with teacher/therapists regarding induction into the education centre programme

At the point of referral, as stated earlier, we assume that whatever intrinsic problems the young person might have, the family/carers and their local network have been overwhelmed by the demands and concerns that the young person is presenting them with. A rapid response is often required, and the service is designed to allow for this. Following a clearly manualized protocol (including risk assessment protocols relevant to any outreach service), the team would make initial contact with the family (by telephone on the day of referral if possible) to begin the process of the initial multilevel assessment.

The assumption is made that from the point of initial contact the assessment forms a powerful intervention in itself, which includes the opportunity to develop engagement. What is required above all is the rapid establishment of some security and containment of the situation, in the hope that internal working models of secure attachment might thus be activated, allowing for the possibility of reflective and exploratory curiosity on the part of the young person and the family. Thus all efforts are focused initially at joining with the family as it is, rather than expecting the family to conform to expected (and often culturally-biased) norms in its mode of engaging with services. For example, at initial telephone contact (if this is possible), the worker will ask 'Whom should I speak to in order to arrange to come and talk to the family about your worries about X?' rather than assuming automatically that one or other parent is the appropriate authority.

The initial tasks are to introduce the team and to clarify their role as well as to keep expectations within appropriate limits, and to arrange the first face-to-face meeting, taking account, for instance, of which family members (and other members of the existing network) are intending or able to be present. The keyworkers will tend to work in the family's home, except when the young person attends the educational/vocational centre, which in any case is likely to occur somewhat 'downstream' from the initial multilevel assessment and engagement phase.

The multilevel assessment aims, in a structured way, to develop a coherent map of the young person's problems, vulnerabilities, strengths and resiliencies, covering all the major functional domains in which multimodal interventions may be deployed. One tool that facilitates this task of assessment is the structured, clinician-rated, adolescent module of the FACE assessment tool (functional assessment of caring environments). This offers domain-based (individual, family, social-ecology, educational, etc.) assessments that are quantifiable and sensitive to change, as well as including risk assessments. This tool also allows the highlighting of key problems that can then be reassessed after specific interventions have been applied. The capacity to provide ongoing measurement of change is a key feature of the intervention as a whole, and it is envisaged that different components of the multimodal 'toolkit' of interventions may be adapted, added, or replaced, as the available evidence-base of effectiveness grows. Moreover, using scales such as this offers to some families and young people a reassurance of the team's commitment to deploy treatments with efficacy, and of the effectiveness of their own efforts to change poorly-adaptive coping mechanisms.

An essential feature of our approach to early intervention will be the routine monitoring of outcomes. As well as FACE (see above), self-report measures from the young person (YSR), and family measures for the young person (SFBT) and for the service (your treatment and care measure) will also be utilized. The aim is to move the young person from the crisis range on these instruments to a more acceptable clinical rating.

The treatment manual allows for flexibility in the unfolding of the multilevel assessment, in recognition of the fact that different families and young people will be able to proceed at different rates. The emphasis from the beginning is on engagement, and on emphasizing the family's expertise-by-experience about the young person in question. However, in pursuit of containment, the first meeting will include in its primary tasks the formation of clear contingency plans, to be triggered in the event of further deterioration. The exercise of timetabling again emphasizes the self-efficacy of the family as well as recognizing the 'real world' aspects of family life; the keyworkers and family members work out a shared 'rota' of care and input that is calculated to be the amount likely to support the young person at home successfully.

Of course there are times when admission would be required in spite of the high intensity of available daily home-based input. Keyworkers are trained in risk assessment, which would support such judgements. In such eventualities, which should be the exception rather than the rule, the preferred solution would be for the young person to be admitted to a local 'family apartment.' This would occur along with member(s) of the family who would be expected to work alongside trained staff in managing the crisis. It is recognized that this may be difficult to arrange, especially if there is no extant adolescent unit to which such an apartment might conceivably be 'appended'. Such an arrangement, by using the support of family members, may somewhat lessen the demand for nursing, but more importantly it retains the involvement and asserts the efficacy of the existing network (family) rather than wholly replacing it by 'professionals'. Such admissions would be construed as emergency responses to crisis, and as soon as the situation was adequately contained a return home would be appropriate. Admissions in these circumstances would ideally be for days rather than weeks or months.

Trial interventions, even if these consist of something as simple as a 'reframing' of the young person's dilemma to family members, are part of the multilevel assessment. The success or failure of such early interventions guides the preparation for more substantive interventions, according to what modalities of intervention are perceived as the most likely to offer opportunities for adaptive change for the young person and the system. At a certain point in the process, psychiatric assessment and medical investigations are likely to be relevant. Medication may well be introduced, using a systemic context by involving the family for instance in 'supporting the tablets to do their job', by helping to encourage adherence in the young person.

Supervision in the team is a prominent feature in this model and through this, and team discussions, a series of priorities will be established and initial interventions started. One key to the model is the capacity to intervene simultaneously in multiple modalities and multiple domains, and to do so 'on the spot' and flexibly. So for instance, in discussing medication the worker may also address the issue of parental boundaries and limit-setting, as well as providing basic psychoeducation for the young person and their family. It may be that individual work with the young person would only take place later in the course of the intervention, or alternatively that a young person who is anxious about perceived parental intrusiveness would insist only on individual sessions at first, with the work with the parents occurring separately and only later expanding into work with the family as a whole. The supervisory 'steer' from the team provides a meta-perspective on the treatment, helping the barefoot therapist to maintain a trajectory into the more settled middle intervention phase.

## Stage 2 (Middle Phase): Short-Term Interventions

The middle phase of a multimodal intervention consists of a combination of short-term interventions, as appropriate to that individual and their family. These are as follows:

1. A systemic family intervention to restore the family's containing function.
2. A multifamily intervention to help overcome individual families' sense of isolation and to share experiences.
3. An individual intervention to give the young person a sense of being someone who matters within the social matrix, to help integrate his/her experience of other aspects of the intervention, and to help him or her to become aware of thoughts, feelings, and behaviour, which impact negatively on his/her well-being. These may be:
   (a) psychodynamic
   (b) neurobiological/medical
   (c) cognitive–behavioural
4. Group work to facilitate peer interaction.
5. Educational intervention, via attendance at a specially established education centre
6. Socio-cultural interventions to engage the young person in appropriate, normative activities.

The 'toolkit' of multimodal interventions has been briefly described above. As the initial crisis is brought under control, the opportunity for more focused work arises, and rather than the initial worker handing this over to other professionals, they would continue to offer the majority of the input. Further 'timetabling' might be required to establish fixed tasks around which the flexible work continues.

In conventional models the multiplication of different professionals involved in a case establishes a tendency for splitting, and in particular those staff members who are closest to the patients (those who spend most of the time in face-to-face contact, who usually do not have offices into which they can retire) may easily be construed as less important/powerful/valid than the more inaccessible 'experts'. This is an unhelpful dynamic, and one which is largely sidestepped in this model. The barefoot therapist has access to a large specialist supervisory team, but remains the major attachment figure for young person and family from the very beginning and sees the case through to its conclusion.

The exception to this would be in the young person and family members' attendance for regular periods at the educational/vocational centre, although the key-worker would introduce them and establish work with them in that setting too, when the time for such an intervention was right. According to the age spread of the young people, the educational/vocational centre may take a variety of forms (for instance younger adolescents may only attend in the mornings, older ones in the afternoons), but essentially the 'model' is designed to be closer in outward appearance to that of an educational/training setting than that of a day hospital, even though functionally there may be great similarities with the latter. The emphasis is on the educational/vocational centre as a normative and thus reassuringly 'ordinary' institution (a quality that mental health settings often fail to achieve). However, it would be highly flexible in its capacity to accommodate different cultural and sub-cultural expectations. Family members would have the opportunity (and would be expected) to work alongside staff in supporting young people in a variety of educational/vocational or occupational activities, as well as being able to share their experiences and feed back to one another, thus emphasizing their expertise and self-efficacy. Opportunities for group and multifamily work would be available in this setting.

In summary, the barefoot practitioner would be working in a truly multisystemic context, ranging from working with the young person's inner world, building up their mentalizing function, through to working with the family, developing new modes of communication and capacities for containment, and subsequently working with the local ecology, setting up and practicing normative activities and liaising with schools and training institutions.

## Stage 3 (Ending Phase): Handover and Relapse Prevention

The final phase of the intervention strategy consists of the following:

1. Negotiation with educational agencies;
2. Handover to local services; and
3. Relapse prevention sessions for spotting signs of relapse and rehearsing strategies for dealing with them.

The current proposal is for a short-term intervention to stabilize a crisis and allow (re-)establishment of links with existing local services. In this sense it would work as an alternative to acute hospitalization. We acknowledge that the model could quite easily be adapted to provide a longer-term 'maintenance' arm for young people needing higher levels of intensive treatment and support. For instance this might be required in the case of first episode psychosis, providing the requisite three-year follow-up as recommended by Early Intervention in Psychosis Services. Young people on trajectories towards, or demonstrating emergent traits of, severe personality disorder, might similarly benefit from longer-term input, but this is beyond the scope of the present proposal.

The final phase of the intervention is thus focussed on the establishment of sustainable meaningful activity (education or vocational training, for instance) and on facilitating a smooth handover to local services. Work with the young person and family in this stage would be focussed on relapse prevention—spotting the 'early warning signs' of an impending crisis, and in establishing a clearly agreed series of responses according to the severity of the problem, as well as clarifying roles and responsibilities within the various elements of the young person's family, social, and professional matrices.

## THE MULTIMODAL TEAM AND TRAINING ISSUES

Given the nature of the work, it is our view that a full-time consultant psychiatrist, with specific interest and expertise in adolescent psychiatry and psychology, needs to lead the team, which is built around a strong supervisory structure. She/he is assisted by a senior clinician, recruited from a background in psychiatric nursing or social work. Each team should have 8–10 full-time keyworkers, with previous experience and qualifications in psychiatric nursing, social work, or psychology. In addition, the team requires five part-time teachers to staff the education centre. Two full-time members of administrative staff are also required.

Treatment lasts for three months on average. It is composed of three phases: intensive (4–6 weeks), middle (4–6 weeks), and ending (two weeks), as described above. Each keyworker has a caseload of one shared intensive case and three 'ongoing' cases. There are two allocated keyworkers per case in the intensive phase, and one keyworker per case during the middle and ending phases. We estimate that a team of this size would be able to work with 100 adolescents and their families each year. Keyworkers receive a skills-based training, which is delivered by senior practitioners working in the field. The formal training programme consists of 12 whole days, spread out over 12 weeks, and aims to equip key workers with the concepts, techniques and skills specific to working in an integrative way with this client group, their families, and the larger network.

## IMPLEMENTATION AND EVALUATION

The 'barefoot practitioner' model proposed in this chapter is, at the time of writing, not yet practiced in this form. However, great interest has been shown and the first training programme is now under way. One of the major hurdles impeding its implementation would seem to be the proliferation of Early Intervention in Psychosis services, targeting first episode psychosis rather than the full spectrum of adolescent crises, which in terms of their effect on long-term developmental, social, and educational trajectories, can be just as costly in economic terms as in human suffering. Thus, this project—ironically because it is so comprehensive—would 'interfere' or compete with a whole range of pre-existing services, fragmented though they tend to be. Furthermore, the traditional divisions between adolescent and adult psychiatric services appear to produce further obstacles. For instance there are 'boundary issues' if an adult-trained psychiatrist treats under-16 year olds, just as there are if a child and adolescent psychiatrist treats over-18 year olds.

The requirement for a 'footprint' in the form of the educational/vocational centre, not to mention the possibility of a 'family apartment' for crisis admissions, will be seen as a major hurdle, especially at a time when capital expenditure is difficult to justify. The current trend for establishing 'virtual' services, comprised of sessional time from a diverse and dispersed group of professionals who act as a 'functional module' (often without even having a team base), is attractive to commissioners for obvious reasons, but anecdotal evidence suggests that these arrangements are unlikely to provide the robustness and containment that a patient group such as the hard-to-reach one that we have described would require.

Start-up costs are extremely onerous to trusts and commissioning bodies, whose commitment to providing (and paying for) existing services for these young people will not go away during the period of recruitment and training of a new team. The 'invest to save' argument is only valid if there are funds available to invest, although in the long term if this intervention reduces reliance on expensive admissions it is likely to save money.

There may be resistance from existing inpatient adolescent units, who may see a service such as this as a direct threat to their existence. At present, many acute admissions to such units are commissioned from the private sector, as (available) acute admission beds are scarce in the public sector. Many of these crises do not require long stays in hospital, and as a rule it is only a minority of young people who are subsequently transferred from private sector beds on to public sector facilities. Those that are, tend to have extreme, complex, and chronic problems, including collapsed or pathological family support systems. Therefore it may be that the primary impact from a commissioning point of view would be the reduction in acute private sector admissions, rather than a reduction in local NHS adolescent inpatient beds.

Finally, there are resistances from established professionals who may feel that hard-won competencies and specialist skills are being undermined in the approach that we suggest, in using 'barefoot practitioners' rather than a range of appropriately qualified professionals. In reply to this we would argue that there remains a vital role for these specialists, not least in supervising and training. What is not on offer—and never will be—are the funds and the numbers of trained personnel to provide an equitable service to the many young people who need and deserve it; in holding out for adequate specialists we risk inadvertently supporting an exclusionary agenda.

There is a need to think more radically about the delivery of mental health services. It is not reasonable, and perhaps not even ethical, to pursue evermore specialized and expensive interventions, if in so doing we reduce our capacity to reach the hardest to reach. Moreover, whilst there are signs of convergences in the spectrum of academic specialties that address themselves to the territory of developing mental disorders in adolescence, in reality the integration of these often contradictory (and sometimes frankly rivalrous) fields will always happen at ground level, in the private interstices between patients and their therapists. Our model takes responsibility for this integrative function of the therapist at a training level, and also in the structural organization of the intervention itself. We suggest that moving away from multiple specialty-defined interventions to a flexible, multimodal, 'single-point-of-delivery' response, with access to multi-family work and, reassuringly, to 'ordinary' people (who themselves have access to strong, expert supervisory structures), offers a simpler and perhaps more humanly understandable intervention that may (to misquote a phrase) reach parts that others have not.

# CHAPTER 6

# Developing an Enhanced Care Model for Depression Using Primary Care Mental Health Workers: Implications for The Care and Management of Young Men with Depression

Stephen Pilling, Judy Leibowitz, John Cape, Jemma Simmons, Pamela Jacobsen and Irwin Nazareth

## INTRODUCTION

This chapter describes a primary care-based pilot project, which attempts to apply the knowledge gained from a range of international programmes on the enhanced care of depression to the treatment and management of depression in the UK National Health Service. It describes the background to the project, the challenges in establishing an enhanced-care model within primary care in the UK, the specific aspects of the programme devoted to young men, some initial indications of the outcomes achieved, and the implications of the study for the future development of the model within the UK.

## THE PROBLEM OF DEPRESSION

Depression is the most common psychiatric disorder, with the potential to affect everyone—men, women, old and young. For example, in primary care settings rates of depression of up to 10% have been reported (Katzelnick et al., 2000), and in the

*Reaching the Hard to Reach: Evidence-based Funding Priorities for Intervention and Research.* Edited by G. Baruch, P. Fonagy and D. Robins. © 2007 John Wiley & Sons Ltd.

UK one in four women and one in ten men suffer at least one episode of depression requiring treatment during their lifetimes (National Depression Campaign, 1999). Depression impacts negatively on an individual's quality of life and daily functioning, and also has wider societal effects with the consequence of extra demands being placed on healthcare resources and a loss of productivity (Katzelnick et al., 2000). It is currently the fourth leading cause of burden among all diseases, and is projected to be the highest ranking cause of burden of disease in developed countries by the year 2020 (World Health Organization, 2001).

The average age of onset of depression is the mid 20s, although a substantial proportion of people with depression have their first depressive episode in childhood or adolescence (Fava & Kendler, 2000). Rates of depression are significantly affected by a variety of socio-demographic factors, including gender, social class, education, and employment (Meltzer et al., 1995a, 1995b). Although often thought of as an acute disorder, evidence suggests that this is not the case. A WHO study of mental disorders from 14 centres across the world demonstrated that 50% of people identified with a mental disorder in the initial phase of the study still met diagnostic criteria for depression one year later (Goldberg et al., 1998). This finding is confirmed by a number of studies, which also show that following their first episode of major depression, at least 50% of people will go on to have at least one more episode (e.g. Kupfer, 1991). Of particular importance for the work described in this chapter is the finding that early-onset depression (depression occurring on or before 20 years) is associated with a significantly increased vulnerability to relapse (Giles et al., 1989).

In addition to the social and occupational burdens imposed by depression, it also has a significant impact on general morbidity and mortality. For example, death rates from myocardial infarction (MI) are significantly greater for those who are depressed, not only in the immediate post-MI period, but also for at least one year following the MI (Lesperance & Frasure-Smith, 2000). In a range of other physical illnesses evidence also suggests an increased mortality rate when co-morbid depression is present (Cassano & Fava, 2002). Depression is also the leading cause of suicide, which accounts for just under 1% of all deaths, of which nearly two-thirds occur in depressed people (Sartorius, 2001). Marital and family relationships are frequently affected in a negative manner, and parental depression may lead to the neglect of and to significant disturbances in the children (Ramachandani & Stein, 2003).

Effective pharmacological, psychological and psychosocial treatments exist for depression (National Institute for Clinical Excellence, 2004), but a number of factors may limit access to such treatments. First, many people with depression do not seek help. Reasons given for not seeking help (Meltzer et al., 2000a) include:

- not believing that any help could be provided (28%);
- thinking that one should be able to cope with the problem oneself (28%);
- thinking that it was not necessary to contact a doctor (17%);
- thinking that the problem would get better by itself (15%);
- being too embarrassed to discuss the problem with anyone (13%); and
- being afraid of the consequences of the treatment, for example hospitalization or being formally admitted to hospital (10%).

Second, the problem of non-recognition of depression by healthcare professionals is considerable, even when a person presents with problems in a health-care setting. Although the annual rate of depression in primary care may exceed 10%, studies indicate that the annual rate of depression recognized by the general practitioner is only about 3% (Goldberg, 1994). A major reason behind this is that many people with depression may seek consultation for physical conditions and do not consider themselves to have any psychological problems, despite the presence of depressive symptoms. Third, for identified patients there may be limited treatment options available (for example, the difficulty in accessing psychological treatments), or those which are available may be judged not to be acceptable (for example, although patients may be offered antidepressant medication, a significant proportion decline the offer, fail to obtain the antidepressants from the pharmacist, or do not complete the treatment as prescribed (Hansen et al., 2004)). Finally, the stigma associated with mental health problems in general (Sartorius, 2002) may account for the reluctance of some depressed people to seek help. However, even when people are identified as being depressed, treatment often falls short of recommended practice (Donoghue & Tylee, 1996; Katon, Korff, Lin, Bush & Ormel, 1992) and outcomes are correspondingly below what is possible (Rost, Williams, Wherry & Smith, 1995).

## DEPRESSION IN YOUNG PEOPLE

So far this chapter has concentrated on the prevalence of, and problems presented by, adults with depression. However, the antecedents of a significant proportion of adult depression can be traced to depressive episodes in childhood and adolescence. As with adults, depression is also common in children and young people, with approximately 1% of pre-pubertal children and 3% of post-pubertal adolescents demonstrating 12-month periods of major depression (Angold & Costello, 2001). Once again, as with adults a considerable proportion of adolescents with depression remain chronically depressed; for example, at 12 months 50% remain clinically depressed and this rate remains at around 20 to 30% at two years (Goodyer, Herbert & Tamplin, 2003; Harrington & Dubicka, 2001). The most serious complication of adolescent depression is suicide (a risk of about 3% over the next 10 years) (Harrington, 2001). Recurrence of depression within five years of the first episode is around 30% and many may go on to experience depression in adult life (Fombonne et al., 2001).

In addition to a significant prevalence of depression in young people and its under-recognition by primary healthcare professionals, young people, in particular young men, are far less likely to ask for help (Royal College of Psychiatrists, 1998). Young men typically present with physical complaints even when the primary problem is an emotional one; they also report a greater difficulty in talking about their problems, and even where depression is identified and treatment offered, they often fail to turn up for subsequent appointments (this reached 60% in one study, Jenkins et al., 1997). As a consequence depression often goes unrecognized, with the result that young men are less likely to be identified and offered treatment. This is of considerable concern since depression is consistently the most prevalent disorder, ranging from 49 to 64% among adolescent suicide victims (Del Piccolo, Saltini & Zimmerman, 1998; Raine et al., 2000; HDA, 2004) as well as in adolescents engaging in non-fatal self-harm (Hawton & James, 2005). Since 1997, suicide rates for young men (15–34) in England have decreased; from 1997 to 2003 there was a drop of 18% to 16.2 per 100000. Nevertheless suicides in the 15–34 age range still represent 20% of all deaths in males, compared to 12–13% in females, and suicide remains the most common cause of death in men under 35 (Department of Health, 2002). The National Suicide Prevention Strategy (2002) recommends that initiatives should focus on this age group. The above information suggests that strategies for identifying and treating depression in young men may contribute to a reduction in suicide rates. This is borne out by a recent systematic review of suicide reduction strategies (Mann et al., 2005), which concluded that the most effective strategies for suicide reduction were probably those that concentrated on the identification and treatment of depression in vulnerable groups.

## ENHANCED CARE MODELS FOR THE TREATMENT OF DEPRESSION

In recent years a number of models designed to improve the outcomes for depression in primary care have been developed (Von Korff & Goldberg, 2001). Often referred to as enhanced care or collaborative care, these models seek to improve outcomes through providing additional staff and resources to enhance the care provided. Improved outcomes have been found where the additional staff facilitate antidepressant medication uptake and adherence (Katon et al., 1995; Simon, VonKorff, Rutter & Wagner, 2000), provide or facilitate referral to psychological therapies (Schulberg et al., 1996; Ward et al., 2000), or both (Katon et al., 1996; Wells, Sherbourne, Schoenbaum et al., 2000). In many studies the additional staff member acts as a care coordinator in liasing with the GP, providing educational materials to the patient and also informal support, as well as encouraging the patient to take up and adhere to treatment (Katon et al., 1995, 1996; Simon et al., 2000; Wells et al., 2000). The emphasis in such studies is often on depression as a potentially chronic condition requiring disease management strategies in primary care and between primary and secondary care, similar to those developed for other chronic diseases; in particular, a consistent care management approach (Von Korff, Grunssan, Schaefer, Curry & Wagner, 1997).

In many of the earlier studies, mental health professionals provided the additional staff input and undertook the role of care coordinator (Katon et al., 1995, 1996; Unutzer et al., 2001). However, more recently others including primary care nurses (Hunkeler et al., 2000; Mann et al., 1998; Rost, Nutting, Smith, Werner & Duan, 2001), or graduates without a core mental health professional training (Katzelnick et al., 2000; Simon et al., 2000), have taken this role. Most studies have been from the USA. In the UK one published study has used practice nurses in the role of care coordinator, and this did not improve either patient antidepressant uptake or outcomes compared to usual GP care (Mann et al., 1998). More recently, however, a pilot study has shown some promising results for practice nurse-coordinated care of patients with depression recruited by sending a letter advertising the practice nurse depression service to all patients on the practice list (Symons et al., 2004). They found that while people can be encouraged to contact their GP by sending them a letter advertising nurse-led depression services, there were not suffici-ent practice nurses to administer this service and to provide subsequent care co-ordination.

In the UK, there are not enough mental health professionals to provide enhanced input and care coordination for all primary care patients with depression. Primary care nurses also have multiple and increasing demands on their time and, with many also uninterested in working with patients with psychological problems (Nolan, Murray & Dallender, 1999), are unlikely to provide a significant role in the routine care coordination for patients with depression, except in a few practices. Graduate primary care mental health workers (PCMHWs) represent a major new NHS staff-ing initiative for primary care mental health (Department of Health, 2000, 2003); 1000 of these new workers (graduates with a brief general training in mental health) have since been employed by primary care trusts nationwide, and work is still con-tinuing to develop and evaluate the range of roles that they can undertake to support primary care in the management of mental health problems.

This project therefore sought to build on the opportunities provided by the arrival of these new workers, the results of the Lewisham trial (Symons et al., 2004), and the work of the groups led by Katon, Simon and others in the United States (Katzelnick et al., 2000; Simon et al., 2000), to set out a potential new role for PCMHWs in which they would contribute to case finding and provide care coordi-nation and enhanced care to primary care patients with depression. The Depart-ment of Health (2003) best practice guideline for the PCMHWs highlighted the need for a stepped-care approach to the management of depression in primary care, and suggested roles for PCMHWs as part of this model. An essential feature of a stepped-care approach is the provision of low intensity, low cost treatment, includ-ing what is referred to as 'supported self-help'. Supported or guided self-help has a reasonable base for its efficacy, and a number of models for its delivery have been developed and evaluated (Lewis et al., 2003; National Institute for Clinical Excel-lence, 2004). It is suggested that where clinically appropriate this type of care could be offered to patients prior to more intense, more intrusive, and higher cost treat-ments; a suggestion that was taken up in the project described here.

## THE CAMDEN ENHANCED CARE PROJECT FOR DEPRESSION

The Camden Enhanced Care Project for Depression is one of a number of projects established in Camden to look at mental health in primary care and community services. This includes studies to evaluate the roles of PCMHWs in delivering guided self-help, such as computerized cognitive behavioural therapies (CBT) (Leibowitz, Wallace, King, Cape & Rudge, 2006, in preparation), and a community links service aimed at helping people with psychosocial problems to access appropri-ate community-based resources (Grant et al., 2000; Grayer, Buszewicz, Orpwood, Cape & Leibowitz, 2006), as well as a suicide prevention project. This later project ('Sort out Stress') focuses specifically on young men and has developed a range of training and educational materials, (including a website, www.sort-out-stress.co.uk)

on mental health, which can be delivered to young men and staff working with them in a wide range of community settings.

The Camden Enhanced Care Project for Depression involved joint working between the Camden and Islington Mental Health and Social Care Trust, Camden Primary Care Trust, the Centre for Outcomes Research and Effectiveness (CORE) at University College London, the Department of Primary Care and Population Sciences at University College London, and the Charlie Waller Memorial Trust who formed the steering group for the project. The overall aim of the project was to assess the feasibility of establishing an enhanced care programme for depression (including young men) in primary care settings in the NHS. It also sought to explore and evaluate the role of PCMHWs.

## THE DEVELOPMENT OF THE PROJECT

The project described here was part of a larger study, including a pilot randomized controlled trial designed to assess the feasibility of conducting a larger multicentre trial of enhanced care for depression. The trial focused on a number of issues, including the feasibility and practicality of establishing the programme within a primary care setting in an inner-city area, the appropriateness of trial recruitment methods and outcome measures, and the experience of primary care staff and patient participants in the trial. The outcomes of the trial are described in a separate publication (Pilling et al., 2006, in preparation); this chapter will concentrate on describing the delivery of the service.

The focus of the work reported in this chapter is primarily on the role of PCMHWs in providing an enhanced care service for depression within primary care, the methods of recruitment to the programme (including elements of the programme that focus specifically on the needs of young men with depression), and the experience of participants in the programme. It describes the success of the recruitment strategy, the challenges experienced in integrating the programme into routine practice in primary care, the experience of training and development of the PCMHWs, and some early indication of the outcomes achieved so far.

The project was carried out in two GP practices in the London borough of Camden, with a combined list size of 14700. The practices were of similar size, but were contrasting in that one was in an affluent part of Camden and one was in a much more socially-deprived area. The more deprived practice had a higher level of unemployment (6.7 vs. 3.3%), a higher proportion of people from black and minority ethnic communities (38 vs. 16%), a higher index of multiple deprivation (54 vs. 1.9%), a lower level of substantial educational achievement (38 vs. 73%), and an increased incidence of life-limiting illnesses (20 vs. 12%).

The first two phases of the project are reported here:

1. The development of protocols and associated materials for the delivery of enhanced care in the practices, including agreeing 'case-finding' approaches to targeting vulnerable groups.
2. Training PCMHWs and associated primary care staff in the delivery of enhanced care for depression.

**Establishing robust protocols** for the implementation of the programme in primary care was led by one of the authors (JL) who had a central role in primary care mental health development in the borough, with support from members of the steering group and the PCMHWs. Key GPs (including one of the authors, IN) in both practices supported the project, but it was felt to be very important for all GPs to be fully in agreement with the protocols before they could be implemented.

Specific protocols that were developed during the course of the project included:

1. Case finding and recruitment procedures using the electronic patient registers of the two practices.
2. Content, format, and method for distribution of the individual patient recruitment flyers.
3. Care and treatment protocols, including:
   (a) the provision of guided self-help;
   (b) the provision of an antidepressant medication support programme;
   (c) the management of risk (including suicidality);
   (d) communication and record-keeping procedures; and
   (e) the provision of support to access other services referred to.

Further details of the agreed protocols are described below, and the full protocols are available from the authors.

The development of each of these protocols involved considerable time even though, in many cases, they were adapted from pre-existing protocols (for example, the guided self-help material drew on material developed by the Northumberland Psychology Service, previously piloted in Camden and Islington).

## THE PRIMARY CARE MENTAL HEALTH WORKERS

One PCMHW worked closely with each of the two practices involved, spending about three sessions per week on direct clinical work for the project, with additional time devoted to case finding, communication, and meeting the demands of the research study. The PCMHWs had a psychology degree and some relevant, but limited previous experience, and no professional qualification in mental health. They were trained, as part of the project development, specifically to offer guided self-help (using CBT-based booklets), in delivering support to people in relation to their use of antidepressants, and in understanding local referral systems in relation to secondary care mental health services. Experienced clinical psychologists and general practitioners delivered the training. Weekly clinical supervision was offered during the course of the project by one of the clinical psychologists (JL) involved. In addition to this training in guided self-help and medication management, the PCMHWs underwent a significant period of induction within the practices to ensure that they had a good grasp of the organizational systems in place, and so that the practice staff became familiar with them and with the project. Initial scepticism on the part of many primary care staff meant that establishing a strong working relationship with the practices was essential in order to overcome the teething problems that the project inevitably faced.

The initial establishment of the protocols in the two practices took approximately six months, including an extended pilot of the system in which both the operational systems and the ability of the PCMHWs to work effectively with depressed patients was piloted and carefully monitored.

## Case Finding and Recruitment Procedures

The service was available to all new presentations of depression, including those presenting with a first episode of depression or those with recurrent depression who had not had any active treatment in the previous four months.

The majority of patients were referred to the study directly by their GPs. In order to facilitate the identification of young men with depression, one of the practices used a system whereby GPs were 'reminded', using electronic 'pop-ups', whenever they had a consultation with a young man, which prompted them to consider the possibility of depression, and also to consider asking two screening questions. Recruitment was supplemented by searches (by the PCMHWs) of the electronic patient record for new presentations of depression that had not been referred by GPs. These searches were carried out on a weekly basis and, if new patients were identified by this method, then the GP's agreement to offering the patients entry into the project was sought. Patients were eligible for the service if they were over 16, had a diagnosis of depression from their GP, and scored above 10 on the Beck Depression Inventory (BDI) (administered by the PCMHW). They were also required not to have had any active treatment for depression in the previous four months (i.e. not to have been prescribed medication or referred to mental health professionals).

## Patient Recruitment Flyers

It is well established that many patients with depression either do not present at all to primary care services, or do so with somatic complaints such that the underlying depressive disorder is not recognized. There was a particular concern among the study group that young men were at particular risk of not having their depression identified (see above). Other groups, such as those with previous episodes of depression and those with chronic physical illnesses likely to involve some associated physical disability or chronic pain, for example chronic rheumatoid arthritis or long-standing cardiovascular disease, were also considered to be at significant risk of depression.

Following on from the method developed by Symons et al. (2004), a direct contact approach with these vulnerable groups was initiated. For example, the method used to develop the flyers for one group—young men (aged 16–35)—initially involved generating ideas on possible designs and wording from focus groups consisting of young men from a number of local youth organizations, with the aim being to develop a flyer that young men were more likely to respond to. The design was then reviewed and agreed with practice staff, along with a letter addressed to the selected individuals (from the practices' electronic patient record), which was signed by the practice. The list of young men who were to receive a letter was also reviewed by the practice medical staff in order to ensure that no individual known to the practice would be in receipt of information that was considered to be inappropriate. The flyer (see Figure 6.1) provided brief information about depression and about the new service to be offered at the practice, and it also explained that that this would be evaluated as part of a research study. Patients were encouraged to contact the primary care worker on the number provided if they had noticed any of the symptoms outlined in the flyer.

Despite the considerable efforts that the group put into both the development and distribution of the leaflets, the number of young men identified by this means was small. Out of 2017 leaflets distributed, less than 20 young men responded, and only five were eventually recruited to the service. In addition, a further five young men were recruited to the project by referral from their GP. This low rate of recruitment is consistent with other studies (Symons et al., 2004), but may have been further reduced in this study by the requirements of the research design, which necessitated informed consent from any participant. The flyer for those with chronic physical illnesses produced a similarly low response. In contrast, the flyer sent to patients who had a previous history of depression produced over 50 responses from

**Figure 6.1**   Don't let it drag you down

just over 1000 flyers sent, and over 20 of these responders were recruited to the study. Overall, almost half of those recruited to the project had responded to flyers.

Despite the low number of young men who entered the study as a result of responding to the flyer, qualitative interviews indicated that there was a good response to the flyer from all of them in general. Those who responded to the flyer said that it had prompted them into seeking help for their psychological problems, which they had previously not requested help for. For example, a 35-year-old man reported that he had been 'battling against his own demons' for some considerable time, and that the flyer gave him the opportunity to make a start to help himself. Another patient, a 26 year old, said that he had been feeling depressed for some time but had found it hard to admit this, even to himself. Things got on top of him during exams, and he finally told someone after having an anxiety attack. He also told his mother and she suggested he saw the doctor, but he couldn't pluck up the courage. Then the flyer came—'which prompted me to do something'—and at this point he contacted the PCMHW. In addition, the flyer sent to young men appears to have had an indirect and positive effect on presentations in primary care (see below).

## The Care and Treatment Provided

This section describes the detail of the provision of the enhanced care model and combines a description of the care provided, along with accounts of the experience of intervention participants. Given the focus of this chapter, the cases are drawn from young men who participated in the study.

### *Initial Meeting with the PCMHW*

All patients who entered the study were offered an initial contact with the PCMHW. For those recruited by the flyer this may have been preceded by a brief explanation of the project over the phone. In describing the nature of the services on offer it was also made clear that, although the interventions may be of value within their own right, they were also intended to enhance the care already provided.

The initial meeting lasted for approximately 45 minutes and was built around a structured clinical interview, which covered current problems, any previous history of depression and current and past treatments. The interview also contained a risk assessment protocol with a particular focus on suicidal risk. The protocol, which was agreed with both practices, set out clear guidelines on the action to be taken by PCMHWs if overt suicidal ideas or behaviour were reported, or other behaviours were identified that suggested a significant suicidal risk. All patients offered enhanced care had between two and six contacts with the PCMHW, made available to them over a four-month period. These contacts could either be face-to-face at the primary care site or over the telephone.

Contact with the PCMHW could involve the provision of guided self-help, support with adherence to medication, help in accessing other services and support, and liaison with the GP. Further details of participants' experience of the interventions are described below, where fuller descriptions of individual elements of enhanced care are also given.

**Guided self-help (GSH)** (support to use CBT-based self-help booklets): where a patient opted to take up the offer of guided self-help, three booklets were used—one on depression, one on stress and anxiety, and one on panic. All booklets were based on CBT principles with a strong psychoeducational component and, in the case of the depression booklet, an emphasis on behavioural activation. In discussion with the PCMHW, individual patients were encouraged to identify specific goals and use the appropriate booklets in order to enable them to achieve these goals. There was high take-up of the offer of GSH (34 out of 43). The qualitative evaluation of the study so far conducted suggests that although the GSH was valued and was generally associated with greater satisfaction, the opportunity to talk and discuss their difficulties with an individual (the PCMHW) was also highly valued. Positive comments provided on GSH included comments on the practical exercises that arose from the use of the self-help booklets, introducing a common sense or normalizing element to an understanding of their problems, helping to avoid being trapped in a circle of negative thinking, the flexibility of the approach (the booklet could be picked up at any time), and the opportunities that were provided by the GSH sessions to discuss their problems with the PCMHWs. The experience of one individual in receipt of enhanced care is described in Case Study 6.1.

## Case Study 6.1
### Lee—delivering enhanced care. (Beck Depression Inventory Second Edition)

### Initial contact with the service

Lee is a 26-year-old British-born Chinese male who had never previously sought help for depression or any mental health-related issue. Nevertheless, he had been depressed for over a year and had thought about speaking to the doctor, but it was not until the flyer came through the door that he felt able to take action. Despite previous discussions of problems with family and friends it was the flyer that finally 'prompted me to do something'. He described a history of mixed depression and anxiety with, at the present time, moderate to severe depressive symptoms (he scored 34 on the BDI-II), but disclosed no suicidal ideas. In line with the study protocol an appointment was arranged with the GP, in this case three days after the initial appointment.

### Initial treatment and management

Lee's GP confirmed the diagnosis and he was allocated to receive enhanced care. The GP was very concerned about his depression and grateful that Lee had responded to the flyer. He was prescribed an antidepressant and was followed-up by the PCMHW. For two weeks he took himself to bed (he said he felt horrible—which he attributed to the side effects of the medication) and the only contact with the PCMHW was via telephone contact with his family. After two weeks he began to feel better and saw the PCMHW four weeks after the initial assessment. A significant proportion of the session was devoted to discussing his antidepressants, and providing psychoeducation and advice on the importance of taking them, following the agreed protocol. In this session guided self-help was also introduced and a number of options for its use were discussed with him. Given his problems with lack of motivation and withdrawal, an activity-scheduling approach was encouraged. He was noted still to be quite depressed, despite his feeling that matters had improved considerably.

## Follow-up sessions

The first follow-up session was arranged after four weeks and there was continued improvement in his depression. He had seen his GP and had a slight increase in the dose of his antidepressant, which he had found to be helpful. He discussed in some detail the benefits of the guided self-help. He reported that he had found sticking with the activity schedules difficult at times but that he had persevered. He also reported that the advice on negative thinking was of some value; he saw it as 'common-sense', but did go back to reading it as he found being reminded of this helpful. At the second follow-up meeting four weeks later he reported feeling much better and more engaged with life. He was, however, experiencing some withdrawal effects having 'run out of medication' a week previously. Problems of withdrawal were discussed (he was taking paroxetine), and he was advised to restart his medication. (He did this and a follow-up call two weeks later was arranged to see if all was well with the medication). He was again advised on the use of guided self-help. He said he had stopped using the exercises as frequently when he began to feel better. He reported that he found the explanation of his physical symptoms helpful (he needed to be reassured that his problems were not physical ones), and that he used the activity schedule if he found himself getting too caught up in what he described as 'vicious cycles of thinking'. He was reassured that some of the symptoms that had re-occurred were likely to have been withdrawal effects related to stopping the medication so suddenly.

The intervention from the PCMHW comprised of four direct contacts totalling 90 minutes, along with five brief telephone calls. There were three contacts with the GP in the same period. His score on the BDI-II at four months was seven.

**Support to promote adherence to prescribed antidepressant medication** (based on a protocol developed by Katon and colleagues (Ludman et al., 2002): patients were given a separate booklet that also had a strong psychoeducational component and was designed to support adherence to a prescribed antidepressant regime. It also provided information on potential side effects, and there was an agreed protocol whereby if any difficulties arose the PCMHW and/or the patient, as appropriate, would contact the GP to seek further advice. Not all patients in the project were in receipt of antidepressants (approximately 65%). Where patients were taking medication clear benefits could be identified associated with the role of the PCMHW in supporting this aspect of care. Some indication of the kind of work done can be seen in Case Study 6.1, where the PCMHW spent considerable time discussing antidepressants with Lee. In this particular aspect of the programme the potential impact of the work of the PCMHW may have been reduced because the PCMHW would not often see the patient until 10 to 14 days after the prescription of antidepressant medication, as a result of the requirement to obtain consent for entry to the trial. This meant that many patients who might have benefited from the programme had already made a decision either to discontinue or never start antidepressant treatment (see Case Study 6.2—where Graham decided very early on in his antidepressant treatment that he would not tolerate the side effects).

## Case Study 6.2
### Graham—using guided self help

Graham was a twenty-nine year old man who had had significant relationship and work problems over the past nine months and had become moderately depressed (BDI-II score of 23) with marked anxiety symptoms. He had tried medication on entering the study but quickly stopped taking it as he found the side effects too difficult to tolerate. Initially he used the guided self-help (GSH) in discussion with the PCMHW to agree some clear goals for himself, which centred on improving his position at work, in particular how he managed his relationships with his colleagues, who had he had begun to think were too critical and unsupportive. As things improved at work he continued to use the GSH to develop techniques for manageing his anxiety symptoms using a range of relaxation and visualization techniques, and also used GSH to help identify triggers for anxiety or low mood. After the initial assessment his discussions of the GSH centred on advice from the PCMHW on how he might use it, and reinforcing and validating the techniques he used. He had four face-to-face contacts with the PCMHW totalling 105 minutes, and one brief telephone contact. He had no further contacts with his GP following the initial assessment. His score on the BDI-II at four months was eight.

**Support in accessing other services**: a number of individuals referred to the study had also been referred to other mental health or psychosocial intervention programmes. PCMHWs could facilitate access to such services; this may include, for example, telephone calls to remind individuals of appointments and, where appropriate, escorting people to appointments with the other services. The experience of the study was that this service was relatively little-used (the majority of referrals to mental health specialists were to the in-house counsellors, with only three referrals to psychiatry), with only limited telephone contacts, and more limited direct facilitation of contact with these services.

**General support and liaison with the GP**: a general protocol for effective communication and support between the GPs and the PCMHW was established for the project, and this was further refined for individual practices. A number of methods were used, including direct contact, reminder notes, entry into patient medical records, and regular attendance at appropriate practice meetings. This allowed for effective communication about patients and also crucially supported the development of effective working relationships. A number of benefits stemmed from this that enhanced the general care provided. These included the identification of people at high risk, including young men such as Lee (and a number identified through the flyer who had significant mental health problems other than depression), and in one case the children of the identified patient who were felt to be at risk.

## Reviewing the Progress of the Project

The major aim of the programme was to see if it was possible to establish a model for the provision of enhanced care for depression in a UK primary care setting, using non-professional staff (in this case PCMHWs). In meeting this aim the project has been successful, although the development time (over six months) was considerable. It was demonstrated that it is possible to offer enhanced care, including the provision of GSH, medication adherence protocols, community referrals facilitation, and protocol-driven communication. Results for the trial (Pilling et al., 2006, in preparation) show moderate and promising effects.

### The Response of the Primary Care Team

At the end of the intervention phase of the project a series of qualitative interviews were held with primary care staff, predominantly GPs. They raised a number of issues concerning the project. On the positive side, the GPs valued the role of the PCMHWs in supporting the implementation of agreed treatment plans, for example adherence to antidepressant medication. They also reported positively on the integration of the PCMHW into the primary care team and the communication with the team. The GPs also raised a number of difficulties concerning the programme; prominent amongst them, in one practice, was a perceived significant increase in the number of individuals presenting with general mental health complaints to the practice. Part of this increased demand was as a direct response to the flyers; PCMHWs identified a number of people with mental health problems who responded to flyers and were asked to see their GP to confirm the diagnosis and develop an appropriate treatment plan. However, the feeling among the GPs was that the flyers had also alerted a significant number of their patients (in particular, young men) to their own health needs generally, and had prompted them to go and see the GPs (not necessarily specifically about mental health issues). An examination of presentation rates for mental health problems in young men prior to and subsequent to the introduction of the flyers demonstrated that, in one of the practices, there was an increase in the overall number of consultations in the months following, in support of the GPs' concerns. The practice using the 'pop-up' reminders to consider depression when having consultations with young men, found them generally 'irritating'. There were mixed views on their effectiveness, with one GP saying they had no impact on the consultation, while another felt that they prompted an exploration of psychosocial factors with young men, which might not otherwise have occurred. Finally, the restrictions imposed upon the programme by the requirements of the formal evaluation and its time-limited nature were also acknowledged by both PCMHWs and primary care staff as presenting a challenge to effective implementation of the programme.

## THE PRIMARY CARE MENTAL HEALTH WORKERS

The development of the PCMHW role in the study presented several challenges. Recruiting staff with no formal mental health training to be involved in the care and management of people with depression required considerable work to convince the GPs that they could have a positive role. The relative youth and inexperience of the PCMHWs further reinforced these anxieties on the part of the primary care team. The study group dealt with this in a number of ways: clear protocols for all key aspects of the PCMHWs' role were developed and agreed in conjunction with the primary care teams; the PCMHWs also received careful training in all the interventions and weekly supervision from an experienced clinical psychologist; in addition, before attempting to implement the interventions, extensive pilots were conducted; and senior members of the research team were either appointed from members of one of the primary care health teams (IN), or maintained regular contact with the teams in order to review progress with the project (JL). The PCMHWs also had considerable anxieties about the provision of the interventions and the reception they would get from the rest of the primary care team. Adequate training and supervision, along with ready access to senior staff in case of clinical problems (for example, suicidal patients), addressed these concerns. The major challenge faced by the PCMHWs over the 15 months of the project centred on the establishment of their role within the primary care team. This was achieved, but it took more time than did developing the competences of the individual PCMHW or the implementation of the protocols.

### Case Finding and Recruitment Methods

Recruitment to the study was lower than originally anticipated, largely because of an overestimation based on epidemiological data of the likely presentation rates of new cases of depression. The most efficient method of recruitment into the study was to encourage GPs to mention it to patients during consultations and to refer them at that point (62% of people identified in this way participated in the study). Searching the electronic patient record systems for patients suitable, but not referred by the GP, proved feasible for the PCMHWs to do on a weekly basis, and did identify some additional cases; however, it was difficult to engage them in the study at that point (only 9% were recruited when written to by the practice). The use of the flyers targeted to specific vulnerable groups proved a useful method of case finding for some groups, but less so for others. Overall, 44% of patients recruited into the study had responded to flyers. The best response was from the flyers sent to people with a previous history of depressive disorder; of the 1042 flyers sent out 64 responded (6.1%), and of these 26 (41%) were recruited into the study. A lower response rate was obtained from the flyers targeted at young men (as mentioned previously), and also those targeting people with physical health problems.

## The Development of Specific Treatment Protocols

The study required the development of specific treatment and care protocols. In all cases the protocols represented a development and/or adaptation of protocols developed by other research and development groups, both local to Camden or from other research and development groups (the GSH and medication adherence protocols). The study group developed and refined the protocols in collaboration with the practices and the PCMHWs, but no significant changes were made to the protocols during the course of the programme. The GSH programme was broadly well-received and proved relatively easy for the PCMHWs to implement. The offer of direct face-to-face and telephone contacts was also appreciated by patients and was again feasible for the PCMHWs to deliver. However, the support to engage with other services was less well-used, perhaps reflecting the relatively low numbers that could benefit from this service, as much as problems with the service itself. The medication protocol worked well but, as acknowledged above, problems with the timeliness of the intervention may have limited its value.

## Identifying and Treating Young Men with Depression

The project was designed primarily to test an enhanced care model for the treatment and management of depression in primary care. However, the project also had an explicit aim to try and recruit young men with depression. This was addressed in two ways: the development of flyers aimed specifically at young men, and by prompting GPs through the use of 'pop-ups' to be aware of the possibility of depression in young men who consulted the GP, irrespective of the reason for the initial presentation. Direct evidence for the effectiveness of either of these two measures in prompting identification of depression in young men was limited, although as discussed above, there was a suggestion that the indirect effect of the flyers was important. Of the relatively small number of men who were entered into the study, most reported a positive experience and, crucially, a number of those responding reported that they would not have sought help if it were not for the prompt provided by the flyer.

   This study demonstrated that, even with substantial efforts to encourage young men with depression to present to primary care (using the approaches mentioned above and offering the PCMHWs as an alternative, and possibly less threatening, initial contact), engagement in primary care remained difficult for this group. This may be due to the considerable stigma associated with mental health issues and a lack of conviction from young men that primary care can help. The work of the Sort out Stress project in Camden is currently addressing some of these issues and lessons learnt from this work may lead to the development of community-based interventions that are more accessible and acceptable for young men.

## CONCLUSION

This pilot project has demonstrated that it is possible to introduce an enhanced care model for the treatment of depression into primary care in the NHS. Further, it suggests that non-professional staff—PCMHWs—have the potential to deliver an effective enhanced care programme. The study also provides important pointers to the further development of work in this area, providing information on the refinement of protocols, the routine integration of the approach into primary care, and the potential for the recruitment and identification of vulnerable groups, for example depressed young men, people with previous significant histories of depression, and those with chronic physical health problems. It also has implications for the training and support needed by PCMHWs if they are to provide this type of care. Evidence from related programmes in which the study group are involved suggests that if the needs of vulnerable groups like young men are to be met then alternative routes, such as links with community groups, will also need to be considered in addition to enhanced care interventions in primary care. Perhaps most encouragingly, both practices following completion of the study have elected to continue with PCMHWs providing enhanced care as part of the range of services they offer to people with depression.

## Acknowledgements

The authors would like to thank the Charlie Waller Memorial Trust, John Lyon's Charity, the British Psychological Society and Camden Primary Care Trust for the financial support that made this project possible, Michael Lord for his help in facilitating the establishment of the project, and also the staff and patients of the two practices who participated in the study.

# CHAPTER 7

# The Hard to Reach and the Place2Be

Peter Wilson and Benita Refson

## INTRODUCTION

The term 'hard to reach' is most commonly used to identify those children, young people, and families, who are suffering high levels of difficulty in managing their lives, but who are unable or unwilling to seek or accept any professional help that may be offered to them. Many may be too preoccupied, overwhelmed or defeated to respond to any overtures of professional assistance. Others may be more actively resistant, independent, defiant or suspicious of external scrutiny and involvement. Some may have endured trauma of various kinds in their lives and so experience any form of intervention as a potential repetition of earlier impingement and intrusion. Then again, for some there may be the sheer practical difficulties of transport, money, time and so forth that prevent them from seeking help.

Clearly, a great deal of thought needs to be given to devising ways of making contact with these people, for they are the very ones who may have significant mental health problems and who may be in the greatest need of help. However, the problem of the 'hard to reach' may not reside solely in their court. It may equally be a problem for those who are responsible for providing them with services. The question arises as to how ready or motivated service providers are to make the necessary effort to reach beyond the comforts of their own professional homes—to go more than half way to meet those who are unable to find or accept help in the usual way. Might it not be the case that many professionals and clinicians are disinclined for various reasons to make this effort? Might it not be the case that they themselves feel overburdened by the circumstances of their employment (lack of resources, over-stretched caseload, bureaucratic overload) to bear the particular burden of those who are hard to reach—that they too may wilt in the face of the very problems that 'hard to reach' clients experience and present?

In other words, professional and clinical services may be hard for the 'hard to reach' to reach. They may be so institutionalized in their practice that, from an organizational point of view, they are not set up or prepared to extend beyond their

*Reaching the Hard to Reach: Evidence-based Funding Priorities for Intervention and Research.* Edited by G. Baruch, P. Fonagy and D. Robins. © 2007 John Wiley & Sons Ltd.

traditional procedures. This may be because of their need to follow and meet established professional standards. It may also be a result of organizational direction. In order to become sufficiently adaptable to meet the psychological and practical needs of the hard to reach, it may well be necessary to change an organization's basic mode of operation. It is often not enough for a service to be set up along traditional lines with an add-on provision for the hard to reach. More substantial results may be achieved when the issue of the hard to reach is addressed at the very centre of the organization's mission. Service development, staff recruitment, managerial and supervisory arrangements can all be moulded to make services more accessible to suit the needs of children and families among the hard to reach.

## THE DEVELOPMENT OF THE PLACE2BE

The Place2Be is an organization committed to providing emotional and therapeutic support to primary school children. Its work began in a primary school in Southwark in London where the head teacher had become acutely aware of the extent and depth of the emotional and behavioural difficulties of the children in his school. He recognized that these were problems largely born and sustained within the children's families and neighbourhoods, and that the children required additional attention over and above what he and his school staff could provide. He also knew that the support he was receiving from outside agencies at that time was insufficient to meet the needs of these children and their families. The local child and adolescent mental health services (CAMHS) were unable to respond quickly or adequately enough, mainly because of the inordinate demands made upon them for their own services. They were also unable or unwilling to see children in the school setting; for the most part they expected children and families to come to them. As a result, he found himself in an impasse—he could see so many children with significant emotional and behavioural problems in the daily life of his school and yet he knew that they were being denied the treatment that he thought could make a difference to their lives. It was at this point that the idea of the Place2Be was formed. Its aim was to bring a therapeutic service relevant to children into their schools, the very places where children and their families centred a significant part of their lives—not only in this head teacher's school but over time in many schools throughout the nation.

In the beginning, the main services provided were individual and group counselling for children in particular need. Subsequent developments have broadened the range of service, but the introduction of counsellors into this school at that time was a significant development. However, it was one that met with a mixed reception from the general public. By and large, teachers in the schools responded positively. They felt that at last some degree of support was being provided in the midst of their schools and that some of the burden they were carrying was being shared. Most parents also welcomed the extra attention that was being given to their children, whereas others had misgivings. Some questioned the very idea of counselling for young children; schools, they said, were there for teaching, not therapy—what kind of intrusion into ordinary school life was this that threatened to pry into children's minds and interfere with the lives of their families? Established professionals in CAMHS also expressed considerable suspicion. Who were these Place2Be counsellors? What were their qualifications? What safeguards were in place to deal with possible malpractice? How feasible was it to provide counselling in the midst of a school, outside the more orderly and protected setting of a conventional clinic?

Despite these misgivings, the Place2Be began to grow quite rapidly. In the space of six years, it was operating in 28 schools. During this time, careful consideration was given to the recruitment of suitable counsellors to work with children. Due to financial constraints and the limited supply of established CAMH professionals, it soon became necessary to recruit volunteer counsellors. Not unexpectedly, reservations were expressed about whether volunteers had enough skill or commitment to undertake counselling of sufficient competence to meet the needs of the children referred to the Place2Be.

It is very much to the credit of the Place2Be that it faced this scepticism with a refreshing degree of pragmatism. Its trustees and chief executive could recognize that there was a problem relating to a limited supply of professionals in the field. They also appreciated the positive values of curiosity and enthusiasm among many of the volunteer counsellors. What needed to be done above all else was to make sure that they were sufficiently equipped with the necessary skills and support to carry out their work effectively. This meant that they needed to be carefully selected, adequately trained and inducted, and closely supervized during the course of their work. In turn, this required an organization that could sustain an effective system of management for this purpose.

The situation now is that the majority of volunteer counsellors working in The Place2Be schools are trainees on placement in the second year of their diploma counselling courses. Most of the remainder are qualified adult counsellors or psychotherapists who volunteer their services to the Place2Be to gain experience in working with children. A relatively small but increasing number of volunteers are being trained internally in a special training programme called The Place2Train, designed for people in the community who may not have basic qualifications but have sufficient suitable skills and personal qualities for working with children. Once they have completed the training, they are known as Place2Be practitioners.

All volunteer counsellors and practitioners are recruited through a thorough and rigorous procedure, comprising individual and group interviews. They all undergo an enhanced check by the Criminal Records Bureau. They attend an introductory two-day training course and a further two-day induction programme before they are allowed to begin work with children in a Place2Be school. They are asked to commit themselves to working in a school for a whole school year, one day per week, and are expected to work with up to four children on those days. Once working in a school, they are given supervision by a qualified counsellor in the school on the same day that they are seeing the children. In addition, they are offered dedicated training courses at no charge on specific aspects of working therapeutically with children. This emphasis on training of volunteer counsellors ensures the quality of the Place2Be service and provides something of value in return for the time commitment given by the volunteer counsellors.

# THE CURRENT SERVICE OF THE PLACE2BE

## Organization

The Place2Be is currently working in 106 schools across the UK in organized clusters called hubs. In any given hub there is an average of 10 schools. A Hub manager, who is a qualified counsellor with management skills, manages each hub. In each school there is a school project manager with similar qualifications and experience. The school project manager is based in a school and normally works for two and a half to three days each week, covering a wide range of duties including the assessment of children for counselling, direct counselling of certain children, liaison with school staff and external agencies, and supervision of the volunteer counsellors in his or her school.

Three regional managers oversee the hub activites in their region. They monitor developments, ensure implementation of the Place2Be policies, and serve as a link between local practice and the Place2Be central office. Central core activities include finance, human resources, training, research and evaluation, operations, funding and service development—all essential to sustain and develop the operation of the organization as a whole and to ensure the efficiency of the Place2Be service at local level.

Great care is taken in setting up hubs of schools in various areas. The Place2Be has grown and developed over the years largely as a result of local people in communities wanting to establish the Place2Be in their schools. Certain key people serve as local champions, stimulating interest amongst schools and making contact with potentially supportive organizations. Eventually, a multi-agency steering group is established consisting of all interested parties, such as head teachers, representatives of local authorities and the health authorities themselves.

The initial purposes of the steering group are to find local and regional funding sources to finance the operation of the hub, to ensure that suitable spaces can be found in the schools to house the Place2Be, and to identify local colleges and training establishments with appropriate counselling courses as potential sources of volunteer counsellors. The Place2Be central office works in close collaboration with the steering group, providing assistance in all aspects of setting up a hub. Once funding has been secured, the steering group then plans a timescale for the development of the hub, indicating dates for the service to be operating in all the participating schools. Initially a hub manager is appointed and then, a term later, the school project managers. The steering group continues to meet regularly once the Place2Be is established, to oversee its operation and development.

## Provision

The Place2Be offers a broadly-based support service within the school that engages with the wider issues of mental health in the school community. The individual and group counselling work with children is a central part of the Place2Be's work. However, this is crucially complemented by other direct interventions with children, by work with parents and school staff, and by liaison with the wider multi-agency system. The Place2Be services comprise referral and assessment, individual counselling, group work, circle time, The Place2Talk, The Place2Think, The Place2Learn and work with parents.

## Referral and Assessment

A thorough and systemic referral and assessment procedure is the foundation of the work of the Place2Be and ensures the safety and effectiveness of the service. Referrals for a Place2Be intervention are usually made by the head teacher, teachers or special education needs coordinators (SENCOs). Parents are also able to access the Place2Be through the head teacher or SENCO. External agencies, e.g. CAMHS and social services, also refer children.

Referrals are made to the school project manager in the Place2Be school. The main reasons for referrals can be broadly characterized as relating to behavioural or peer group issues, e.g. extreme impulsive or aggressive behaviour, inability to follow instructions, difficulty in concentrating, bullying, or victimizing behaviour. Some children may be more withdrawn, depressed, and isolated. The majority of children referred come from families in which there is a great deal of distress or discord arising from difficulties in the parents' relationship, economic hardship, and social problems such as unemployment, crime, and asylum seeking.

Once the referral is made the school project manager is responsible for the management of the referral process. This involves extensive liaison with teachers, parents, and other agencies, and obtaining parental consent for the process of assessment and later, if necessary, for counselling. The assessment involves completing the Goodman Strengths and Difficulties Questionnaires (SDQs) with the child, the child's parents, and teachers (Goodman, 1997b). These initial SDQs provide the 'pre-intervention perceptions' of all parties, and are measured against the 'post-intervention perceptions' to provide an indication of the success of the work.

The school project manager takes into account risk and protective factors in the child and family, judges the severity, complexity, and persistence of the child's problems, and assesses the extent to which these problems interfere with the child's learning potential in the school. On the basis of the assessment, the school project manager proposes three types of Place2Be intervention for the child: short- or long-term individual counselling or group work. For some cases, a referral to an external agency, e.g. CAMHS, may be made.

## Individual Counselling

Children who are seen individually meet with a designated counsellor for a set period of time, once every week. Short-term counselling usually lasts for one school term; long-term counselling in most cases lasts for one school year. The counselling takes place in a special room located in the school—a safe and reliable place known as the Place2Be room. It is well-equipped with a wide range of play materials including dolls houses, puppets, soft animals, plastic models, sand tray, paints, coloured pens, plasticine and other toys. Each child has his or her own box in which to keep models, paintings and drawings that he or she may create during the course of the counselling sessions. The box is stored in a lockable cupboard, kept secure by the counsellor. When counselling comes to an end, the child can take away whatever he or she may choose from his or her box.

The counsellor works through forming a reliable and trusting relationship with the child, encouraging them to play with the toys and creative materials in his or her own way, and to talk if necessary about whatever is on his or her mind. It is through play that the children are seen to express themselves most vividly and to relate stories about their experiences. The counsellor's role is to facilitate the process of play and to enable children to explore and make better sense of their worries and concerns.

At the beginning of individual counselling, the counsellor makes a contract with the child in order to help them to understand more about what to expect in the sessions. The contract ensures that the child knows how many sessions there will be, when they will take place, and how to use the Place2Be room. The counsellor also explains the nature of confidentiality, and they make it clear that should the child talk about, or show in their play, that they are in danger of being harmed in some way at home or in the community, then the counsellor has to inform those adults who can protect him or her. The counsellor also makes it clear that, although what goes in the child's sessions will be respected as private, the counsellor or the school project manager may from time to time talk to teachers or hear teachers' concerns about the child, and that the child will be aware of this.

## Group Work

Some children may need the opportunity of a supervized group experience in order to explore and understand better their relationships with other children and with teachers. Others may have more specific worries, e.g. about bullying or making the transition to secondary school, and may benefit from being in groups in which they can share the anxieties they have in common, and learn from each other how to better cope with situations.

Groups differ in size, but usually consist of between six to eight children. Most groups run for eight sessions during the course of one school term. All groups are facilitated by two adults, most commonly by the school project manager and a Place2Be counsellor. The school project manager may also work with suitably experienced members of the teaching staff or with other support staff, such as SENCO's, learning mentors or behavioural support workers. Great care is taken to provide a room that is comfortable and reasonably private and separate in the school. This is not usually the Place2Be room. With each group of children, similar contracts are arranged as in individual counselling, with clear ground rules for how children should behave in the groups.

Circle time is a form of group work usually involving all children in any given class. In many schools, circle time is a regular, formal part of the day. The Place2Be school project manager, and in some cases experienced Place2Be counsellors, join with teachers in facilitating circle time. Circle time covers a wide range of subject matters of relevance to children's and teachers' experience in school. It has a key role in building emotional literacy, helping children to name and understand their feelings, difficulties, and achievements.

## The Place2Talk

The Place2Talk is a self-referral service available during lunch times when children book in for fifteen minutes individually or in small groups to see the school project manager. It is very popular and allows the children the chance to come of their own accord to talk about worries and difficulties they may be having at home or in school. The school project manager makes arrangements so that children can write down on a slip of paper that they would like to come to the Place2Talk and put it in a special posting box. For most children, these brief meetings are sufficient; for others, more time is needed and the school project manager may refer some for assessment and individual or group counselling.

## The Place2Think

The Place2Think is the name given to the school project manager providing opportunities for teachers and other staff in the school to discuss their concerns about and observations of children in the school. The focus is on improving teachers' understanding of children and their relationship with them. Most of the children being discussed are children who are in individual counselling or group work with the Place2Be. The Place2Think may take place in planned and scheduled meetings between the Place2Be staff and teachers and others. It may also happen more informally in brief conversations and discussions during the course of the day.

## Work with Parents

The Place2Be recognizes the importance of the child's family in the course of his or her development. School project managers, in making their assessment of children referred to the Place2Be, interview parents of children receiving counselling and provide further support where necessary. In addition, in some hubs a newly established separate service, known as the Place for Parents, provides parent workers to support parents referred by the school project manager and to improve their understanding of children being seen in counselling.

## The Place2Learn

The Place2Learn provides a wide range of training for school-based professionals. This includes whole school INSET days and training courses for teachers and teaching assistants and for mid-day supervisors. The aim of the training is to improve participants' understanding of children's mental health and their ability to deal with complex situations through teamwork in the school. The Place2Learn courses are validated by the Open College Network. They meet the objectives of the Child Workforce Development Council and contribute to schools carrying out the social, emotional aspects of learning (SEAL).

## THE HARD TO REACH AND THE PLACE2BE

The Place2Be locates its work in areas of England and Scotland suffering considerable socio-economic deprivation. In these areas, there are high rates of poverty and unemployment, with a relatively high proportion of families facing major difficulties in coping with their living circumstances. Parental separation and divorce, criminality, drug and alcohol misuse, are typical problems in families, often with unfavourable effects, such as neglect and physical, sexual and emotional abuse on children.

In the most recent report and clinical audit carried out by the Place2Be evaluation team, 2003–2004 (The Place2Be Evaluation Team, Tiley & White, 2004), a number of significant findings are recorded relating to the socio-demographic profile of the Place2Be population. For example, with reference to ethnic origin, the proportion of non-white children accessing individual or group interventions in the Place2Be was 35% (on average, across all hubs). This compares with 7.5% in the general population, as indicated in the National Statistics Census, 2001. Similarly, with regard to household composition, approximately 44% (on average across all hubs) of the children accessing the Place2Be individual or group interventions came from lone-parent households. The National Statistics Census, 2001, indicates that approximately 10% of households in the United Kingdom are 'lone-parent households'. The proportion of children from lone-parent households in the Place2Be population is therefore unusually large, with more than four times the proportion observed in the general population.

Whilst these findings do not necessarily indicate that lone parents or parents in minority ethnic groups are amongst the hard to reach, it is nevertheless probably true to say that such parents are more hard pressed than others in our society to access help and support from established agencies. It is certainly well-known among teachers and other professionals involved in working in the communities where the Place2Be is based, that many of the families are disinclined for various reasons to seek help from established professional agencies for the emotional problems they are experiencing.

In most of these communities, the primary school assumes a central role. Many parents and children see it as a place of safety and reliability. It is valued not just as a centre for education but also as a source of general support. For some parents, teachers fulfil a very important primary care function. Some seek help directly for themselves, whilst most do so indirectly through entrusting their children to be well cared for. Whatever the nature of the relationship, the primary school is as close as any professional service to the hard to reach with young children, and it is in this context that the value of the Place2Be can be appreciated. Most teachers in the Place2Be schools know that the Place2Be, by virtue of it being so well-established within the primary school, provides a form of therapeutic and emotional support to children and their families, who otherwise are unlikely to receive any.

The problems that the children seen in the Place2Be are experiencing are at the more severe end of the spectrum. The Place2Be report and clinical audit shows for example, that the proportion of children accessing the Place2Be individual and group interventions with special educational needs status was over three times the proportion observed in the general population. In the clinical audit's detailed analysis of Goodman's Strengths and Difficulties Questionnaires (SDQs), of the 1147 children for whom pre-and post-intervention data were available, the significant finding was that more than half of this cohort were identified as falling within Goodman's 'abnormal' category prior to an intervention, compared to only 10% of the general population. This reflects the complexity of many of the cases and illustrates the degree of need of children referred to the Place2Be relative to the general population.

In further analysis of the data, a number of findings indicated the effectiveness of the Place2Be interventions. For example, according to teacher-related SDQs, 62% of the sample showed an improvement in social and emotional behaviour following intervention. Teacher ratings also indicated that boys in the initial SDQ scoring had significantly higher levels of social and emotional difficulties than girls, but post- intervention both groups showed similar levels of improvement in ratings. Children who lived at home with either both or one parent were more likely than children from other groups (step-parent families or 'looked after' by the local authority) to show a significant increase in pro-social behaviour following intervention.

The conclusion of the report was that 'these findings indicate that the Place2Be individual and group interventions are effective at dealing with a broad range of difficulties experienced by primary school-aged children and, importantly, are capable of bringing about changes in social and emotional well-being that are noticeable to teachers, parents, and the children themselves. These changes involve not only a reduction in unwanted behaviour relating to conduct problems, emotional difficulties, hyperactivity, and peer problems, but also an increase in desired behaviour indicative of positive social and emotional well-being in the child'.

It should be added however, that the report also showed that not all children progressed so well, and that the Place2Be interventions were the least successful with children with conduct problems. For example, the SDQ scores of some children decreased following the Place2Be intervention, representing a deterioration in social behaviour. Findings such as this raise important questions about the appropriateness of the counselling approach, the severity of these children's problems, and the influence of other factors in the family, school, and community. However, the meaning of 'deterioration' needs to be thoroughly understood in terms of children's overall progress. A withdrawn child who has been helped in counselling to work through some of their underlying anxieties may begin to display challenging behaviour on the way to finding a new equilibrium in their life. Similarly, 'deterioration' may be observed in a child who, whilst engaged in counselling, temporarily lets go of previous defensive mechanisms before finding new ways of coping with difficulties.

Finally, even though some children failed to show an improvement, the Place2Be intervention often had indirect benefits. With one child, for example, the counsellor noticed some odd moments during the counselling sessions in which the child seemed to suddenly go blank, quite unable to respond to her. The counsellor eventually referred the child to a neurologist who diagnosed a mild form of epilepsy. This had not been picked up by the teachers in the school. As a result, the child received appropriate treatment and her mother, who had been difficult to make contact with, became much more approachable.

## COUNSELLING IN THE PLACE2BE: CASE STUDIES

The counselling that is carried out in the Place2Be is varied, according to the experience and understanding of individual volunteer counsellors, all subject to various influences. They attend different counselling courses, each with their own theoretical and technical preferences and with all mostly focussing on adults. Many follow a person-centred or humanistic approach, others have a more psychoanalytical orientation. There is thus a rich diversity of approach; at best stimulating, at worst sometimes confusing.

There is however one significant unifying factor at the centre of the Place2Be's work, and this resides in the emphasis placed by everyone on the importance of play in working with children. All counsellors and practitioners in the Place2Be are trained to respect and follow carefully the process of the child's play. In different ways, they encourage children to express their thoughts and feelings through play in order to help children gain greater mastery over experiences in their lives that have led them to their problems at home and in the school. The counsellors all work to try to enable children make better sense of their problems, often implicitly through the medium of the metaphor of the play itself, or through direct verbal clarification and interpretation of what is happening in the play. Supervision by qualified counsellors of all counsellors and practitioners is clearly a crucial part of the service. Two case studies illustrate something of the kind of work that is done.

**George**[4] was nine years old. He was referred by his mother, who was worried about his aggressive behaviour and his refusal to communicate with her. His teacher also had a number of concerns. She saw George as a solitary boy who only seemed to come alive when he was playing football. He was not concentrating on his work and not achieving anywhere near his full potential.

His parents came from different countries and met in England. They had difficulty in settling into this country and were afraid of racist attacks in the community in which they lived. They divorced when George was aged six. Since then, his mother has remarried and had another child. George now lives with his mother, stepfather, and half-sister. George misses his father, whom he only sees occasionally at weekends, and worries a great deal about him—fearing that his father might disappear or be abducted and killed.

In the Place2Be counselling sessions, George talked a great deal at first about his father, telling stories of his travels and of the dangers he might be in. Increasingly,

---

[4] In order to protect the children's anonymity all names have been changed and more personal aspects of the children's cases have been removed.

however, he played quietly with the play materials in the Place2Be room. He became absorbed in various kinds of games in which he was aggressive and competitive, making sure he was in charge of the rules so that he could win over the opposition or the counsellor whenever he wished. Occasionally, he changed the way he played, so that he was not in command, and at such times he became quite babyish and giggly.

It became increasingly clear that being in control was very important to him, and that at times he had to act aggressively to reassure himself of his strength and power. Without this, he felt helpless and then had to withdraw. All of this seemed related to his feeling that he had no influence at home in relation to what his parents did or to what might become of his father. The counsellor was able to help George put into words some of his anger and fearfulness and so enable him to gain a clearer understanding of the problems he had at school and at home.

George clearly benefitted from his counselling experience, which lasted for a year. He became more able to speak to his mother about her divorce, saying how much he resented what she had done. He also could share his fears for his father's safety with her and his father. For the first time, he broke down in tears with her. The mother found this very distressing and sought help from the school project manager. After this, George and his mother got on much better and George had more regular contact with his father. At school, he became better able to join in with his peers in various activities and found it easier to concentrate.

**Tina** was aged eight when she was referred to the Place2Be by the SENCO. She was a puzzling little girl, for the most part very quiet and often unwell, with many colds and stomach upsets. However, from time-to-time she quite unexpectedly became very angry and attacked other children quite violently.

Tina came from a very unsettled background. Her mother had suffered serious depression after Tina's birth and was unable to cope with Tina and her three older brothers. All the children were placed in care and were in various foster homes for three years. Tina's father drank heavily and was unemployed (there was a very high level of unemployment in his community). He sometimes tried to look after the children but too often lost his temper and disappeared. Despite this, shortly before Tina started school, the children were returned to live with mother and father in a new flat. They lived well enough with each other, although there were many fights, and the children often looked undernourished.

In her individual sessions with the Place2Be counsellor, Tina spent much of her time playing with the toy farm animals in the sand tray. The counsellor noticed in particular a very prominent theme that ran through all of her play. Tina kept all the children farm animals in a locked cage in the sand tray. No one could go in and no one could go out. Grown-up animals came to visit the children—sometimes they shouted at the children, and sometimes they laughed and sang songs. The children didn't know what to expect and so sometimes they were frightened and sometimes happy. Eventually, a big 'policeman' lion came up and told the other grown-ups to go away. He then unlocked the cage. Some of the children stayed where they were and the others escaped and ran away.

Tina was very proccupied with this play, which she repeated in nearly all of her sessions. Clearly, she was expressing something important on her mind and it was tempting for the counsellor to put into words her own understanding of what was going on in terms of Tina's fears in relation to grown-ups. However, the counsellor chose for the most part not make any interpretations. Instead she respected the metaphor of the play by following its process without interruption or intrusion. This afforded the child some safe distance from the disturbing realities of her life, yet allowed her to work through some of her anxieties contained in the metaphor. As Tina played, the counsellor provided some commentary on the activities of the play and at times alluded to the connections between the activities that were so prominent in her play and the realities of her life at home. Towards the end of counselling, Tina herself began to talk about the frightening and confusing things that happened at home and her conflicting wishes both to stay at home and look after her mother and to just run away.

The outcome of this work was that Tina became gradually more able to take part in various activities with other children. She still looked unwell for much of the time and she was slow in carrying out her work. But she seemed more relaxed in general and her outbursts of violence decreased considerably.

## SUMMARY

The Place2Be provides an early intervention service that aims to support the emotional well-being of children, thus reducing the likelihood of mental health problems and antisocial behaviour later in life. It is an organization whose mission is to make its services available to those in the greatest need. Under the direction of its trustees and chief executive, it has clearly located its services in areas of high socio-economic deprivation and has managed its work in such a way as to be accessible to those who are too unwilling, afraid, suspicious, and unable to seek professional help for the emotional problems of their children.

During the course of its development, the Place2Be has expanded the range of its services so that now its service in a school constitutes a whole package, made up of various interventions in relation to child, teacher, and parent and to the whole school. In effect the Place2Be is an 'external' service that embeds itself in the 'inner' workings of the school; it retains its own authority and standards and yet it fits into the fabric of the school, working alongside teachers and others close to the children. It is because of this very proximity, and the Place2Be's familiarity in the school, that individual and group counselling of children becomes such a realistic possibility. There is little stigma attached to children receiving counselling in the school; if anything, the opposite is true—counselling is seen as some kind of privilege. There are also very few D.N.As (children who do not attend counselling sessions)—an important advantage—in contrast to the relatively high level of D.N.As in clinics based outside the school. Moreover, through the Place2Talk, children can refer themselves for help.

It is this very accessibility that characterizes the Place2Be's strength. The Place2Be clinical audit shows that the majority (64%) of referrals for individual and group counselling come from teachers; 11% come from parents. These figures suggest that both teachers and parents find it relatively easy to refer children that they are concerned about. They are not daunted in the same way as they might be in relation to an outside service. Indeed, they may well be more motivated to refer

in view of their first-hand knowledge of the Place2Be and its staff in the school and
the quicker take-up of concerns and referrals, compared with the likelihood of
encountering long waiting lists elsewhere.

The quality of the Place2Be's work is safeguarded by an organizational system
that ensures adequate supervision and training of staff at all levels and the regular
monitoring of service delivery. The Place2Be report and clinical audit provides a
detailed overview of the service and an examination of the Place2Be interventions
and outcomes.

The evidence from the report and clinical audit indicates that the Place2Be
service benefits a substantial proportion of children who are seen. This may be due
to the effectiveness of the individual and group counselling. It may be further facilitated by the general presence of the Place2Be, offering support for children, teachers and parents at different levels throughout the whole school. Many of these
children come from very disadvantaged backgrounds, both in terms of their family-
life and their communities, and they show significantly higher levels of mental health
problems than the general population. There are strong indications, both from an
examination of the socio-demographic profile of children and families and of their
household composition, and from anecdotal evidence, that a substantial proportion
of these children and families fall within the category of the 'hard to reach', and
that many are reachable through the Place2Be's services in schools.

# Epilogue
# Supporting Programmes Targeting Hard to Reach Young People: The Implications for Charitable Funders

**David Robins**

There are in the region of 190000 charities in the UK and a significant number of them are concerned with the mental health of young people. Many of these charities have played important roles as campaigners and educators, as treatment providers, and as grant-awarding bodies.

In the 1950s, the Richmond Fellowship pioneered the halfway house model to enable young people with severe mental health problems to live within the community. In the 1960s the Philadelphia Association, a charity founded by R. D. Laing, challenged the perception of troubled families as passive victims, with the teenager being the cuckoo in the nest. Halfway houses, child guidance clinics, day and drop in centres, family therapy—all of these advances may not have been possible without the philanthropic support and backing of prominent and enlightened public figures from business, industry, law, local government, the church, and the media, operating through the voluntary sector.

Such liberal, reforming sentiments paved the way for the gradual closure of Victorian mental hospitals and the advent of care in the community, which has been likened as a reform equivalent in its impact to Pinel after the French Revolution, who 'freed the mad from their chains'. Since then, new mental health charities have been formed by committed individuals, acting on a voluntary basis, and responding to shortcomings in the 'care in the community' system. For example, the Zito Trust was established in 1994 following the publication of the report from the inquiry into the care and treatment of Christopher Clunis, a schizophrenia sufferer who killed Jonathan Zito in 1992. The subsequent report into the homicide revealed a catalogue of errors and missed opportunities. The Trust campaigns for better community care for people with mental illness, conducts relevant research, provides training

*Reaching the Hard to Reach: Evidence-based Funding Priorities for Intervention and Research.* Edited by G. Baruch, P. Fonagy and D. Robins. © 2007 John Wiley & Sons Ltd.

for healthcare professionals, and provides a support service for families and carers.

Founded by his family to commemorate Charlie Waller, the Charlie Waller Memorial Trust aims to raise awareness of the nature and dangers of depression, to reduce the stigma associated with this illness, to provide training for primary care staff, and to encourage those who may be depressed, especially young men who are often reluctant to seek help.

Charities also endow academic positions for the furtherance of teaching and research into evidence-led treatment programmes, to ensure a sound academic and scientific basis for future programme development. Waller, for example, has recently agreed to help fund a chair in cognitive behavioural therapy at the University of Reading.

Waller also works in co-operation with local NHS initiatives (see Chapter 6) and has helped to finance a pilot walk-in clinic attached to a GP practice in Lambeth, and a computerized cognitive behavioural therapy programme for two surgeries in Berkshire.

Charities also commission and finance reports into pressing mental health issues. For example, the Camelot Foundation, the charitable arm of the operators of the National Lottery, has recently funded a report on self-harming among young women.

But there is another side to the picture. Today a backlash against Freud and his ideas, breakdowns in the supervision of seriously disturbed people, and confusion over accreditation in the caring professions, have weakened public confidence in the mental health regime. There is, therefore, a general lack of confidence, which is compounded by the worrying thought that anyone can set up as a counsellor.

Peter Fonagy states, earlier in this book, that: 'hard to reach is a child buried under the rubble of cumulative psycho–social risk'. Fonagy refers to 'multiple sources of danger' for the young person, and cites as model practice: 'taking help to the child rather than expecting the child to seek help'. But in this context, 'good intentions are not enough'—the adage that I believe every charity grant maker should have over his desk—is perhaps most relevant, for the view from this grant maker's desk suggests that sometimes a potential source of danger to the hard to reach child is the type of help being proffered.

What are funders to make of the 'tough love' approach, popularized on reality TV shows and based on confrontation theory? Are there significant risks and side effects? And what of therapies using religious indoctrination to claim dramatic improvements in a young person's outlook? There is evidence that in some communities a system of mental health treatment-under-culture has emerged, with faith healers and exorcists who prefer to blame mental health disorders on malevolent spirits. In this regard, charity officers and their trustees need to be alert to what may lie behind the 'catch all' term in counselling, and the potential misuse of their money.

Applications for financial support often chase newspaper headlines. During the height of the moral panic over child abuse, it became a recurrent theme in applications associated with drug taking, school refusal and offending.

The national telephone helpline NSPCC/Childline has increased public awareness of abusive behaviours towards children and has appealed successfully for donations from the general public. But is there a workable network of treatment centres to which the children who phone in are referred? What are the long-term benefits of this 'vulnerable child seeks help' model? There are many examples of damaged young people being referred, i.e. ricocheted, around the system.

To impress funders, applicants often feel compelled to make immodest claims of magical transformations in their client's behaviour. Some appear to assume that troubled young people require their support because they are without family or friends and lack significant others, like teachers, social workers, or medical workers.

Evidence of the level of demand for adolescent services may be misleading. Young people may inquire about a service and may even attend an initial interview, but the rate of non-compliance is high. What funders require is evidence of the frequency and duration of attendance for treatment programmes.

Voluntary groups often cite partnerships with other agencies; however, in many localities the state of inter-agency working is fragile. Child and adolescent psycho-therapists may come at young persons' problems from a very different perspective to that of say, police officers and social workers. And youngsters leading chaotic and careering life styles can become adept at 'playing the system'. On one occasion a young resident of a hostel for the homeless returned from a treatment programme perhaps naturally angered by the feelings aroused by the initial interview. The homeless centre workers actively supported the young person's strategies of non-compliance with the treatment programme.

Finally I believe that funders have a special responsibility to avoid putting coun-selling resources into the hands of inexperienced and untrained adults 'doing psy-chotherapy' with their young clients.

So in the face of such pitfalls, what can be considered 'best practice' for charity funders? It is perhaps unrealistic to expect charity trustees to keep abreast of the latest developments in the cognitive neurosciences, attachment theory, or in neu-roscientific research into brain functioning. Rather, trustees need to be made broadly aware by their advisers and officers of evidence-based treatment programmes like those outlined in this book.

An important message for funders is that in approaching the hard to reach young person there are no quick fixes. Many of the projects commended by Wolpert et al. in their report on child and adolescent mental health services (CAMHS), detailed above, are financed by short-term funding that is often in danger of drying up, in a context of services nationally that are under-resourced. Support by private funders needs to be considered in the form of long-term funding commitments within the continuing constraints of competition for limited financial resources.

Funders may need to be receptive to the cost implications for financially hard-pressed agencies of the requirement for clinical audits and treatment outcome evaluation supervised by appropriately trained and qualified professionals, of which there are several examples in this book. Funders should also be alerted to the train-ing and support needs of the professionals working with often challenging young people.

Charitable grant makers are often interested in pioneering work with troubled young people, for example developing work in non-clinical setting like schools, as described in the chapter on the Place2Be. This support can be crucial in helping to develop services in times of financial stringency and administrative reorganization.

Charitable funders are often sympathetic to specialist agencies. For example, the Women's Therapy Centre (WTC), a registered charity in Islington, London, provides psychotherapy for women in crisis. Around half of the clients are from black and ethnic minority communities. Many are refugees seeking to overcome the trauma of their past experiences. Problems include depression, eating disorders, phobias, anxiety and self-harming. The WTC is one of a very small number of agencies offering therapy in languages other than English, and it is cited by the Department of Health as 'an example of good practice in the provision of gender-sensitive therapy'. The Department of Health acknowledges a shortfall in the availability of psychological therapies appropriate to this client group, and here charitable funders can offer additional help.

There are also occasions when charities themselves take a proactive approach and help set the agenda. For example problems of depression affecting young men occur across the social spectrum, but there are people existing at the very margins of society who are under particular pressure. They have arrived in the UK from all over the world as refugees and asylum seekers. The City Parochial Foundation (CPF), a London grant-awarding charity, identifies them as 'the new poor of London', appropriate beneficiaries of charitable monies designed for 'the alleviation of poverty'. Recently the CPF and John Lyon's Charity, another London funder, joined forces to set up a project involving young men who were refugees and asylum seekers in West London. The majority of the young men, even those who had been in the UK for some time, were extremely isolated. Many exhibited symptoms of mental distress, including anxiety, insomnia, depression, poor concentration, poor appetite, and forgetfulness. Many were on antidepressant medication. Clearly a lot of the current asylum system procedures impact negatively on refugee's mental health. There is a case here for targeted charitable support through organizations like the Medical Foundation for the Care of Victims of Torture.

As Wolpert et al. point out, funding emerging, positive practice needs to be considered in the context of increased policy attention focused on vulnerable groups against a background of continued under-resourcing. Although charitable funds are not intended to replace statutory support, it is the under-resourcing—the gaps in state provision—that are created, perhaps inevitably, with every new turn in health policy, which should be of interest to charities. Since the advent of the 'contract culture', the system of competitive tendering by local authorities for cost-effective services, the core income of mental health providers is usually comprised of contracts and service agreements with central and local government and statutory bodies—primary care trusts, the Youth Justice Board, the Department of Health, and local and regional authorities. Shortfalls in income are often supplemented by contributions from charities. Sometimes around half of a mental health agency's income is derived from charities, including the Lottery.

Increased funding from a primary care trust (PCT) may reflect an agency's success in developing mental health service models appropriate to the needs of young people. But gaps in provision persist. For example, an arbitrary cut-off point of the age of 18 means that PCT-funded specialist child services can only be accessed below that age. But teenagers do not pass neatly into adulthood on a particular birthday, and an adult treatment regime is not always appropriate. There may, therefore, be a case for looking for support from an independent charitable source towards, say, a specialized therapy programme for young people aged 18–23.

Examples of what may be considered by many charities as positive outcomes from their funding include a child and adolescent psychotherapist who developed her work in a voluntary agency entirely supported by a charity, and who is now being funded directly by the local CAMHS to continue the work. And the following is my own example of a successful outcome from the funder's perspective. Based in Kentish Town, London, the Brandon Centre for Counselling and Psychotherapy for Young People offers treatments in clinical settings, as well as though outreach in schools and in a pupil referral unit. An acknowledged 'centre of excellence', Brandon's facilities include a contraceptive and sexual health service, and it has been cited by the Department of Health as a model of good practice, combining service delivery with the rigorous evaluation of mental health outcomes. A few years ago John Lyon's Charity provided support to Brandon for the placement, supervised by the centre, of a psychotherapist at an EBD School. This was the sole mental health provision in the school for some of the most damaged boys imaginable, children who rejected treatments in more formal settings. The charity's grants committee judged this an exceptional case, and support beyond the usual funding period of three years was agreed. Towards the end of the funding period the chairman of the charity wrote to the health authority urging statutory mental health provision for the school. The Director of Brandon later reported: 'There has been an excellent outcome. I am pleased to report that the Camden Primary Care Trust has taken over the funding and employment of the post on a permanent basis'. I was delighted to convey this message to the trustee.

# Bibliography

Achenbach, T. M., Howell, C. T., Aoki, M. F., & Rauh, V. A. (1993). Nine-year outcome of the Vermont intervention programme for low birth weight infants. *Pediatrics, 91*, 45–55.

Achenbach, T. M., Phares, V., Howell, C. T., Rauh, V. A., & Nurcombe, B. (1990). Seven-year outcome of the Vermont Intervention Programme for Low-Birthweight Infants. *Child Development, 61*, 1672–1681.

Acheson, S. D. (1998). *Independent Inquiry into Inequalities in Health*. London: Stationery Office.

Ackerman, S. (1980). Early life events and peptic ulcer susceptibility: An experimental model. *Brain Research Bulletin, 5*(Suppl.), 43–49.

Adelstein, A. M. (1980). Life style in occupational cancer.

Adler, N. E., Boyce, W. T., Chesney, M., Folkman, S., & Syme, L. (1993). Socioeconomic inequalities in health: No easy solution. *Journal of the American Medical Association, 269*(24), 3140–3145.

Advocacy in Somerset. (2005). *The Headspace Toolkit*. Advocacy in Somerset.

Affleck, G., Tennen, H., Rowe, J., Roscher, B., & Walker, L. (1989). Effects of formal support on mothers' adaptation to the hospital-to-home transition of high-risk infants: The benefits and costs of helping. *Child Development, 60*, 488–501.

Ahnert, L., Gunnar, M. R., Lamb, M. E., & Barthel, M. (2004). Transition to childcare: Associations with infant-mother attachment, infant negative emotion, and cortisol elevations. *Child Development, 75*(3), 639–650.

Ainsworth, M. D. S., Bell, S. M., & Stayton, D. J. (1974). Infant mother attachment and social development: Socialisation as a product od reciprocal responsiveness to signals. In M. J. M. Richards (Ed.), *The Integration of a Child into the Social World* (pp. 99–135). London: Cambridge University Press.

Allen, J., Markowitz, J., Jacobs, D. R., & Knox, S. S. (2001). Social support and health behavior in hostile black and white men and women in CARDIA. Coronary Artery Risk development in Young Adults. *Psychosomatic Medicine, 63*, 609–618.

Anderson, C. M., Reiss, D. J., & Hogarty, G. E. (1986). *Schizophrenia and the Family: A Practitioner's Guide to Psychoeducation and Management*. New York: Guilford Press.

Anderson, N. B., & Armstead, C. A. (1995). Toward understanding the association of socioeconomic status and health: A new challenge for the biopsychosocial approach. *Psychosomatic Medicine, 23*, 3726–3751.

Andrews, S. R., et al. (1982). The skills of mothering: A study of parent child development centers. *Monographs of the Society for Research in Child Development, 47*, 1–83.

Angerer, P., Siebert, U., Kothny, W., Muhlbauer, D., Mudra, H., & von Schaden, C. (2000). Impact of social support, cynical hostility and anger expression on progression of coronary atherosclerosis. *Journal of the American College of Cardiology, 36*, 1781–1788.

Angold, A., & Costello, E. J. (2001). The epidemiology of depression in children and adolescents. In I. M. Goodyer (Ed.), *The Depressed Child and Adolescent*, 2nd edn. *Cambridge Child and Adolescent Psychiatry series* (pp. 143–178). Cambridge: Cambridge University Press.

Anisman, H., Zaharia, M. D., Meaney, M. J., & Merali, Z. (1998). Do early life events permanently alter behavioral and hormonal responses to stressors? *International Journal of Developmental Neuroscience, 16*, 149–164W.

Antonucci, T. C., Akiyama, H., & Takahashi, K. (2004). Attachment and close relationships across the lifespan. *Attachment & Human Development, 6*(4), 353–370.

Arsenault, L., et al. (2003). Strong genetic effects on cross-situational antisocial behaviour among 5-year-old children according to mothers, teachers, examiner-observers, and twins' self-reports. *Journal of Child Psychology and Psychiatry, 44*, 832–848.

Arsenio, W. F., Cooperman, S., & Lover, A. (2000). Affective predictors of preschoolers' aggression and peer acceptance: Direct and indirect effects. *Developmental Psychology, 36*(4), 438–448.

Asen, E. (1998). On the brink: Managing suicidal teenagers. In P. Sutcliffe, G. Tufnell, & U. Cornish (Eds.), *Death and the Family: Systemic Approaches to Therapeutic Work*. London: Macmillan.

Asen, E. (2002). Multiple family therapy: An overview. *Journal of Family Therapy, 24*, 3–16.

Asen, E., Dawson, N., & McHugh, B. (2001). *Multiple Family Therapy. The Marlborough Model and its Wider Applications*. London: Karnac.

Asen, E., Stein, R., Stevens, A., McHugh, B., Greenwood, J., & Cooklin, A. (1982). A day unit for families. *Journal of Family Therapy, 4*, 345–358.

Audit Commission. (1999). *Children in Mind: Child and Adolescent Mental Health Services*. London: Audit Commission.

August, G. J., Realmuto, G. M., Hektner, J. M., & Bloomquist, M. L. (2001). An integrated components preventive intervention for aggressive elementary school children: The early risers programme. *Journal of Consulting and Clinical Psychology, 69*(4), 614–626.

Avishai-Eliner, S., Eghbal-Ahmadi, M., Tabachnik, E., Brunson, K. L., & Baram, T. Z. (2001). Down-regulation of hypothalamic corticotrophin releasing hormone messenger ribonucleic acid (mRNA) preceeds early life experience induced changes in hippocampal glucocorticoid receptor mRNA. *Endocrinology, 142*, 89–97.

Baldwin, M. W., Keelan, J., Fehr, B., Enns, V., & Koh-Rangarajoo, E. (1996). Social cognitive conceptualisation of attachmetn styles: Availability and accessibility effects. *Journal of Personality and Social Psychology, 71*, 94–109.

Barker, D. J. (1990). The fetal and infant origins of adult disease. *British Medical Journal, 301*, 111.

Barkley, R. A., et al. (2000). Multi-method psychoeducational intervention for preschool children with disruptive behavior: Preliminary results at post-treatment. *Journal of Child Psychology and Psychiatry, 41*, 319–332.

Barnes, D., Wistow, R., Dean, R., Appleby, C., Glover, G., & Bradley, S. (2004). National child and adolescent mental health service mapping exercise 2004. Available at: http://www.camhsmapping.org.uk/2004/atlas/CAMHS_MAPPING_Booklet.pdf

Barnett, W. S. (1995). Long term effects of early childhood programmes on cognitive and school outcomes. *The Future of Children, 5*, 25–50.

Barrera, M. E., Rosenbaum, P. L., & Cunningham, C. E. (1986). Early home intervention with low-birth-weight infants and their parents. *Child Development, 57*, 20–33.

Barth, R. P., Blythe, B. J., Schinke, S. P., & Schilling, R. F. 2nd. (1983). Self-control training with maltreating parents. *Child Welfare, 62*, 313–324.

Barth, R. P., Fetro, J. V., Leland, N., & Volkan, K. (1992). Preventing adolescent pregnancy with social and cognitive skills. *Journal of Adolescence Research, 7*, 208–232.

Barth, R. P., Hacking, S., & Ash, J. R. (1988). Preventing child abuse: An experimental evaluation of the Child Parent enrichment Project. *Journal of Primary Prevention, 8*, 201–217.

Bartholomew, K., & Horowitz, L. M. (1991). Attachment styles among young adults: A test of a four-category model. *Journal of Personality and Social Psychology, 61*, 226–244.

Bateman, A. W., & Fonagy, P. (2004). *Psychotherapy for Borderline Personality Disorder: Mentalization Based Treatment*. Oxford: Oxford University Press.

Baumrind, D. (1991). The influence of parenting style on adolescent competence and substance use. *Journal of Early Adolescence, 11*, 56–95.

Beckwith, L., Cohen, S. E., & Hamilton, C. E. (1999). Maternal sensitivity during infancy and subsequent life events relate to attachment representation at early adulthood. *Development and Psychopathology, 35*, 693–700.

Beland, K. (1997). *Second Step: A Violence Prevention Curriculum. Teachers Manual.* Seattle, WA: Committee for Children.

Belsky, J. (1996). Parent, infant, and social-contextual antecedents of father-son attachment security. *Developmental Psychology, 32,* 905–913.

Belsky, J. (1999). Modern evolutionary theory and patterns of attachment. In J. Cassidy, & P. R. Shaver (Eds.), *Handbook of Attachment: Theory, Research and Clinical Applications* (pp. 141–161). New York: Guilford.

Benes, F. M. (2006). The development of the prefrontal cortex: The maturation of neuro-transmitter systems and their interactions. In D. Cicchetti, & D. J. Cohen (Eds.), *Developmental Psychopathology,* 2nd edn. *Volume II: Developmental Neuroscience* (pp. 216–258). New York: Wiley.

Benoit, D., & Parker, K. (1994). Stability and transmission of attachment across three generations. *Child Development, 65,* 1444–1457.

Berkman, L. F. (1988). The changing and heterogeneous nature of ageing and longevity: A social and biomedical perspective. *Annual Review of Gerontology and Geriatrics, 8,* 37–68.

Berkman, L. F. (2000). Social networks and health: The bonds that heal. In A. R. Tarlov, & R. F. St. Peter (Eds.), *The Society and Population Health Reader: A state and community perspective* (Vol. II, pp. 259–277). New York: The New Press.

Berkman, L. F., & Syme, S. L. (1979). Social networks, host resistance and mortality: A nine year follow-up study of Alameda County residents. *American Journal of Epidemiology, 109,* 186–204.

Berlin, L. J., Brooks-Gunn, J., McCarton, C., & McCormick, M. C. (1998). The effectiveness of early intervention: Examining risk factors and pathways to enhanced development. *Preventive Medicine, 27,* 238–245.

Beveridge, W. L. (1942). *Social Insurance and Allied Services* (Vol. Cmnd. 6404). London: HMSO.

Birditt, K., & Fingerman, K. (2003). Age and gender differences in adults' descriptions of emotional reactions to interpersonal problems. *Journal of Gerentology: Psychological Sciences, 58,* P237–P245.

Bishop, P., Clilverd, A., Cooklin, A., & Hunt, U. (2002). Mental health matters: A multi-family framework for mental health intervention. *Journal of Family Therapy, 24,* 46–56.

Bjorklund, D. F., & Pellegrini, A. D. (2000). Child developmetn and evolutinary psychology. *Child Development, 71,* 1687–1708.

Black, D. [1980 (1982)]. *The Black Report.* London: Penguin Books.

Blair, C. (2002). Early intervention for low birth weight, preterm infants: the role of negative emotionality in the specification of effects. *Development and Psychopathology, 14*(2), 311–332.

Blair, C., & Ramey, C. (1997). Early intervention for low birth weight infants and the path to second generation research. In M. Gurlanick (Ed.), *The Effectiveness of Early Intervention* (pp. 77–98). Baltimore, MD: Paul Brookes.

Blane, D., Brunner, E., & Wilkinson, R. G. (1996). *Health and Social Organization: Towards a Health Policy for the 21st century.* London: Routledge.

Blazer, D. G. (1982). Social support and mortality in an elderly community population. *American Journal of Epidemiology, 115*(5), 684–694.

Bobak, M., Pikhart, H., Rose, R., Hertzman, C., & Marmot, M. (2000). Socioeconomic factors, material inequalities, and perceived control in self-rated health: Cross-sectional data from seven post-communist countries. *Social Sciecne & Medicine, 51,* 1343–1350.

Bobak, M., et al. (2005). The association between psychosocial characteristics at work and problem drinking: A cross-sectional study of men in three Eastern European urban populations. *Occup Environ Med, 62*(8), 546–550.

Bosma, H., Marmot, M. G., Hemingway, H., Nicholson, A., Brunner, E. J., & Stansfeld, S. A. (1997). Low job control and risk of coronary heart disease in the Whitehall II (prospective cohort) study. *British Medical Journal, 314,* 235–239.

Bowlby, J. (1969). *Attachment and Loss, Vol. 1: Attachment*. London: Hogarth Press and the Institute of Psycho-Analysis.

Bowlby, J. (1973). *Attachment and Loss, Vol. 2: Separation: Anxiety and Anger*. London: Hogarth Press and Institute of Psycho-Analysis.

Bowlby, J. (1980). *Attachment and Loss, Vol. 3: Loss: Sadness and Depression*. London: Hogarth Press and Institute of Psycho-Analysis.

Boyce, W. T., O'Neill-Wagner, P. L., Price, C. S., Haines, M., & Suomi, S. J. (1998). Crowding stress and violent injuries among behaviorally inhibited rhesus macaques. *Health Psychology, 17*, 285–289.

Bremner, J. D., & Vermetten, E. (2001). Stress and development: Behavioral and biological consequences. *Development and Psychopathology, 13*, 473–489.

Bremner, J. D., et al. (1997). Elevated CSF corticotropin-releasing factor concentrations in posttraumatic stress disorder. *American journal of Psychiatry, 154*, 624–629.

Brennan, K., Clark, C., & Shaver, P. (1998). Self report measurement of adult attachment: An integrative overview. In J. Simpson, & W. Rholes (Eds.), *Attachmetn theory and close relationships*. New York: Guilford.

Brotman, L. M., Gouley, K. K., Klein, R. G., Castellanos, F. X., & Pine, D. S. (2003a). Children, stress, and context: Integrating basic, clinical, and experimental prevention research. *Child Development, 74*(4), 1053–1057.

Brotman, L. M., Klein, R. G., Kamboukos, D., Brown, E. J., Coard, S. I., & Sosinsky, L. S. (2003b). Preventive intervention for urban, low-income preschoolers at familial risk for conduct problems: A randomized pilot study. *Journal of Clinical Child and Adolescent Psychology, 32*(2), 246–257.

Broussard, E. R. (1995). Infant attachment in a sample of adolescent mothers. *Child Psychiatry and Human Development, 25*, 211–219.

Browne, K., & Herbert, M. (1997). *Preventing family Violence*. Chichester: Wiley.

Bryant, D., & Maxwell, K. (1997). The effectiveness of early intervention for disadvantaged children. In M. Guralnick (Ed.), *The Effectiveness of Early Intervention* (pp. 23–46). Baltimore, MD: Brookes.

Burch, G., & Mohr, V. (1980). Evaluating a child abuse intervention programme. *Social Casework: The Journal of Contemporary Social Work, 61*, 90–99.

Burnett, A., & Peel, M. (2001). Health needs of asylum seekers and refugees. *British Medical Journal, 322*, 544–547.

Caldji, C., Diorio, J., Anisman, H., & Meaney, M. J. (2004). Maternal behavior regulates benzodiazepine/GABAA receptor subunit expression in brain regions associated with fear in BALB/c and C57BL/6 mice. *Neuropsychopharmacology, 29*(7), 1344–1352.

Caldji, C., Diorio, J., & Meaney, M. J. (2000a). Variations in maternal care in infancy regulate the development of stress reactivity. *Biological Psychiatry, 48*, 1164–1174.

Caldji, C., Frances, D., Sharma, S., Plotsky, P. M., & Meaney, M. J. (2000b). The effects of early rareing environement on the development of GABA-A and central benzodiazepine receptor levels and novelty induced fearfulness in the rat. *Neuropsychopharmacology, 22*, 219–229.

Caldji, C., Tannenbaum, B., Sharma, S., Frances, D., Plotsky, P. M., & Meaney, M. J. (1998). Maternal care during infancy regulates the development of neural systems mediating the expression of fearfulness in the rat. *Proceedings of the National Academy of Sciences, 95*, 5335–5340.

Cameron, N. M., Champagne, F. A., Parent, C., Fish, E. W., Ozaki-Kuroda, K., & Meaney, M. J. (2005). The programmeming of individual differences in defensive responses and reproductive strategies in the rat through variations in maternal care. *Neuroscience and Biobehavioral Reviews, 29*(4–5), 843–865.

CAMHS Outcome Research Consortium (CORC). (2002). Available at: http://www.camhoutcomeresearch.org.uk/

Campbell, F. A., & Ramey, C. (1995). Cognitive and school outcomes for high risk African American students at middle adolescence: Positive effects of early intervention. *American Educational Research journal, 32*, 743–772.

Campbell, F. A., & Ramey, C. T. (1994). Effects of early intervention on intellectual and academic achievement: A follow-up study of children from low-income families. *Child Development, 65*, 684–698.

Carlson, V., Cicchetti, D., Barnett, D., & Braunwald, K. (1989). Disorganised/disoriented attachment relationships in maltreated infants. *Developmental Psychology, 25*, 525–531.

Carpendale, J., & Lewis, C. (2006). *How Children Develop Social Understanding.* Oxford: Blackwell.

Case, R. B., et al. (1992). Living alone after myocardial infarction. *Journal of the American Medical Association, 267*, 515–519.

Caspi, A., Taylor, A., Moffitt, T. E., & Plomin, R. (2000). Neighborhood deprivation affects children's mental health: Environmental risks identified in a genetic design. *Psychological Science, 11*(4), 338–342.

Caspi, A., et al. (2002). Role of genotype in the cycle of violence in maltreated children. *Science, 297*(5582), 851–854.

Caspi, A., et al. (2003). Influence of life stress on depression: Moderation by a polymorphism in the 5-HTT gene. *Science, 301*(5631), 386–389.

Cassano, P., & Fava, M. (2002). Depression and public health: An overview. *Journal of Psychosomatic Research, 53*(4), 849–857.

Cauce, A. M., Stewart, A., Rodriguez, M. D., Cochran, B., & Ginzler, J. (2003). Overcoming the odds? Adolescent development in the context of urban poverty. In S. S. Luthar (Ed.), *Resilience and vulnerability: Adaptation in the context of childhood adversities* (pp. 452–481). New York: Cambridge University Press.

Champagne, F. A., Weaver, I. C., Diorio, J., Sharma, S., & Meaney, M. J. (2003). Natural variations in maternal care are associated with estrogen receptor alpha expression and estrogen sensitivity in the medial preoptic area. *Endocrinology, 144*(11), 4720–4724.

Chisolm, K. (1998). A three year follow-up of attachment and indiscriminate friendliness in children adopted from Russian orphanages. *Child Development, 69*, 1092–1106.

Chugani, H. T., Behen, M. E., Muzik, O., Juhasz, C., Nagy, F., & Chugani, D. C. (2001). Local brain functional activity following early deprivation: A study of postinstitutionalized Romanian orphans. *Neuroimage, 14*(6), 1290–1301.

Cicchetti, D., & Curtis, W. J. (2005). An event-related potential study of the processing of affective facial expressions in young children who experienced maltreatment during the first year of life. *Development and Psychopathology, 17*(3), 641–677.

Cicchetti, D., Rogosch, F. A., & Toth, S. L. (2000). The efficacy of toddler-parent psychotherapy for fostering cognitive development in offspring of depressed mothers. *Journal of Abnormal Child Psychology, 28*(2), 135–148.

Cicchetti, D., Toth, S. L., & Rogosch, F. A. (1999). The efficacy of toddler-parent psychotherapy to increase attachment security in offspring of depressed mothers. *Attachment & Human Development, 1*, 34–66.

Cicirelli, V. (1989). Feelings of attachmetn to siblings and well-being in later life. *Psychology and Ageing, 4*, 211–216.

Ciechanowski, P. S., Katon, W. J., Russo, J. E., & Walker, E. A. (2001). Patient-provider relationship: Attachmetn theory and adherence to treatment in diabetes. *American Journal of Psychiatry, 158*, 29–35.

Clark, A., Seidler, A., & Miller, M. (2001). Inverse association between sense of humor and coronary heart disease. *International Journal of Cardiology, 80*, 87–88.

Cohen, S., Tyrrell, D. A., & Smith, A. P. (1991). Psychological stress and susceptibility to the common cold. *New England Journal of Medicine, 325*, 606–612.

Conduct Problems Prevention Research Group. (2002). Predictor variables associated with positive fast track outcomes at the end of the third grade. *Journal of Abnormal Child Psychology, 30*, 37–52.

Conger, R. D., Wallace, L. E., Sun, Y., Simons, R. L., McLoyd, V. C., & Brody, G. H. (2002). Economic pressure in African American families: A replication and extension of the family stress model. *Developmental Psychology, 38*, 179–193.

Consedine, N. S., & Magai, C. (2003). Attachment and emotion experience in later life: the view from emotions theory. *Attachment & Human Development*, 5(2), 165–187.

Constantino, J. N. (1996). Intergenerational aspects of the development of aggression: A preliminary report. *Journal of Developmental and Behavioral Pediatrics*, *17*, 176–182.

Cooklin, A., Miller, A., & McHugh, B. (1983). An institution for change: Developing a family day unit. *Family Process*, *22*, 453–468.

Cooper, P. J., Murray, L., Wilson, A., & Romaniuk, H. (2003). Controlled trial of the short- and long-term effect of psychological treatment of post-partum depression. I. Impact on maternal mood. *British Journal of Psychiatry*, *182*, 412–419.

Coplan, J. D., et al. (1996). Persistent elevations of cerebrospinal fluid concentrations of corticotropin-releasing factor in adult nonhuman primates exposed to early life stressors: Implications for the pathophysiology of mood and anxiety disorders. *Proceedings of the National Academy of Sciences*, *93*, 1619–1623.

Cowan, P. A., & Cowan, C. P. (2002). Interventions as tests of family systems theories: marital and family relationships in children's development and psychopathology. *Development and Psychopathology*, *14*(4), 731–759.

Cowen, E. L., Wyman, P. A., Work, W. C., Kim, J. Y., Fagen, D. B., & Magnus, K. B. (1997). Follow-up study of young stress-affected and stress-resilient urban children. *Development and Psychopathology*, *9*, 564–577.

Craig, F. W., Lynch, J. J., & Quartner, J. L. (2000). The perception of available social support is related to reduced cardiovascular reactivity in Phase II cardiac rehabilitation patients. *Integrated Physiological and Behavioral Science*, *35*, 272–283.

Crittenden, P. M. (1994). Peering into the black box: An exploratory treatise on the development of self in young children. In D. Cicchetti, & S. L. Toth (Eds.), *Disorders and Dysfunctions of the Self. Rochester Symposium on Developmental Psychopathology* (Vol. 5, pp. 79–148). Rochester, NY: University of Rochester Press.

Crowell, J. A., Frayley, R. C., & Shaver, P. R. (1999). Measurement of individual differences in adolescent and adult attachment. In J. Cassidy, & P. R. Shaver (Eds.), *Handbook of Attachment: Theory, Research and Clinical Applications* (pp. 434–465). New York: Guilford.

Cuipers, P. (2003). Examining the effects of prevention programmes on the incidence of new cases of mental disorders: The lack of statistical power. *American Journal of Psychiatry*, *160*, 1385–1391.

Das Eiden, R., Teti, D. M., & Corns, K. M. (1995). Maternal working models of attachment, marital adjustment, and the parent-child relationship. *Child Development*, *66*, 1504–1518.

David, P. A. (1991). Computer and Dynamo: The Modern Productivity Paradox in a Not-Too-Distant Mirror, in *OECD, Technology and Productivity: The Challenge for Economic Policy*. Paris: OECD, 315–348.

Davis, C. H., MacKinnon, D. P., Schultz, A., & Sandler, I. (2003). Cumulative risk and population attributable fraction in prevention. *Journal of Clinical Child and Adolescent Psychology*, *32*(2), 228–235.

Dawson, N., & McHugh, B. (2000). Family relationships, learning and teachers—Keeping the connections. In R. Best, & C. Watkins (Eds.), *Tomorrow's Schools*. London: Routledge.

De Wolff, M. S., & van IJzendoorn, M. H. (1997). Sensitivity and attachment: A meta-analysis on parental antecedents of infant attachment. *Child Development*, *68*, 571–591.

Del Piccolo, L., Saltini, A., & Zimmerman, C. (1998). Which patients talk about stressful life events to the general practitioner? *Psychological Medicine*, *28*, 1289–1299.

Dellu, F., Mayo, W., Vallee, M., Le Moal, M., & Simon, H. (1994). Reactivity to novelty during youth as a predictive factor of cognitive impairment in the elderly: A longitudinal study in rats. *Brain Research*, *653*, 51–56.

Department for Education & Skills. (2003). *Every Child Matters*. London: Stationery Office.

Department for Education & Skills. (2004). *Every Child Matters: Next Steps*. London: Department for Education & Skills.

Department of Health. (1995). *A Handbook on Child and Adolescent Mental Health*. London: Department of Health.

Department of Health. (1999). *Saving Lives: Our Healthier Nation*. London: HMSO.

Department of Health. (2000). *The NHS Plan: A Plan for Investment, A Plan for Reform*. London: Department of Health.

Department of Health. (2002a). *Improvement, Expansion and Reform: The Next 3 Years. Priorities and Planning Framework 2003–2006*. London: Department of Health.

Department of Health. (2002b). *Safeguarding Children: A Joint Chief Inspector's Report on Arrangements to Safeguard Children*. London: Department of Health.

Department of Health. (2003). *Fast-forwarding Primary Care Mental Health: Graduate Primary Care Mental Health Workers*. London: Department of Health.

Department of Health. (2004). *The Mental Health and Psychological Well-being of Children and Young People. Standard Nine of the National Service Framework for Children, Young People and Maternity Services*. London: Department of Health.

Department of Health. (2005). *Delivering a Comprehensive Child and Adolescent Mental Health Service by 2006*. London: Department of Health.

Department of Health & Department for Education & Skills. (2004). *National Service Framework for Children, Young People and Maternity Services*. Available at: http://www.dh.gov.uk/PublicationsandStatistics/Publications/PublicationsPolicyandGuidance/Publications
PolicyandGuidanceArticle/fs/en?CONTENT_ID=4089100&chk=Egpznc

Department of Health, Home Office, & Department for Education & Skills. (2003). *Keeping Children Safe: The Government's Resonse to the Victoria Climbié Inquiry Report and Joint Chief Inspectors' Report Safeguarding Children*. London: Stationery Office.

Deutsch, M., Deutsch, C. P., Jordan, T. J., & Grallo, R. (1983). The IDS programme: An experiment in early and sustained enrichment. In C. f. L. Studies (Ed.), *As the Twig is Bent. Lasting Effects of Preschool Programmes*. Hillsdale, NJ: Lawrence Erlbaum Associates Inc.

Donoghue, J. M., & Tylee, A. (1996). The treatment of depression: Prescribing patterns of antidepressants in primary care in the UK. *British Journal of Psychiatry, 168*, 164–168.

Drever, F., Whitehead, M., & Roden, M. (1996). Current patterns and trends in male mortality by social class (based on occupation). *Population Trends, 86*, 15–20.

Dunn, V., & Goodyer, I. M. (2006). Longitudinal investigation into childhood- and adolescence-onset depression: Psychiatric outcome in early adulthood. *British Journal of Psychiatry, 188*, 216–222.

Durham University Mapping Team. (2002). CAMHS Mapping website. Available at: http://www.camhsmapping.org.uk/

Durlak, J. A., & Wells, A. M. (1997). Primary prevention mental health programmes for children and adolescents: A meta-analytical review. *American Journal of Community Psychology, 25*, 115–152.

Dyer, A. R., Stamler, J., Shekelle, R. B., & Schoenberger, J. (1976). The relationship of education to blood pressure: findings on 40,000 employed Chicagoans. *Circulation*. Dec; *54*(6), 987–992.

Eckenrode, J., et al. (2001). Child maltreatment and the early onset of problem behaviors: Can a programme of nurse home visitation break the link? *Development and Psychopathology, 13*(4), 873–890.

Elder, G. H., & Caspi, A. (1988). Economic stress in lives: Developmental perspectives. *Journal of Social Issues, 44*, 25–45.

Elicker, J., Englund, M., & Sroufe, L. A. (1992). Predicting peer competence and peer relationships in childhood from early parent-child relationships. In R. Parke, & G. Ladd (Eds.), *Family-Peer Relationships: Modes of Linkage* (pp. 77–106). Hillsdale, NJ: Erlbaum.

Englund, M. M., Levy, A. K., Hyson, D. M., & Sroufe, L. A. (2000). Adolescent social competence: effectiveness in a group setting. *Child Development, 71*(4), 1049–1060.

Falloon I. R., Boyd, J. L., McGill, C. W., Williamson, M., Razani, J., Moss, H. B., Gilderman, A. M. & Simpson, G. M. (1985). Family management in the prevention of morbidity of schizophrenia. *Archives of General Psychiatry, 42*, 887–896.

Farmer, I. P., et al. (1996). Higher levels of social support predict greater survival following accute myocardial infarction: The Corpus Christi Heart Project. *Behavioral Medicine, 22*, 59–66.

Fava, M., & Kendler, K. (2000). Major depressive disorder. *Neuron, 28*(2), 335–341.

Felitti, V. J. (2002). The relation between adverse childhood experiences and adult health: Turning gold into lead. *The Permanente Journal, 6*, 44–47.

Felitti, V. J., et al. (1998). Relationship of childhood abuse and household dysfunction to many of the leading causes of death in adults: The Adverse Childhood Experiences (ACE) study. *American Journal of Preventive Medicine, 14*, 245–258.

Fergusson, D. M., & Lynskey, M. T. (1996). Adolescent resiliency to family adversity. *Journal of Child Psychology and Psychiatry, 37*, 281–292.

Ferrie, J. E. (2001). Is job insecurity harmful to health? *Journal of the Royal Society of Medicine, 94*, 71–76.

Ferrie, J. E., Martikainen, P., Shipley, M. J., Marmot, M. G., Stansfeld, S. A., & Davey Smith, G. (2001). Employment status and health after privatisation in white collar civil servants: Prospective cohort study. *British Medical Journal, 322*, 647–651.

Ferrie, J. E., Shipley, M. J., Davey Smith, G., Stansfeld, S. A., & Marmot, M. (2002a). Change in health inequalities among British civil servants: The Whitehall II study. *Journal of Epidemiology and Community Health, 56*, 922–926.

Ferrie, J. E., Shipley, M. J., Marmot, M. G., Stansfield, S., & Davey Smith, G. (1995). Health effects of anticipation of job change and non-employment: Longitudinal data from the Whitehall II study. *British Medical Journal, 311*, 1264–1269.

Ferrie, J. E., Shipley, M. J., Newman, K., Stansfeld, S. A., & Marmot, M. (2005). Self-reported job insecurity and health in the Whitehall II study: Potential explanations of the relationship. *Social Science & Medicine, 60*(7), 1593–1602.

Ferrie, J. E., Shipley, M. J., Stansfeld, S. A., Davey Smith, G., & Marmot, M. (2003). Future uncertainty and socioeconomic inequalities in health: The Whitehall II study. *Social Science & Medicine, 57*, 637–646.

Ferrie, J. E., Shipley, M. J., Stansfeld, S. A., & Marmot, M. G. (2002b). Effects of chronic job insecurity and change in job security on self reported health, minor psychiatric morbidity, physiological measures and health related behaviors in British civil servants: The Whitehall II Study. *Journal of Epidemiology and Community Health, 56*(6), 405–406.

Field, T. M., Widmayer, S., Greenberg, R., & Stoller, S. (1982). Effects of parent training on teenage mother and their infants. *Pediatrics, 69*, 703–707.

Field, T. M., et al. (1986). Tactile/kinesthetic stimulation effects on preterm neonates. *Pediatrics, 77*, 654–658.

Fiese, B. H., Tomcho, T. J., Douglas, M., Josephs, K., Poltrock, S., & Baker, T. (2002). A review of 50 years of research on naturally occurring routines and rituals: Cause for celebration? *Journal of Family Psychology, 16*, 381–390.

Finkelhor, D. (1986). *A Sourcebook on Child Sexual Abuse.* Beverly Hills: Sage Publications.

Floeter, M. K. (1979). Cerebellar plasticity: Modifications of purkinje cell structure by diferential raring in monkeys. *Science, 206*, 227–229.

Fogel, R. W. (1994). *Economic Growth, Population Theory and Physiology: The Bearing of Long-Term Processes on the Making of Economic Policy.* Cambridge, Mass.: National Bureau of Economic Research.

Fombonne, E., et al. (2001). The Maudsley long-term follow-up of child and adolescent depression: 1. Psychiatric outcomes in adulthood. *British Journal of Psychiatry, 179*, 210–217.

Fonagy, P. (1991). Thinking about thinking: Some clinical and theoretical considerations in the treatment of a borderline patient. *International Journal of Psycho-Analysis, 72*, 1–18.

Fonagy, P. (2003). The development of psychopathology from infancy to adulthood: The mysterious unfolding of disturbance in time. *Infant Mental Health Journal, 24*(3), 212–239.

Fonagy, P., Gergely, G., Jurist, E., & Target, M. (2002a). *Affect Regulation, Mentalization and the Development of the Self.* New York: Other Press.

Fonagy, P., Steele, H., & Steele, M. (1991). Maternal representations of attachment during pregnancy predict the organization of infant-mother attachment at one year of age. *Child Development, 62,* 891–905.

Fonagy, P., & Target, M. (1997). Attachment and reflective function: Their role in self-organization. *Development and Psychopathology, 9,* 679–700.

Fonagy, P., Target, M., Cottrell, D., Phillips, J., & Kurtz, Z. (2000). *A Review of the Outcomes of All Treatments of Psychiatric Disorder in Childhood* (No. MCH 17–33). London: National Health Service Executive.

Fonagy, P., Target, M., Cottrell, D., Phillips, J., & Kurtz, Z. (2002b). *What Works For Whom? A Critical Review of Treatments for Children and Adolescents.* New York: Guilford.

Ford, T., Hamilton, H., Goodman, R., & Meltzer, H. (2005). Service contacts among the children participating in the British child and adolescent mental health surveys. *Child and Adolescent Mental Health, 10*(1), 2–9.

Forgatch, M. S., & DeGarmo, D. S. (1999). Parenting through change: An effective prevention programme for single mothers. *Journal of Consulting and Clinical Psychology, 67*(5), 711–724.

Francis, D. D., Caldji, C., Champagne, F., Plotsky, P. M., & Meaney, M. J. (1999). The role of corticotropine-releasing factor-norepinephrine systems in mediating the effects of early experience on the development of behavioral and endocrine responses to stress. *Biological Psychiatry, 46,* 1153–1166.

Fredrickson, B. L. (2001). The role of positive emotions in positive psychology. The broaden-and-build theory of positive emotions. *American Psychologist, 56*(3), 218–226.

Fride, E., Dan, Y., Feldon, J., Halevy, G., & Weinstock, M. (1986). Effects of prenatal stress on vulnerability to stress in prepubertal and adult rats. *Physiology and Behavior, 37,* 681–687.

Funkenstein, D., King, S., & Drolette, M. (1957). *Mastery of Stress.* Cambridge, MA: Harvard University Press.

Gale, F., Dover, S., Edwards, J., & Flemming, A. (2004). *The Role of the Child Primary Mental Health Worker (PMHW).* National (UK) Committee for Primary Mental Health Workers in CAMHS, National CAMHS Support Service, and Department of Health.

Garber, H. L. (1988). *The Milwaukee Project: Preventing Mental retardation in Children at Risk.* Washington, DC: American Association on Mental Retardation.

Gergely, G. (2002). The development of understanding of self and agency. In U. Goshwami (Ed.), *Handbook of Childhood Cognitive Development* (pp. 26–46). Oxford: Blackwell.

Giles, D. E., et al. (1989). Clinical predictors of recurrence in depression. *American Journal of Psychiatry, 146*(6), 764–767.

Gilligan, J. (1997). *Violence: Our Deadliest Epidemic and Its Causes.* New York: Grosset/Putnam.

Goldberg, D., et al. (1998). The effects of detection and treatment on the outcome of major depression in primary care: A naturalistic study in 15 cities. *British Journal of General Practice, 48*(437), 1840–1844.

Goldberg, S., Benoit, D., Blokland, K., & Madigan, S. (2003). Atypical maternal behavior, maternal representations, and infant disorganized attachment. *Development and Psychopathology, 15*(2), 239–257.

Goldstein, M. J., et al. (1978). Drug and family therapy in the after-care of acute schizophrenics. *Archives of General Psychiatry, 35,* 1169–1177.

Goodman, R. (1997a). *Child and Adolescent Mental Health Services: Reasoned Advice to Commissioners and Providers.* London: Institute of Psychiatry, South London and Maudsley NHS Trust.

Goodman, R. (1997b). The strengths and difficulties questionnaire: A research note. *Journal of Child Psychology and Psychiatry, 38*, 581–586.

Goodyer, I. M., Herbert, J., & Tamplin, A. (2003). Psychoendocrine antecedents of persistent first-episode major depression in adolescents: A community-based longitudinal enquiry. *Psychological Medicine, 33*, 601–610.

Goodyer, I. M., Herbert, J., Tamplin, A., & Altham, P. M. (2000). Recent life events, cortisol, dehydroepiandrosterone and the onset of major depression in high-risk adolescents. *British Journal of Psychiatry, 177*, 499–504.

Gottman, J. M., Katz, L., & Hooven, C. (1997). *Meta-emotion: How Families Communicate Emotionally.* Mahwah, NJ: Erlbaum.

Graham, E., MacLeod, M. D., Johnston, M., Dibben, C., & Briscoe, S. (2000). Individual deprivation, neighbourhood and recovery from illness. In H. Graham (Ed.), *Understanding Health Inequalities* (pp. 170–185). Buckingham: Open University Press.

Gray, J., Cutler, C., Dean, J., & Kempe, C. H. (1979). Prediction and prevention of child abuse and neglect. *Journal of Social Issues, 35*, 127–139.

Gray, S. W., & Klaus, R. A. (1965). An experimental preschool programme for culturally deprived children. *Child Development, 36*, 887–898.

Gray, S. W., & Klaus, R. A. (1970). The early training project: A seventh-year report. *Child Development, 41*, 909–924.

Grayer, J., Buszewicz, M., Orpwood, L., Cape, J., & Leibowitz, J. (2006). A Primary Care Mental Health Worker pilot study: Facilitating access to voluntary and community sector services. A description of the 'Community Link Service', patient characteristics, and primary care staff's perceptions. *Primary Care Mental Health* (in press).

Greenberg, M. T., Kusche, C. A., Cook, E. T., & Quamma, J. T. (1995). Promoting emotional competence in school-aged children: The effects of the PATHS Curricululm. *Development and Psychopathology, 7*, 117–136.

Griffin, D., & Bartholomew, K. (1996). Models of the self and other: Fundamental dimensions underlying measures of adult attachment. *Journal of Personality and Social Psychology, 67*, 430–445.

Grossman, K. E., Grossman, K., Winter, M., & Zimmerman, P. (2002). Attachment relationships and appraisal of partnership: From early experience of sensitive support to later relationship representation. In L. Pulkkinen, & A. Caspi (Eds.), *Paths to Succesful Development*. Cambridge: Cambridge University Press.

Grossman, K. E., Grossman, K., & Zimmermann, P. (1999). A wider view of attachment and exploration. In J. Cassidy, & P. R. Shaver (Eds.), *Handbook of Attachment: Theory, Research and Clinical Applications* (pp. 760–786). New York: Guilford.

Grossman, K. E., Grossmann, K., & Schwan, A. (1986). Capturing the wider view of attachment: A reanalysis of Ainsworth's Strange Situation. In C. E. Izard, & P. B. Read (Eds.), *Measuring Emotions in Infants and Children* (Vol. 2, pp. 124–171). New York: Cambridge University Press.

Grossmann, K. E., Grossmann, K., & Waters, E. (Eds.). (2005). *The Power of Longitodinal Atachment Research: From Infancy and Childhood to Adulthood.* New York: Guilford.

Gunnar, M., & Vazquez, D. (2006). Stress neurobiology and developmental psychopathology. In D. Cicchetti, & D. J. Cohen (Eds.), *Developmental Psychopathology*, 2nd edn. *Volume II: Developmental Neuroscience* (pp. 533–577). New York: Wiley.

Gutelius, M. F., Kirsch, A. D., MacDonald, S., Brooks, M. R., McErlean, T., & Newcomb, C. (1972). Promising results from a cognitive stimulation programme in infancy. A preliminary report. *Clinical Pediatrics, 11*, 585–593.

H M Treasury. (2004). *Child Poverty Review.* London: H M Treasury.

Hagel, A. (2004). *Time Trends in Adolescent Well-being.* London: Nuffield Foundation.

Hamilton, C. E. (2000). Continuity and discontinuity of attachment from infancy through adolescence. *Child Development, 71*(3), 690–694.

Hansen, D. G., Vach, W., Rosholm, J. U., Søndergaard, J., Gram, L. F., & Kragstrup, J. (2004). Early discontinuation of antidepressants in general practice: Association with patient and prescriber characteristics. *Family Practice, 21*(6), 623–629.

Hardy, J. B., & Streett, R. (1989). Family support and parenting education in the home: an effective extension of clinic-based preventive health care services for poor children. *Journal of Pediatrics, 115*, 927–931.

Harrington, R. (2001). Depression, suicide and deliberate self-harm in adolescence. *British Medical Bulletin, 57*, 47–60.

Harrington, R., & Dubicka, B. (2001). Natural history of mood disorders in children and adolescents. Cambridge Child and Adolescent Psychiatry series. In I. M. Goodyear (Ed.), *The Depressed Child and Adolescent* (pp. 311–343). Cambridge: Cambridge University Press.

Harris, J. R. (1998). *The Nurture Assumption: Why Children Turn out the Way They Do. Parents Matter Less than You Think and Peers Matter More.* New York: Free Press.

HAS 2000. (2000). *Standards for Child and Adolescent Mental Health Services.* Brighton: Pavilion Publishing.

Hauser-Cram, P., Sirin, S. R., & Stipek, D. (2003). When teachers' and parents' values differ: Teachers' ratings of academic competence in children from low-income families. *Journal of Educational Psychology, 95*, 813–820.

Hawton, K., & James, A. (2005). Suicide and deliberate self harm in young people. *British Medical Journal, 330*, 891–894.

Hebert, T. P. (2002). Educating gifted children from low socioeconomic backgrounds: Creating visions of a hopeful future. *Exceptionality, 10*, 127–138.

Heffelfinger, A. K., & Newcomer, J. W. (2001). Vlucocorticoid effects on memory function over the human lifespan. *Development and Psychopathology, 13*, 491–513.

Heffernan, K., & Cloitre, M. (2000). A comparison of posttraumatic stress disorder with and without borderline personality disorder among women with a history of childhood sexual abuse: Etiological and clinical characteristics. *Journal of Nervous and Mental Disease, 188*(9), 589–595.

Heinicke, C. M., Fineman, N. R., Ponce, V. A., & Guthrie, D. (2001). Relation based intervention with at-risk mothers: Outcome in the second year of life. *Infant Mental Health Journal, 22*, 431–462.

Heinicke, C. M., Fineman, N. R., Ruth, G., Recchia, S. L., Giuthrie, D., & Rodning, C. (1999). Relationship-based intervention with at-risk mothers: Outcome in the first year of life. *Infant Mental Health Journal, 20*, 349–374.

Heinicke, C. M., & Ponce, V. A. (1999). Relation-based early family intervention. In D. Cicchetti, & S. L. Toth (Eds.), *Rochester Symposium on Developmental Psychopathology. Vol. 9: Developmental Approaches to Prevention and Intervention.* Rochester: University of Rochester Press.

Heinicke, C. M., et al. (2000). Relationship-based intervention with at-risk mothers: Factors affecting variations in outcome. *Infant Mental Health Journal, 21*(3), 133–155.

Hemingway, H., & Marmot, M. G. (1999). Psychosocial factors in the aetiology and prognosis of coronary heart disease: A systematic review of prospective cohort studies. *British Medical Journal, 318*, 1460–1461.

Henggeler, S. W., & Borduin, C. M. (1990). *Family Therapy and Beyond: A Multisystermic Approach to Treating the Behavior Problems of Children and Adolescents.* Pacific Grove, CA: Brooks/Cole.

Henggeler, S. W., Melton, G. B., Smith, L. A., Schoenwald, S. K., & Hanley, J. H. (1993). Family preservation using multisystemic treatment: Long-term follow-up to a clinical trial with serious juvenile offenders. *Journal of Child and Family Studies, 2*, 283–293.

Hertzman, C. (1995). *Environment and Health in Central and Eastern Europe.* Washington, DC: World Bank.

Hertzman, C., & Wiens, M. (1996). Child development and long-term outcomes: A population health perspective and summary of successful interventions. *Social Science and Medicine, 43*, 1083–1095.

Heslop, P., Davey Smith, G., Carroll, D., Macleod, J., & Hart, C. (2001). Perceived stress and coronary heart disease risk-factors: The contribution of socio-economic position. *British Journal of Health Psychology, 6*, 167–178.

Hesse, E., & Main, M. (2000). Disorganized infant, child, and adult attachment. *Journal of the American Psychoanalytical Association, 48*, 1097–1127.

Hetherington, E. M., & Kelly, J. (2002). *For Better or for Worse: Divorce Reconsidered.* New York: W.W. Norton.

Hill, J., Fonagy, P., Safier, E., & Sargent, J. (2003). The ecology of attachment in the family. *Fam Process, 42*(2), 205–221.

Hobson, P., Patrick, M., Crandell, L. E., Garcia-Perez, R., & Lee, A. (2005). Personal relatedness and attachment in infants of mothers with borderline personality disorder. *Development and Psychopathology, 17*, 329–347.

Hodes, M., Garralda, M. E., Rose, G., & Schwartz, R. (1999). Maternal expressed emotion and adjustment in children with epilepsy. *Journal of Child Psychology and Psychiatry, and Allied Disciplines, 40*(7), 1083–1093.

Hofer, M. A. (1995). Hidden regulators: Implications for a new understanding of attachment, separation and loss. In S. Goldberg, R. Muir, & J. Kerr (Eds.), *Attachment Theory: Social, Developmental, and Clinical Perspectives* (pp. 203–230). Hillsdale, NJ: The Analytical Press, Inc.

Hofer, M. A. (1996). On the nature and consequences of early loss. *Psychosomatic Medicine, 58*, 570–581.

Hoffman, M. L. (2000). *Empathy and Moral Development. Implications for Caring and Justice.* Cambridge: Cambridge University Press.

Hoffman, S., & Hatch, M. C. (1996). Stress, social support and pregnancy outcomes: A reassessment based on recent research. *Paediatric and Perinatal Epidemiology, 10*(4), 380–405.

House, J. S., Robbins, C., & Metzner, H. L. (1982). The association of social relationships and activities with mortality: Prospective evidence from the Tecumseh community health study. *American Journal of Epidemiology, 116*, 123–140.

Howell, J. C. (1997). *Juvenile Justice and Youth.* Thousand Oaks, CA: Sage.

Hunkeler, E. M., et al. (2000). Efficacy of nurse telehealth care and peer support in augmenting treatment of depression in primary care. *Archives of Family Medicine, 9*, 700–708.

Huston, A. C., et al. (2001). Work-based antipoverty programmes for parents can enhance the school performance and social behavior of children. *Child Development, 72*(1), 318–336.

Infante-Rivard, C., Filion, G., Baumgarten, M., Bourassa, M., Labelle, M., & Messier, M. (1989). A public health home intervention among families of low socio-economic status. *Children's Health Care, 18*, 102–107.

Inoue, T., Tsuchiya, K., & Koyama, T. (1994). Regional changes in dopamine and serotonin activation with various intensity of physical and psychological stress in the rat brain. *Pharmacology, Biochemistry and Behavior, 49*, 911–920.

Insel, T. R. (2003). Is social attachment an addictive disorder? *Physiology & Behavior, 79*(3), 351–357.

Insel, T. R., & Fernald, R. D. (2004). How the brain processes social information: Searching for the social brain. *Annual Reviews of Neuroscience, 27*, 697–722.

Izard, C. E. (2002). Translating emotion theory and research into preventive interventions. *Psychological Bulletin, 128*(5), 796–824.

Izard, C. E., Fine, S., Mostow, A., Trentacosta, C., & Campbell, J. (2002). Emotion processes in normal and abnormal development and preventive intervention. *Development and Psychopathology, 14*(4), 761–787.

Jackson, A. P. (2000). Maternal self-efficacy and children's influence on stress and parenting among single black mothers in poverty. *Journal of Family Issues, 21*, 3–16.

Jackson, J. J. (1988). Social determinatns of the health of ageing black populations in the United States. In J. Jackson (Ed.), *The bloack American Elderly: Research on Physical and Psychosocial Health.* New York: Springer.

Jackson, R. W., Treiber, F. A., Turner, J. R., Davis, H., & Strong, W. B. (1999). The effects of race sex and socionomic status on cardiovascular responsivity and recovery in youth. *International Journal of Psychophysiology, 31*, 111–119.

Jenkins, R., et al. (1997). The National Psychiatric Morbidity surveys of Great Britain—initial findings from the household survey. *Psychological Medicine, 27*, 775–789.

Jester, R. E., & Guinagh, B. J. (1983). The Gordon parent education infant and toddler programme. In T. C. f. L. Studies (Ed.), *As the Twig is Bent. Lasting Effects of Preschool Programmes* (pp. 103–132). Hhillsdale, NJ: Lawrence Erlbaum Associates Inc.

Johnson, D. L., & Walker, T. (1991). A follow-up evaluation of the Houston Parent-Child Development Center: School performance. *Journal of Early Intervention, 15*, 226–236.

Jones, E., & Asen, E. (2000). *Systemic Couple Therapy and Depression*. London: Karnac.

Jorgensen, R. S., Frankowski, J. J., Lantinga, L. J., Phadke, K., Sprafkin, R. P., & Abdul-Karim, K. W. (2001). Defensive hostility and coronary heart disease: A preliminary investigation of male veterans. *Psychosomatic Medicine, 63*, 463–469.

Kaehler, S. T., Singewald, N., Sinner, C., Thurner, C., & Phillipu, A. (2000). Conditioned fear and inescapable shock modify the release of serotonin in the locus coeruleus. *Brain Research, 859*, 249–254.

Kahn, H. S., Williamson, D. F., & Stevens, J. A. (1991). Race and weight change in US women: the roles of socioeconomic and marital status. *American Journal of Public Health, 81*, 319–323.

Kalynchuk, L. E., & Meaney, M. J. (2003). Amygdala kindling increases fear responses and decreases glucocorticoid receptor mRNA expression in hippocampal regions. *Progress in Neuropsychopharmacology and Biological Psychiatry, 27*, 1225–1234.

Kalynchuk, L. E., Pinel, J. P., & Meaney, M. J. (2006). Serotonin receptor binding and mRNA expression in the hippocampus of fearful amygdala-kindled rats. *Neuroscience Letters, 396*(1), 38–43.

Kam, C. M., Greenberg, M. T., & Walls, C. T. (2003). Examining the role of implementation quality in school-based prevention using the PATHS curriculum. Promoting Alternative THinking Skills Curriculum. *Prevention Science, 4*(1), 55–63.

Kaplan, G. A., et al. (1996). Inequality in income and mortality in the United States: Analysis of mortality and potential pathways. *British Medical Journal, 312*, 999–1253.

Karlsen, S., & Nazroo, J. Y. (2000). The relationship between racism, social class and health amongst ethnic minority groups. *Health Variations: Official newsletter of the ESRC Health Variations Programme, 5*, 8–9.

Karlsen, S., & Nazroo, J. Y. (2002a). Agency and structure: The impact of ethnic identity and racism on the health of ethnic minority people. *Sociology of Health and Illness, 24*(1), 1–20.

Karlsen, S., & Nazroo, J. Y. (2002b). The relationship between racial discrimination, social class and health among ethnic minority groups. *American Journal of Public Health, 92*(4), 624–631.

Karlsen, S., & Nazroo, J. Y. (2002c). The relationship between racial discrimination, social class and health among ethnic minority groups. *American Journal of Public Health, 92*, 624–631.

Karlsen, S., & Nazroo, J. Y. (2004). Fear of racism and health. *Journal of Epidemiology and Community Health, 58*(12), 1017–1018.

Karnes, M. B., Teska, J. A., & Hodgins, A. S. (1970). The effects of four programmes of classroom intervention on the intellectual and language development of 4-year-old disadvantaged children. *American Journal of Orthopsychiatry, 40*, 58–76.

Karoly, L. A., et al. (1998). *Investing in Our Children: What We Know and Don't Know About the Costs and Benefits of Early Childhood Interventions*. Santa Monica, CA: RAND Corp.

Katon, W., Von Korff, M., Lin, E., Bush, T., & Ormel, J. (1992). Adequacy and duration of antidepressant treatment in primary care. *Medical Care, 30*, 67–76.

Katon, W., et al. (1995). Collaborative management to achieve treatment guidelines. Impact on depression in primary care. *Journal of the American Medical Association, 273*, 1026–1031.

Katon, W., et al. (1996). A multifaceted intervention to improve treatment of depression in primary care. *Archives of General Psychiatry, 53*, 924–932.

Katzelnick, D., et al. (2000). Randomized trial of a depression management programme in high utilizers of medical care. *Archives of Family Medicine, 9*, 345–351.

Kaufman, J., & Charney, D. F. (2001). Effects of early stress on brain structure and function: Implications for understanding the relationship between child maltreatment and depression. *Development and Psychopathology, 13*, 451–471.

Kawachi, I., Kennedy, B. P., & Protrow-Stith, D. (1996). Income distribution and mortality: Cross-sectional ecological study of the Robin Hood Index in the United States. *British Medical Journal, 312*, 1004–1007.

Kellam, S. G., Ling, X., Merisca, R., Brown, C. H., & Ialongo, N. (1998). The effect of the level of aggression in the first grade classroom on the course and malleability of aggressive behavior into middle school. *Development and Psychopathology, 10*(2), 165–185.

Kellam, S. G., Rebok, G. W., Mayer, L. S., Ialongo, N., & Kalodner, C. R. (1994). Depressive symptoms over first grade and their response to a developmental epidemiologically based preventive trial aimed at improving achievement. *Development and Psychopathology, 6*, 463–481.

Kelvin, R. G. (2005). Capacity of tier 2/3 CAMHS and service specification: A model to enable evidence based service development. *Child and Adolescent Mental Health, 10*(2), 63–73.

Kendrick, D., et al. (2000). Does home visiting improve parenting and quality of the home environment? A systematic review and meta-analysis. *Archives of Diseases in Childhood, 86*, 443–451.

Kiecolt-Glaser, J. K., & Glaser, R. (1995). Psychoneuroimmunology and health consequences: Data and shared mechanisms. *Psychosomatic Medicine, 57*, 269–274.

Kim-Cohen, J., Caspi, A., Moffitt, T. E., Harrington, H.-L., & Milne, B. J. P., R. (2003). Prior juvenile diagnoses in adults with mental disorder: Developmental follow-back of a prospective longitudinal cohort. *Archives of General Psychiatry, 60*, 709–717.

Kitzman, H., et al. (1997). Effect of prenatal and infancy home visitation by nurses on pregnancy outcomes, childhood injuries, and repeated childbearing: A randomized controlled trial. *Journal of the American Medical Association, 278*, 644–652.

Kivimaki, M., et al. (2005). Justice at work and reduced risk of coronary heart disease among employees: the Whitehall II Study. *Archives of Internal Medicine, 165*(19), 2245–2251.

Klein, M. (1945). The Oedipus complex in the light of early anxieties. In *Love, Guilt and Reparation: The Writings of Melanie Klein* (Vol. I, pp. 370–419). London: Hogarth Press.

Klerman, G. L., Weissman, M. M., Rounsaville, B. J., & Chevron, E. S. (1984). *Interpersonal Psychotherapy of Depression*. New York: Basic Books.

Klohaen, B., & John, O. (1998). Working models of attachment: A theory based prototype approach. In J. Simpson, & W. Rholes (Eds.), *Attachmetn theory and close relationships*. New York: Guilford.

Knox, S. S., Adelman, A., Ellison, R. C., & Arnett. (2000). Hostility, social support and carotid artery atherosclerosis in National Heart, Lung and Blood Institute Family Heart Study. *American Journal of Cardiology, 86*, 1086–1089.

Kochanska, G. (2001). Emotional development in children with different attachment histories: The first three years. *Child Development, 72*, 474–490.

Kochanska, G., Murray, K., & Harlan, E. (2000). Effortful control in early childhood: Continuity and change, antecedents, and implications for social development. *Developmental Psychology, 36*, 220–232.

Kochanska, G., & Murray, K. T. (2000). Mother-child mutually responsive orientation and conscience development: From toddler to early school age. *Child Development, 71*, 417–431.

Kraemer, G. W. (1992). A psychobiological theory of attachment. *Behavior and Brain Sciences, 15*, 493–511.

Kristenson, M. (1998). *Possible Causes for the Differences in Coronary Heart Disease Mortality between Lithuania and Sweden: The LiVicordia Study*. Unpublished Linkoping University Medical Dissertations No 547, Linkoping University.

Kuipers, L., Leff, J., & Lam, D. (1992). *Family Work for Schizophrenia: A Practical Guide.* London: Gaskell.

Kupfer, D. J. (1991). Long-term treatment of depression. *Journal of Clinical Psychiatry,* 52(Suppl. 5), 28–34.

Kurtz, Z., Thornes, R., & Wolkind, S. (1995). *Services for the Mental Health of Children and Young People in England: A National Review.* London: Department of Health.

Lakoff, G., & Johnson, M. (1999). *Philosophy in the Flesh: The Embodied Mind and its Challenge to Western Thought.* New York: Basic Books.

Langford, H. G., Watson, R. L., & Douglas, B. H. (1968). Factors affecting blood pressure in population groups. *Transactions of the Association of American Physician,* 8(1), 135–145.

Laqueur, H. P., La Burt, H. A., & Morong, E. (1964). Multiple family therapy: Further developments. *International Journal of Social Psychiatry,* 10, 69–80.

Larson, C. P. (1980). Efficacy of prenatal and postpartum home visits on child health and development. *Pediatrics,* 66, 191–197.

Larson, M., Gunnar, M., & Hertsgaard, L. (1991). The effectsof morning naps, car trips, and maternal separation onadrenocortical activity in human infants. *Child Development,* 62, 362–372.

Laucht, M., Esser, G., & Schmidt, M. H. (1994). Parental mental disorder and early child development. *European Child and Adolescent Psychiatry,* 3, 124–137.

Le Grange, D., Eisler, I., Dare, C., & Hodes, M. (1992). Family criticism and self-starvation: A study of expressed emotion. *Journal of Family Therapy,* 14, 177–192.

Lealman, G. T., Haigh, D., Phillips, J. M., Stone, J., & Ord-Smith, C. (1983). Prediction and prevention of child abuse—an empty hope? *Lancet,* 1(8339), 1423–1424.

LeBar, K. S., & LeDoux, J. E. (2003). Fear conditioning in relation to affective neuroanatomy. In R. J. Davidson & K. R. Scherer (Eds.), *Handbook of Affective Sciences.* London: Oxford University Press.

Lee, V. E., Brooks-Gunn, J., & Schnur, E. (1988). Does Head Start work? A 1-year follow-up comparison of disadvantaged children attending Head Start, no preschool, and other preschool programmes. *Developmental Psychology,* 24, 210–222.

Lee, V. E., Brooks-Gunn, J., Schnur, E., & Liaw, F. R. (1990). Are Head Start effects sustained? A longitudinal follow-up comparison of disadvantaged children attending Head Start, no preschool, and other preschool programmes. *Child Development,* 61, 495–507.

Leerkes, E. M., & Siepak, K. J. (2006). Attachment linked predictors of women's emotional and cognitive responses to infant distress. *Attachment & Human Development,* 8(1), 11–32.

Leff, J., & Vaughn, C. (1982). The role of maintenance therapy and relatives' expressed emotion in the relapse of schizophrenia: A two-year follow-up. *British Journal of Psychiatry,* 139, 102–104.

Leff, J. P., & Vaughn, C. (1985). *Expressed emotion in families.* New York: Guilford Press.

Leib, S. A., Benfield, D. G., & Guidubaldi, J. (1980). Effects of early intervention and stimulation on the preterm infant. *Pediatrics,* 66, 83–90.

Lesperance, F., & Frasure-Smith, N. (2000). Depression in patients with cardiac disease: A practical review. *Journal of Psychosomatic Research,* 48(4–5), 379–391.

Levenstein, P., & Sunley, R. (1968). Stimulation of verbal interaction between disadvantaged mothers and children. *American Journal of Orthopsychiatry,* 38, 116–121.

Lewis, G., et al. (2003). *Self-Help Interventions for Mental Health Problems. Report to the Department of Health R & D Programme.* London: Department of Health.

Liu, D., et al. (1997a). Maternal care, hippocampal glucocorticoid receptors, and hypothalamic-pituitary-adrenal responses to stress. *Science,* 277, 1659–1662.

Liu, D., et al. (1997b). Maternal care, hippocampal glucocorticoid receptors, and hypothalamic-pituitary-adrenal responses to stress. *Science,* 277, 1659–1662.

Lochman, J. E., & Wells, K. C. (2002). The Coping Power programme at the middle-school transition: Universal and indicated prevention effects. *Psychology of Addictive Behaviors,* 16(4 Suppl.), S40–S54.

Loeber, R., Farrington, D. P., & Waschbusch, D. A. (1998). Serious and violent juvenile offenders. In R. Loeber, & D. P. Farrington (Eds.), *Serious and Violent Juvenile Offenders: Risk Factors and Successful Interventions* (pp. 13–29). Thousand Oaks, CA: Sage.

Lord Laming. (2003). *The Victoria Climbié Inquiry*. London: Stationery Office.

Lupien, S., King, E., Meaney, M., & McEwan, B. (2001). Can poverty get under your skin? Basal cortisol levels and cognitive function in children from low and high socioeconomic status. *Development and Psychopathology, 2001*(13), 653–676.

Luthar, S. S. (Ed.). (2003). *Resilience and vulnerability: Adaptation in the context of childhood adversities*. Cambridge: Cambridge University Press.

Luthar, S. S., & Becker, B. E. (2002). Privileged but pressured: A study of affluent youth. *Child Development, 73*, 1593–1610.

Luthar, S. S., & Latendresse, S. J. (2005). Comparable 'risks' at the socioeconomic status extremes: Preadolescents' perceptions of parenting. *Development and Psychopathology, 17*(1), 207–230.

Luthar, S. S., & Suchman, N. E. (2000). Relational Psychotherapy Mothers' Group: A developmentally informed intervention for at-risk mothers. *Development and Psychopathology, 12*(2), 235–253.

Lutzker, J. R., & Rice, J. M. (1984). Project 12-ways: Measuring outcome of a large in-home service for treatment and prevention of child abuse and neglect. *Child Abuse and Neglect, 8*, 519–524.

Lyons-Ruth, K. (1996). Attachment relationships among children with aggressive behavior problems: The role of disorganized early attachment patterns. *Journal of Consulting and Clinical Psychology, 64*, 32–40.

Lyons-Ruth, K., Bronfman, E., & Parsons, E. (1999). Atypical attachment in infancy and early childhood among children at developmental risk. IV. Maternal frightened, frightening, or atypical behavior and disorganized infant attachment patterns. In J. Vondra, & D. Barnett (Eds.), *Typical Patterns of Infant Attachment: Theory, Research and Current Directions* (Vol. 64, pp. 67–96). Monographs of the Society for Research in Child Development.

Lyons-Ruth, K., & Jacobovitz, D. (1999). Attachment disorganization: Unresolved loss, relational violence and lapses in behavioral and attentional strategies. In J. Cassidy, & P. R. Shaver (Eds.), *Handbook of Attachment Theory and Research* (pp. 520–554). New York: Guilford.

Macfie, J., McElwain, N. L., Houts, R. M., & Cox, M. J. (2005). Intergenerational transmission of role reversal between parent and child: Dyadic and family systems internal working models. *Attachment & Human Development, 7*(1), 51–65.

MacIntyre, S. (1997). The Black Report and beyond: What are the issues? *Social Science and Medicine, 44*, 723–745.

MacLeod, M. D., Graham, E., & Johnston, M. (2001). Relative deprivation and recovery from first acute myocardial infarction. *Research Findings from the Health Variations Programme, 8*, 1–4.

Magai, C., Consedine, N. S., Gillespie, M., O'Neal, C., & Vilker, R. (2004). The differential roles of early emotion socialization and adult attachment in adult emotional experience: Testing a mediator hypothesis. *Attachment & Human Development, 6*(4), 389–417.

Main, M., & Cassidy, J. (1988). Categories of response to reunion with the parent at age 6: Predictable from infant attachment classifications and stable over a 1-month period. *Developmental Psychology, 24*, 415–426.

Main, M., & Solomon, J. (1990). Procedures for identifying infants as disorganized/disoriented during the Ainsworth Strange Situation. In M. Greenberg, D. Cicchetti, & E. M. Cummings (Eds.), *Attachment during the Preschool Years: Theory, Research and Intervention* (pp. 121–160). Chicago: University of Chicago Press.

Makino, S., Schulkin, J., Smith, M. A., Pacak, K., Palkovits, M., & Gold, P. W. (1995). Regulation of corticotrophin releasing hormone receptor messenger-ribo-nucleic acid in the rat-brain and pituitary by glucocorticoids and stress. *Endocrinology, 136*, 4517–4525.

Malphurs, J. E., Field, T. M., Larrain, C., Pickens, J., & Pelaez-Nogueras, M. (1996). Altering withdrawn and intrusive interaction behaviors of depressed mothers. *Infant Mental Health Journal, 17*, 152–160.

Mann, A., et al. (1998). An evaluation of practice nurses working with general practitioners to treat people with depression. *British Journal of General Practice, 48*, 875–879.

Marchenko, M. O., & Spence, M. (1994). Home visitation services for at-risk pregnant and post-partum women: A randomized trial. *American Journal of Orthopsychiatry, 64*, 468–478.

Marmot, M. (1995). Sickness absence as a measure of health status and functioning: From the Whitehall II Study. *Journal of Epidemiology and Community Health, 49*, 124–130.

Marmot, M. (1998). Improvement of social environment to improve heallth. *Lancet, 351*, 57–60.

Marmot, M., Ben-Shlomo, Y., & White, I. (1996). Does the variation in the socioeconomic characteristics of an area affect mortality? *British Medical Journal, 312*, 1013–1014.

Marmot, M., Bobak, M., & Davey Smith, G. (1995). Explanations for social inequalities in health. In B. C. Amick, S. Levine, A. R. Tarlov, & D. C. Welsh (Eds.), *Society and Health*. New York: Oxford University Press.

Marmot, M., Bosma, H., Hemingway, H., Brunner, E., & Stansfeld, S. (1997). Contribution of job control and other risk factors to social variations in coronary heart disease incidence. *Lancet, 350*, 235–239.

Marmot, M., Ferrie, J., Newman, K., & Stansfeld, S. (2001). The contribution of job insecurity to socio-economic inequalities. *Research Findings from the Health Variations Programme, 11*, 1–5.

Marmot, M. G. (2006). Status syndrome: A challenge to medicine. *Journal of the American Medical Association, 295*(11), 1304–1307.

Marmot, M. G., Adelstein, A. M., & Bulusu, L. (1984). *Immigrant Mortality in England and Wales, 1970–1978: Causes of Death by Country of Birth*. London: HMSO.

Marmot, M. G., & Shipley, M. J. (1996). Do socioeconomic differences in mortality persist after retirement? 25 year follow-up of civil servants from the first Whitehall study. *British Medical Journal, 313*, 1177–1180.

Marshall, P. J., & Fox, N. A. (2004). A comparison of the electroencephalogram between institutionalized and community children in Romania. *Journal of Cognitive Neuroscience, 16*(8), 1327–1338.

Matthews, K. A., Kelsey, S. F., Meilahn, E. N., Muller, L. H., & Wing, R. W. (1989). Educational attainment and behavioral and biologic risk factors for coronary heart disease in middle aged women. *American Journal of Epidemiology, 129*, 1132–1144.

Maughan, B., Rowe, R., Messer, J., Goodman, R., & Meltzer, H. (2004). Conduct disorder and oppositional defiant disorder in a national sample: Developmental epidemiology. *Journal of Child Psychology and Psychiatry, 45*(3), 609–621.

McFarlane, W. R. (2002). *Multifamily Groups in the Treatment of Severe Psychiatric Disorders*. New York: Guilford Press.

McGuigan, W. M., Katzev, A. R., & Pratt, C. C. (2003). Multi-level determinants of retention in a home-visiting child abuse prevention programme. *Child Abuse & Neglect, 27*(4), 363–380.

McKeown, T. (1988). *The Origins of Human Disease*. New York: Basil Blackwell.

McKinnon, W., et al. (1989). Chronic stress, leukocyte subpopulations, and humoral response to latent viruses. *Health Psychology, 8*, 389–402.

McLennan, J. D., & Offord, D. R. (2002). Should postpartum depression be targeted to improve child mental health? *Journal of the American Academy of Child and Adolescent Psychiatry, 41*(1), 28–35.

McLoyd, V. C. (1989). Socialization and development in a changing economy: The effects of paternal job and income loss on children. *American Psychologist, 44*, 293–302.

McLoyd, V. C. (1990). The impact of economic hardship on black families and children: Psychological distress, parenting, and socioemotional development. *Child Development, 61*, 311–346.

McLoyd, V. C. (1998). Socioeconomic disadvantage and child development. *American Psychologist, 53,* 185–204.

Meaney, M. J., Aitken, D., Bhatnager, S., van Berkel, C., & Sapolsky, R. M. (1988). Effect of neonatal handling on age-related impairments associated with the hippocampus. *Science, 239,* 766.

Meaney, M. J., Aitken, D. H., Sharma, S., & Sarrieau, A. (1989). Neonatal handling alters adrenocortical negative feedback sensitivity and hippocampal type II glucocorticoid receptor binding in the rat. *Neuroendocrinology, 50,* 597–604.

Meaney, M. J., & Szyf, M. (2005). Environmental programmeming of stress responses through DNA methylation: Life at the interface between a dynamic environment and a fixed genome. *Dialogues Clinical Neuroscience, 7*(2), 103–123.

Meltzer, H., et al. (2000a). The reluctance to seek treatment for neurotic disorders. *Journal of Mental Health, 9*(3), 319–327.

Meltzer, H., Gatward, R., Goodman, R., & Ford, T. (2000b). *The Mental Health of Children and Adolescents in Great Britain.* London: Stationery Office.

Meltzer, H., et al. (1995a). *Economic Activity and Social Functioning of Adults with Psychiatric Disorders. OPCS Surveys of Psychiatric Morbidity, Report 3.* London: HMSO.

Meltzer, H., et al. (1995b). *The Prevalence of Psychiatric Morbidity Among Adults Living in Private Households. OPCS Surveys of Psychiatric Morbidity, Report 1.* London: HMSO.

Mental Health Foundation. (1999). *Bright Futures: Promoting Children and young People's Mental Health.* London: Mental Health Foundation.

Merrison, S. A. (1979). *Royal Commission on the National Health Service.* London: HMSO.

Metcalfe, C., Davey Smith, G., Sterne, J. A. C., Heslop, P., Macleod, J., & Hart, C. (2001). Individual employment histories and subsequent cause specific hospital admissions and mortality: A prospective study of a cohort of male and female workers with 21 years follow-up. *Journal of Epidemiology and Community Health, 55,* 503–504.

Metropolitan Area Child Study Research Group. (2002). A cognitive-ecological approach to preventing aggression in urban settings: Initial outcomes for high risk children. *Journal of Consulting and Clinical Psychology, 70,* 179–194.

Meyer, E. C., Coll, C. T., Lester, B. M., Boukydis, C. F., McDonough, S. M., & Oh, W. (1994). Family-based intervention improves maternal psychological well-being and feeding interaction of preterm infants. *Pediatrics, 93,* 241–246.

Mistry, R. S., Vandewater, E. A., Huston, A. C., & McLoyd, V. C. (2002). Economic well-being and children's social adjustment: The role of family process in an ethnically diverse low-income sample. *Child Development, 73,* 935–951.

Monk, C. S., et al. (2003). Adolescent immaturity in attention-related brain engagement to emotional facial expressions. *NeuroImage, 20,* 420–428.

Montgomery, S. M., Bartley, M., & Wilkinson, R. G. (1997). Family conflict and slow growth. *Archives of the Diseases of Childhood, 77,* 326–330.

Montgomery, S. M., Bartley, M. J., Cook, D. G., & Wadsworth, M. E. J. (1996). Health and social precursors of unemployment in young men. *Journal of Epidemiology and Community Health, 50,* 415–422.

Mrazek, P. J., & Brown, C. H. (2002). An evidence-based literature review regarding outcomes in psychosocial prevention and early intervention in young children. In P. J. Mrazek, & R. J. Haggerty (Eds.), *Reducing Risks for Mental Disorders: Frontiers for Preventive Intervention Research* (pp. 215–313). Washington, DC: National Academy press.

Munck, A., Guyere, P. M., & Holbrock, M. J. (1984). Physiological functions of glucocorticoids in stress and their relations to pharmacological actions. *Endocrinology Review, 93,* 9783–9799.

Murray, L., Cooper, P. J., Wilson, A., & Romaniuk, H. (2003). Controlled trial of the short- and long-term effect of psychological treatment of post-partum depression: 2. Impact on the mother-child relationship and child outcome. *British Journal of Psychiatry, 182,* 420–427.

Murray, L., Fiori-Cowley, A., Hooper, R., & Cooper, P. (1996). The impact of postnatal depression and associated adversity on early mother-infant interactions and later infant outcome. *Child Development*, *67*, 2512–2526.

Mustard, J. F. (2000). Healthy societies: An overview. In A. R. Tarlov, & R. F. S. Peter (Eds.), *The Society and Population Health Reader: A State and Community Perspective* (Vol. II, pp. 3–14). New York: The New Press.

Myrtek, M. (2001). Meta-analyses of prospective studies on coronary heart disease, type a personality and hostility. *International Journal of Cardiology*, *79*, 245–251.

Nachmias, M., Gunnar, M. R., Mangelsdorf, S., Parritz, R. H., & Buss, K. (1996). Behavioral inhibition and stress reactivity: Moderating role of attachment security. *Child Development*, *67*, 508–522.

Naliboff, B. D., et al. (1991). Immunological changes in young and old subjects during brief laboratory stress. *Psychosomatic Medicine*, *53*, 121–132.

National Depression Campaign. (1999). National Depression Campaign Survey.

National Institute for Clinical Excellence. (2004). *Depression: Management of Depression in Primary and Secondary Care*. London: National Institute for Clinical Excellence.

Nazroo, J. Y. (1998). Genetic, cultural or socio-economic vulnerability? Explaining ethnic inequalities in health. In M. Bartley, D. Blane, & G. Davey Smith (Eds.), *The Sociology of Health Inequalities* (pp. 151–170). Oxford: Blackwell.

Nazroo, J. Y. (2001). South Asian people and heart disease: An assessment of the importance of socioeconomic position. *Ethnicity & Disease*, *11*, 401–411.

Neisser, U., Boodo, G., & Bouchard, T. (1996). Intelligence knowns and unknowns (report of a task force established by the American Psychological Association). *American Psychologist*, *51*, 77–101.

Nelson, E. E., Leibenluft, E., McClure, E. B., & Pine, D. S. (2005). The social re-orientation of adolescence: A neuroscience perspective on the process and its relation to psychopathology. *Psychological Medicine*, *35*, 163–174.

Nelson, K. E., & Landsman, M. J. (1992). *Alternative Models of Family Preservation: Family-based Services in Context*. Springfield, IL: Charles C. Thomas Publ.

NICHD Early Childcare Research Network. (1997). The effects of infant childcare on infant-mother attachment: security: Results of the NICHD study of early childcare. *Child Development*, *68*, 860–879.

Nicholson, A., Bobak, M., Murphy, M., Rose, R., & Marmot, M. (2005). Socio-economic influences on self-rated health in Russian men and women—A life course approach. *Social Science & Medicine*, *61*(11), 2345–2354.

Nolan, P., Murray, E., & Dallender, J. (1999). Practice nurses' perceptions of services for clients with psychological problems in primary care. *International Journal of Nursing Studies*, *36*, 97–104.

O'Connor, T. (2006). The persisting effects of early experiences on social development. In D. Cicchetti, & D. J. Cohen (Eds.), *Developmental Psychopathology*, 2nd ed. *Vol. 3: Risk, Disorder and Adaptation* (pp. 202–234). New York: Wiley.

O'Herlihy, A., et al. (2002). *National Inpatient Child and Adolescent Psychiatry Study (NICAPS)*. London: Royal College of Psychiatrists' Research Unit.

Olds, D. L., Henderson, C., Kitzman, H., Eckenrode, J., Cole, R., & Tatelbaum, R. (1998). The promise of home visitation: Results of two randomized trials. *Journal of Community Psychology*, *26*(1), 1–21.

Olds, D. L., Henderson, C. R., Chamberlin, R., & Tatelbaum, R. (1986). Preventing child abuse and neglect: A randomized trial of nurse home visitation. *Pediatrics*, *78*, 65–78.

Olds, D. L., et al. (1997). Long-term effects of home visitation on maternal life course and child abuse and neglect: Fifteen-year follow-up of a randomized trial. *Journal of the American Medical Association*, *278*, 637–643.

Ontiveros, J., Miller, T., Markides, K. S., & Espino, D. V. (1999). Physical and psychosocial consequences of strokes in elderly Mexican Americans. *Ethnicity and Disease*, *9*, 212–217.

Owen, M. T., & Cox, M. J. (1997). Marital conflict and the development of infant-parent attachment relationships. *Journal of Family Psychology*, *11*, 152–164.

Ozonoff, S., Pennington, B. F., & Solomon, M. (2006). Neuropsychological perspectives on developmental psychopathology. In D. Cicchetti, & D. J. Cohen (Eds.), *Developmental Psychopathology*, 2nd edn. *Vol. II: Developmental Neuroscience* (pp. 332–380). New York: Wiley.

Pappas, G., Queen, S., Hadden, W., & Fisher, G. (1993). The increasing disparity in mortality between socioeconomic groups in the United States, 1960 and 1986. *New England Journal of Medicine, 329*(2), 103–109.

Parker, S. J., Zahr, L. K., Cole, J. G., & Brecht, M. L. (1992). Outcome after developmental intervention in the neonatal intensive care unit for mothers of preterm infants with low socioeconomic status. *Journal of Pediatrics, 120,* 780–785.

Parker, S. W., & Nelson, C. A. (2005a). An event-related potential study of the impact of institutional rearing on face recognition. *Development and Psychopathology, 17*(3), 621–639.

Parker, S. W., & Nelson, C. A. (2005b). The impact of early institutional rearing on the ability to discriminate facial expressions of emotion: An event-related potential study. *Child Development, 76*(1), 54–72.

Patterson, G. R., Reid, J. B., & Dishion, T. J. (1992). *Antisocial Boys.* Eugene, OR: Castalia.

Pei, Q., Zetterstrom, T., & Fillenz, M. (1990). Tail pinch induces changes in the turnover and release of dopamine and 5-hydroxytrptamine in different brain regions of the rat. *Neuroscience, 35,* 133–138.

Penninx, B. W., et al. (1997). Effects of social support and personal coping resources on mortality in older age: The Longitudinal Ageing Study Amsterdam. *American Journal of Epidemiology, 146*(6), 510–519.

Peterson, L., Tremblay, G., Ewigman, B., & Saldana, L. (2003). Multilevel selected primary prevention of child maltreatment. *Journal of Consulting and Clinical Psychology, 71*(3), 601–612.

Petersen, L., et al. (2005). A randomized multicentre trial of integrated versus standard treatment for patients with a first episode of psychotic illness. *British Medical Journal, 331,* 602–605.

Petty, F., Kramer, G., & Wilson, L. (1992). Prevention of learned helplessness: In vivo correlation with cortical serotonin. *Pharmacology, Biochemistry and Behavior, 43,* 361–367.

Pincus, T., Callahan, L. F., & Burkhauser, R. V. (1987). Most chronic diseases are reported more frequently by individuals with fewer than 12 years of formal education in the age 18–64 United States population. *Journal of Chronic Disease, 40*(9), 865–874.

Plomin, R., & McGuffin, P. (2003). Psychopathology in the postgenomic era. *Annual Review of Psychology, 54,* 205–228.

Plotsky, P. M., Thrivikraman, K. V., Nemeroff, C. B., Caldji, C., Sharma, S., & Meaney, M. J. (2005). Long-term consequences of neonatal rearing on central corticotropin-releasing factor systems in adult male rat offspring. *Neuropsychopharmacology, 30,* 2192–2204.

Pollak, S. (2005). Early adversity and mechnisms of plasticity: Integrating affective neuroscience with developmental approaches to psychopathology. *Development and Psychopathology, 17,* 735–752.

Pollak, S. D., Cicchetti, D., Klorman, R., & Brumaghim, J. T. (1997). Cognitive brain event-related potentials and emotion processing in maltreated children. *Child Development, 68,* 773–787.

Pollak, S. D., Klorman, R., Thatcher, J. E., & Cicchetti, D. (2001). P3b reflects maltreated children's reactions to facial displays of emotion. *Psychophysiology, 38*(2), 267–274.

Posada, G., et al. (1995). The secure based phenomenon across cultures Children's behavior, mothers' preferences and experts' concepts. *Monographs of the Society for Research in Child Development, 60,* 27–48.

Poulton, R., et al. (2002). Association between children's experience of socioeconomic disadvantage and adult health: A life-course study. *Lancet, 360*(9346), 1640–1645.

Powell, L. F. (1974). The effect of extra stimulation and maternal involvement on the development of low-birth-weight infants and on maternal behavior. *Child Development, 45,* 106–113.

Powell, C., & Grantham-McGregor, S. (1989). Home visiting of varying frequency and child development. *Pediatrics, 84,* 157–164.

Power, C., & Hertzman, C. (1997). Social and biological pathways linking early life and adult disease. *British Medical Bulletin, 53,* 210–221.

Power, C., Manor, O., & Fox, J. (1991). *Health and Class: The Early Years.* Chapman and Hall.

Power, C., Matthews, S., & Manor, O. (1998). Inequalities in self-related health: explanations from different stages of life. *Lancet, 351,* 1009–1014.

Putnam, R. D. (1993). *Making Democracy Work: Traditions in Modern Italy.* Princeton: Princeton University Press.

Radojevic, M. (1992). *Predicting quality of infant attachment to father at 15 months from prenatal paternal representations of attachment: an Australian contribution.* Paper presented at the 25th International Congress of Psychology, Brussels, Belgium.

Raine, A., Venables, P. H., Dalais, C., Mellingen, K., Reynolds, C., & Mednick, S. A. (2001). Early educational and health enrichment at age 3–5 years is associated with increased autonomic and central nervous system arousal and orienting at age 11 years: Evidence from the Mauritius Child Health Project. *Psychophysiology, 38*(2), 254–266.

Raine, R., Lewis, L., Sensky, T., Hutchings, A., Hirsch, S., & Black, N. (2000). Patient determinants of mental health interventions in primary care. *British Journal of General Practice, 50,* 620–625.

Rainford, L., Mason, V., Hickman, M., & Morgan, A. (2000). *Health in England 1998: Investigating the Links between Social Inequalities and Health.* London: Stationery Office.

Ramachandani, P., & Stein, A. (2003). The impact of parental psychiatric disorder on children. *British Medical Journal, 327*(7409), 242–243.

Ramey, C. T., & Campbell, F. A. (1991). Poverty, early childhood education and academic competence: The Abecedarian experiment. In A. C. Huston (Ed.), *Children in Poverty.* Cambridge: Cambridge University press.

Rauh, V. A., Achenbach, T. M., Nurcombe, B., Howell, C. T., & Teti, D. M. (1988). Minimizing adverse effects of low birthweight: Four-year results of an early intervention programme. *Child Development, 59,* 544–553.

Ravaja, N., Katainen, S., & Keltikangas-Jarvinen, L. (2001). Perceived difficult temperament, hostile maternal child-rearing attitudes and insulin resistance syndrome precursors among children: A 3-year follow-up study. *Psychotherapy and Psychosomatics, 70,* 66–77.

Reid, J. B., Eddy, J. M., Fetrow, R. A., & Stoolmiller, M. (1999). Description and immediate impacts of a preventive intervention for conduct problems. *American Journal of Community Psychology, 27*(4), 483–517.

Rende, R., & Waldman, I. (2006). Behavioral and molecular genetics and developmental psychopathology. In D. Cicchetti, & D. J. Cohen (Eds.), *Developmental Psychopathology,* 2nd edn. *Volume II: Developmental Neuroscience* (pp. 427–464). New York: Wiley.

Resnick, G. (1985). Enhancing parental competencies for high risk mothers: An evaluation of prevention effects. *Child Abuse and Neglect, 9,* 479–489.

Resnick, M. B., Armstrong, S., & Carter, R. L. (1988). Developmental intervention programme for high-risk premature infants: Effects on development and parent-infant interactions. *Journal of Developmental and Behavioral Pediatrics, 9,* 73–78.

Resnick, M. B., Eyler, F. D., Nelson, R. M., Eitzman, D. V., & Bucciarelli, R. L. (1987). Developmental intervention for low birth weight infants: Improved early development outcome. *Pediatrics, 80,* 68–74.

Richardson, G., & Partridge, I. (Eds.). (2003). *Child and Adolescent Mental Health Services: An Operational Handbook.* London: Gaskell.

Roisman, G. I., Collins, W. A., Sroufe, L. A., & Egeland, B. (2005). Predictors of young adults' representations of and behavior in their current romantic relationship: Prospective tests of the prototype hypothesis. *Attachment & Human Development, 7*(2), 105–121.

Ronan, P. J., Steciuk, M., Kramer, G. L., Kram, M., & Petty, F. (2000). Increased septal 5-HIAA efflux in rats that do not develop learned helplessness after inescapable stress. *Journal of Neuroscience Research, 61*, 101–106.

Rose, R. J., Kaprio, J., Winter, T., Koskenvuo, M., & Viken, R. J. (1999). Familial and socio-regional environmental effects on abstinence from alcohol at age sixteen. *Journal of Studies on Alcohol. Supplement, 13*, 63–74.

Rose, R. J., Viken, R. J., Dick, D. M., Bates, J. E., Pulkkinen, L., & Kaprio, J. (2003). It does take a village: Nonfamilial environments and children's behavior. *Psychological Science, 14*(3), 273–277.

Rost, K., Nutting, P., Smith, J., Werner, J., & Duan, N. (2001). Improving depression outcomes in community primary care practice. *Journal of General Internal Medicine, 16*, 143–149.

Rost, K., Williams, C., Wherry, J., & Smith, G. R. (1995). The process and outcomes of care for major depression in rural family practice settings. *Journal of Rural Health, 11*, 114–121.

Rothbaum, F., Pott, M., Azuma, H., Migake, K., & Weisz, J. (2000). The development of close relationships in Japan and the United States: Paths of symbiotic harmony and generative tension. *Child Development, 71*, 1121–1142.

Rotheram-Borus, M. J., & Duan, N. (2003). Next generation of preventive interventions. *Journal of the American Academy of Child and Adolescent Psychiatry, 42*(5), 518–526.

Royal College of Psychiatrists. (1998). *Men Behaving Sadly*. London: Royal College of Psychiatrists.

Russek, L. G., & Schwartz, G. E. (1997). Perceptions of parental caring predict health status in midlife: A 35-year follow-up of the Harvard Mastery of Stress Study. *Psychosomatic Medicine, 59*(2), 144–149.

Russell, G. F. M., Szmukler, G., Dare, C., & Eisler, I. (1987). An evaluation of family therapy in anorexia nervosa and bulimia nervosa. *Archives of General Psychiatry, 44*, 1047–1056.

Rutter, M., Giller, H., & Hagell, A. (1998). *Antisocial Behaviour by Young People*. Cambridge: Cambridge University Press.

Rutter, M., & O'Connor, T. G. (2004). Are there biological programmeming effects for psychological development? Findings from a study of Romanian adoptees. *Developmental Psychology, 40*(1), 81–94.

Rutter, M., Pickles, A., Murray, R., & Eaves, L. (2001). Testing hypotheses on specific environmental causal effects on behavior. *Psychological Bulletin, 127*(3), 291–324.

Sander, L. W. (1970). Regulation and organization of behavior in the early infant-caretaker system. In R. Robinson (Ed.), *Brain and Early Behavior*. London: Academic Press.

Sanders, M. R., Markie-Dadds, C., Tully, L., & Bor, B. (2000). The Triple P-Positive Parenting Programme: A comparison of enhanced, standardm and self-directed behavioral family intervention for parents of children with early onset conduct problems. *Journal of Consulting and Clinical Psychology, 68*, 624–640.

Sapolsky, R. M. (1994). *Why Zebras Don't Get Ulcers. A Guide to Stress, Stress-Related Disease and Coping*. New York: W H Freeman.

Sapolsky, R. M. (1996). Why stress is bad for your brain. *Science, 273*, 749–750.

Sapolsky, R. M., Krey, L. C., & McEwen, B. S. (1983). The adrenocortical stress-response in the aged male rat: Impairment of recovery from stress. *Experimental Gerontology, 18*, 55–64.

Sapolsky, R. M., Krey, L. C., & McEwen, B. S. (1984). Stress down-regulates corticosterone receptors in a site specific manner in the brain. *Endocrinology, 114*, 287–292.

Sartorius, N. (2001). The economic and social burden of depression. *Journal of Clinical Psychiatry, 62*(Suppl. 15), 8–11.

Sartorius, N. (2002). Eines der letzen Hindernisse einer verbesserten psychiatrischen Versorgung: Das Stigma psychisher Erkrankung [One of the last obstacles to better mental health care: the stigma of mental illness]. *Neuropsychiatrie, 16*(1–2), 5–10.

Scarr-Salapatek, S., & Williams, M. L. (1973). The effects of early stimulation on low-birth-weight infants. *Child Development, 44*, 94–101.

Schieche, M., & Spangler, G. (2005). Individual differences in biobehavioral organization during problem-solving in toddlers: The influence of maternal behavior, infant-mother attachment, and behavioral inhibition on the attachment-exploration balance. *Developmental Psychobiology, 46*(4), 293–306.

Schlegel, A., & Barry, H. (1991). *Adolescence: An Anthropological Enquiry*. New York: Free Press (Macmillan).

Schoenbach, V. J., et al. (1986). Social ties and mortality in Evans County, Georgia. *American Journal of Epidemiology, 123*, 577–591.

Schore, A. (1993). *Affect Regulation and the Origin of the Self: The Neurobiology of Emotional Development*. Hillsdale, NJ: Erlbaum.

Schore, A. N. (2001). Contributions from the decade of the brain to infant mental health: An overview. *Infant Mental Health Journal, 22*, 1–6.

Schulberg, H. C., et al. (1996). Treating major depression in primary care practice. Eightmonth clinical outcomes. *Archives of General Psychiatry, 53*, 913–919.

Schultz, D., Izard, C. E., Ackerman, B. P., & Youngstrom, E. A. (2001). Emotion knowledge in economically disadvantaged children: Self-regulatory antecedents and relations to social difficulties and withdrawal. *Development and Psychopathology, 13*(1), 53–67.

Schweinhart, L. J., Berrueta-Clement, J. R., Barnett, W. S., Epstein, A. S., & Weikart, D. P. (1985). Effects of the Perry Preschool Programme on youths through age 19: A summary. *Topics in Early Childhood Special Education, 5*, 26–35.

Scott, K. G. (2003). Commentary: Individual risk prediction, individual risk, and population risk. *Journal of Clinical Child and Adolescent Psychology, 32*(2), 243–245.

Seeman, T. E., Berkman, L. F., Blazer, D. G., & Rowe, J. W. (1994). Social ties and support and neuroendocrine function: The MacArthur Studies of Successful Ageing. *Annals of Behavioral Medicine, 16*, 95–106.

Seeman, T. E., et al. (1993). Intercommunity variations in the association between social ties and mortality in the elderly: A comparative analysis of three communities. *Annals of Epidemiology, 3*, 325–335.

Sege, R. D., et al. (1997). Short-term effectiveness of anticipatory guidance to reduce early childhood risks for subsequent violence. *Archives of Pediatric and Adolescent Medicine, 151*, 392–397.

Shannon, C., et al. (2005). Maternal absence and stability of individual differences in CSF 5-HIAA concentrations in rhesus monkey infants. *American Journal of Psychiatry, 162*(9), 1658–1664.

Shaw, D. S., & Vondraa, J. I. (1993). Chronic family adversity and infant attachment security. *Journal of Child Psychology and Psychiatry, 34*, 1205–1215.

Simon, G. E., VonKorff, M., Rutter, C., & Wagner, E. (2000). Randomised trial of monitoring, feedback, and management of care by telephone to improve treatment of depression in primary care. *British Medical Journal, 320*, 550–554.

Slaughter, D. T. (1983). Early interventions and their effect on maternal and child development. *Monographs of the Society for research in child development, 48*, 4.

Sloan, R. P., et al. (2001). Hostility, gender and cardiac autonomic control. *Psychosomatic Medicine, 63*, 434–440.

Social Exclusion Unit. (2004). *Mental health and social exclusion: Social Exclusion Unit report*. London: The Office of the Deputy Prime Minister.

Society Exclusion Unit. (2000). *Report of Policy Action Team 12: Young People*. London: Social Exclusion Unit.

Solomon, J., & George, C. (1999). *Attachment Disorganization*. New York: Guilford.

Spangler, G., & Grossman, K. E. (1993). Biobehavioral organization in securely and insecurely attached infants. *Child Development, 64*, 1439–1450.

Spieker, S. J., & Booth, C. L. (1988). Maternal antecedents of attachment quality. In J. Belsky, & T. Nezworski (Eds.), *Clinical Implications of Attachment Theory* (pp. 95–135). Hillsdale, NJ: Erlbaum.

Sroufe, L. A. (1979). Socioemotional development. In J. Osofsky (Ed.), *Handbook of Infant Development* (pp. 462–516). New York: Wiley.

Sroufe, L. A. (1996). *Emotional Development: The Organization of Emotional Life in the Early Years*. New York: Cambridge University Press.

Sroufe, L. A. (2005). Attachment and development: A prospective, longitudinal study from birth to adulthood. *Attachment & Human Development, 7*(4), 349–367.

Sroufe, L. A., Carlson, E., Levy, A. K., & Egeland, B. (1999). Implications of attachment theory for developemntal psychopathology. *Development and Psychopathology, 11*, 1–13.

Sroufe, L. A., Egeland, B., Carlson, E., & Collins, W. A. (2005a). *The Development of the Person: The Minnesota Study of Risk and Adaptation from Birth to Adulthood*. New York: Guilford.

Sroufe, L. A., Egeland, B., Carlson, E., & Collins, W. A. (2005b). Placing early attachment experiences in developmental context. In K. E. Grossmann, K. Grossmann, & E. Waters (Eds.), *The Power of Longitodinal Atachment Research: From Infancy and Childhood to Adulthood* (pp. 48–70). New York: Guilford.

Sroufe, L. A., Egeland, B., & Kreutzer, T. (1990). The fate of early experience following developmental change: Longitudinal approaches to individual adaptation in childhood. *Child Development, 61*, 1363–1373.

Sroufe, L. A., Fox, N., & Pancake, V. (1983). Attachment and dependency in developmental perspective. *Child Development, 54*, 1615–1627.

St. Pierre, R. G., Layzer, J. I., & Barnes, H. V. (1995). Two-generation programmes: Design, cost and short-term effectiveness. *The Future of Children, 5*, 76–93.

Stansfeld, S. A., & Marmot, M. G. (1992). Deriving a survey measure of social support: The reliability and validity of the Close Persons Questionnaire. *Social Science and Medicine, 35*, 1027–1035.

Stanton, M. D., & Shadish, W. R. (1997). Outcome, attrition and family/couples treatment for drug abuse: A meta-analysis and review of the controlled and comparative studies. *Psychological Bulletin, 122*, 170–191.

Stanton, M. E., Gutierrez, Y. R., & Levine, S. (1988). Maternal deprivation potentiates pituitary-adrenal stress responses in infant rats. *Behavioral Neuroscience, 102*, 692–700.

Steele, H., Phibbs, E., & Woods, R. T. (2004). Coherence of mind in daughter caregivers of mothers with dementia: Links with their mothers' joy and relatedness on reunion in a strange situation. *Attachment & Human Development, 6*(4), 439–450.

Steele, H., Steele, M., & Fonagy, P. (1996). Associations among attachment classifications of mothers, fathers, and their infants: Evidence for a relationship-specific perspective. *Child Development, 67*, 541–555.

Stein, H., et al. (2002). Adult attachment: What are the underlying dimensions? *Psychol Psychother, 75*(Pt 1), 77–91.

Stein, M. B. (1997). Hippocampal volume in women victimised by childhood sexual abuse. *Psychological Medicine, 27*, 951–959.

Stolberg, A. L., & Garrison, K. M. (1985). Evaluating a primary prevention programme for children of divorce. *Am J Community Psychol, 13*(2), 111–124.

Stoolmiller, M., Eddy, J. M., & Reid, J. B. (2000). Detecting and describing preventive intervention effects in a universal school-based randomized trial targeting delinquent and violent behavior. *Journal of Consulting and Clinical Psychology, 68*(2), 296–306.

Sucheki, D., Nelson, D. Y., VanOers, H., & Levine, S. (1995). Activation and inhibition of the hypothalamic-pituitary-adrenal axis of the neonatal rat: Effects of maternal deprivation. *Psychoneuroendocrinology, 20*, 169–182.

Sugisawa, H., Liang, J., & Liu, X. (1994). Social networks, social support and mortality among older people in Japan. *J Gerontol, 49*, S3–13.

Suomi, S. J. (1991). Up-tight and laid-back monkeys: Individual differences in the response to social challenges. In S. Brauth, W. Hall, & R. Dooling (Eds.), *Plasticity of Development* (pp. 27–56). Cambridge, MA: MIT Press.

Suomi, S. J. (1999). Attachment in rhesus monkeys. In J. Cassidy, & P. R. Shaver (Eds.), *Handbook of Attachment: Theory, Research and Clinical Applications* (pp. 181–197). New York: Guilford.

Suomi, S. J. (2005). Aggression and social behaviour in rhesus monkeys. *Novartis Foundation Symposium, 268,* 216–222; discussion 222–216, 242–253.

Suomi, S. J., & Levine, S. (1998). Psychobiology of intergenerational effects of trauma. In Y. Danieli (Ed.), *International Handbook of Multigenerational Legacies of Trauma* (pp. 623–637). New York: Plenum Press.

Symons, L., et al. (2004). Improving access to depression care: Descriptive reports of a multidisciplinary primary care pilot service. *BJGP, 54*(506), 679–668.

Teicher, M. H. (2000). Wounds that time won't heal: The neurobiology of child abuse. *Cerebrum, 4,* 50–67.

Teicher, M. H., Andersen, S. L., Polcari, A., Anderson, C. M., & Navalta, C. P. (2002). Developmental neurobiology of childhood stress and trauma. *Psychiatric Clinics of North America, 25*(2), 397–426, vii–viii.

Teicher, M. H., Andersen, S. L., Polcari, A., Anderson, C. M., Navalta, C. P., & Kim, D. M. (2003a). The neurobiological consequences of early stress and childhood maltreatment. *Neuroscience and Biobehavioral Reviews, 27*(1–2), 33–44.

Teicher, M. H., Polcari, A., Andersen, S. L., Anderson, C. M., & Navalta, C. P. (2003b). Neurobiological Effects of Childhood Stress and Trauma. In S. Coates, J. L. Rosenthal, & D. S. Schechter (Eds.), *September 11: Trauma and Human Bonds* (pp. 211–238). Hillsdale, NJ: Analytical Press.

Teti, D., Gelfand, D., & Isabella, R. (1995). Maternal depression and the quality of early attachment: An examination of infants, preschoolers and their mothers. *Developmental Psychology, 31,* 364–376.

The Conduct problems Prevention Research Group. (2002a). Evaluation of the first 3 years of the Fast Track Prevention trial with children at high risk for adolescent conduct problems. *Journal of Abnormal Child Psychology, 30,* 19–35.

The Conduct problems Prevention Research Group. (2002b). The implementation of the Fast track Programme: An example of a large-scale prevention science efficacy trial. *Journal of Abnormal Child Psychology, 30,* 1–17.

The Infant Health and Development Programme. (1990). Enhancing the outcomes of low birth weight premature infants. *Journal of the American Medical Association, 263,* 3035–3042.

The Place2Be Evaluation Team, Tiley, C., & White, J. (2004). *Report and Clinical Audit: Hub Summary Report September 2003—August 2004.* London: Place2Be.

Thomas, C. B., & Duszynski, K. R. (1974). Closeness to parents and the family constellation in a prospective study of five disease states; suicide, mental illness, malignant tumor, hypertension, and coronary heart disease. *Johns Hopkins Medical Journal, 134,* 251.

Tolan, P. H., & Gorman-Smith, D. (2002). What violence prevention research can tell us about developmental psychopathology. *Development and Psychopathology, 14*(4), 713–729.

Tomasello, M. (2005). *Constructing a Language: A Usage-Based Theory of Language Acquisition.* Cambridge, MA: Harvard University Press.

Toth, S. L., Maughan, A., Manly, J. T., Spagnola, M., & Cicchetti, D. (2002). The relative efficacy of two interventions in altering maltreated preschool children's representational models: Implications for attachment theory. *Development and Psychopathology, 14*(4), 877–908.

Tremblay, R. E. (2000). The origins of violence. *ISUMA,* Autumn, 19–24.

Tronick, E. Z., & Gianino, A. F. (1986). The transmission of maternal disturbance to the infant. In E. Z. Tronick, & T. Field (Eds.), *Maternal Depression and Infant Disturbance* (pp. 5–11). San Francisco, CA: Jossey Bass.

Twemlow, S. W., Fonagy, P., & Sacco, F. C. (2001a). An innovative psychodynamically influenced intervention to reduce school violence. *Journal of the American Academy of Child and Adolescent Psychiatry, 40*(3), 377–379.

Twemlow, S. W., Fonagy, P., Sacco, F. C., Gies, M. L., Evans, R., & Ewbank, R. (2001b). Creating a peaceful school learning environment: A controlled study of an elementary school intervention to reduce violence. *American Journal of Psychiatry, 158*(5), 808–810.

Uchino, B., & Garvey, T. (1997). The availability of social support reduces cardiovascular reactivity to acute psychological stress. *Journal of Behavioral Medicine, 20*(1), 15–27.

Unutzer, J., et al. (2001). Improving primary care for depression in late life: The design of a multicenter randomized trial. *Med Care, 39*, 785–799.

van den Boom, D. C. (1994). The influence of temperament and mothering on attachment and exploration: An experimental manipulation of sensitive responsiveness among lower-class mothers with irritable infants. *Child Development, 65*, 1449–1469.

van den Boom, D. C. (1995). Do first-year intervention effects endure? Follow-up during toddlerhood of a sample of Dutch irritable infants. *Child Development, 66*, 1798–1816.

van IJzendoorn, M. H. (1995). Adult attachment representations, parental responsiveness, and infant attachment: A meta-analysis on the predictive validity of the Adult Attachment Interview. *Psychological Bulletin, 117*, 387–403.

van IJzendoorn, M. H., Goldberg, S., Kroonenberg, P. M., & Frenkel, O. J. (1992). The relative effects of maternal and child problems on the quality of attachment: A meta-analysis of attachment in clinical samples. *Child Development, 59*, 147–156.

Vaughn, B. E. (2005). Discovering pattern in developing lives: Reflections on the Minnesota study of risk and adaptation from birth to adulthood. *Attachment & Human Development, 7*(4), 369–380.

Verschueren, K., & Marcoen, A. (1999). Representation of self and socioemotional competence in kindergartners: Differential and combined effects of attachment to mother and father. *Child Development, 70*(1), 183–201.

Vicentic, A., et al. (2006). Maternal separation alters serotonergic transporter densities and serotonergic 1A receptors in rat brain. *Neuroscience, 140*(1), 355–365.

Villarejo, D. (2003). The health of U.S. hired farm workers. *Annual Review of Public Health, 24*, 175–193.

Vitaro, F., Brendgen, M., Pagani, L., Tremblay, R. E., & McDuff, P. (1999). Disruptive behavior, peer association and conduct disorder: Testing the developmental links through early intervention. *Development and Psychopathology, 11*, 287–304.

Von Korff, M., & Goldberg, D. (2001). Improving outcomes in depression—The whole process of care needs to be enhanced. *British Medical Journal, 323*, 948–949.

Von Korff, M., Grunssan, J., Schaefer, J., Curry, S., & Wagner, E. (1997). Collaborative management of chronic illness. *Annals of Internal Medicine, 127*, 1097–1102.

Wadsworth, M. E. J. (1991). *The Imprint of Time: Childhood, History and Adult Life.* Oxford: Clarendon Press.

Wahab, A. (2005). Lib Dem says there is a serious tension between Social Exclusion Unit and Home Office. *YoungMinds Magazine, 79*(Nov/Dec).

Walker, H., Irvin, L. K., & Sprague, J. R. (1997). *Violence Prevention and School Safety: Issues, Problems, Approaches, and Recommended Solutions.* Eugene, OR: Institute on Violence and Destructive Behaviour, University of Oregon.

Wamboldt, M. Z., & Wamboldt, F. S. (2000). Role of the family in the onset and outcome of childhood disorders: Selected research findings. *Journal of the American Academy of Child & Adolescent Psychiatry, 39*, 1212–1219.

Ward, E., et al. (2000). Randomised controlled trial of non-directive counselling, cognitive-behaviour therapy, and usual general practitioner care for patients with depression. I: Clinical effectiveness. *British Medical Journal, 321*, 1383–1388.

Ward, M. J., & Carlson, E. A. (1995). Associations among Adult Attachment representations, maternal sensitivity, and infant-mother attachment in a sample of adolescent mothers. *Child Development, 66*, 69–79.

Warren, N. J., & Amara, I. A. (1984). Educational groups for single parents: The Parenting after Divorce programmes. *Journal of Divorce, 8*, 79–96.

Wartner, U. G., Grossman, K., Fremmer-Bombrik, E., & Suess, G. (1994). Attachment patterns at age six in South Germany: Predictability from infancy and implications for pre-school behaviour. *Child Development, 65*, 1014–1027.

Wasik, B. H., Ramey, C. T., Bryant, D. M., & Sparling, J. J. (1990). A longitudinal study of two early intervention strategies: Project CARE. *Child Development, 61*, 1682–1696.

Watamura, S. E., Donzella, B., Alwin, J., & Gunnar, M. R. (2003). Morning-to-afternoon increases in cortisol concentrations for infants and toddlers at childcare: Age differences and behavioral correlates. *Child Development, 74*(4), 1006–1020.

Waters, E., Merrick, S. K., Treboux, D., Crowell, J., & Albersheim, L. (2000). Attachment security from infancy to early adulthood: A 20 year longitudinal study. *Child Development, 71*(3), 684–689.

Watson, P. (1994). *Explaining rising mortality amongst men in Esatern Europe.* Paper presented at the ESRC Research Seminar on Gender, Class and Ethnicity in Post-Communist States.

Weblin, L., et al. (1985). Prospective study of social influences on mortality: The study of men born in 1913 and 1923. *Lancet, 1*, 915–918.

Webster-Stratton, C. (1996). Early intervention with videotape modelling: Programmes for families of children with Oppositional Defiant Disorder or Conduct Disorder. In E. S. Hibbs, & P. S. Jensen (Eds.), *Psychosocial Treatments for Child and Adolescent Disorders: Empirically based Strategies for Clinical Practice* (pp. 435–474). Washington, DC: American Psychological Association.

Webster-Stratton, C. (1998). Preventing conduct problems in Head Start children: Strengthening parenting competencies. *Journal of Consulting and Clinical Psychology, 66*, 715–730.

Webster-Stratton, C., Reid, M. J., & Hammond, M. (2001). Preventing conduct problems, promoting social competence: A parent and teacher training partnership in head start. *Journal of Clinical Child Psychology, 30*(3), 283–302.

Webster-Stratton, C., & Taylor, T. (2001). Nipping early risk factors in the bud: Preventing substance abuse, delinquency, and violence in adolescence through interventions targeted at young children (0–8 years). *Prevention Science, 2*(3), 165–192.

Weinberg, M. K., & Tronick, E. Z. (1994). Beyond the face: An empirical study of infant affective configurations of facial, vocal, gestural, and regulatory behaviors. *Child Development, 65*(5), 1503–1515.

Weiner, H. (1996). The use of animal models in peptic ulcer disease. *Psychosomatic Medicine, 58*, 524–545.

Weinfield, N., Sroufe, L. A., & Egeland, B. (2000). Attachment from infancy to early adulthood in a high risk sample: Continuity, discontinuity and their correlates. *Child Development, 71*(3), 695–702.

Weinfield, N. S., Sroufe, L. A., Egeland, B., & Carlson, A. E. (1999). The nature of individual differences in infant-caregiver attachment. In J. Cassidy, & P. R. Shaver (Eds.), *Handbook of Attachment: Theory, Research and Clinical Applications* (pp. 68–88). New York: Guilford.

Weiss, M., Zelkowitz, P., Feldman, R. B., Vogel, J., Heyman, M., & Paris, J. (1996). Psychopathology in offspring of mothers with borderline personality disorder: A pilot study. *Canadian Journal of Psychiatry, 41*(5), 285–290.

Wells, K. B., et al. (2000). Impact of disseminating quality improvement programmes for depression in managed primary care: A randomized controlled trial. *Journal of the American Medical Association, 283*(2), 212–220.

Whitfield, K. E., Weidner, G., Clark, R., & Anderson, N. B. (2002). Sociodemographic diversity and behavioral medicine. *Journal of Consulting and Clinical Psychology, 70*, 463–481.

Wilkinson, R. G. (1996). *Unhealthy Societies: From Inequality to Wellbeing.* New York: Routledge.

Wilkinson, R. G. (2000). Social relations, hierarchy and health. In A. R. Tarlov, & R. F. S. Peter (Eds.), *The Society and Population Health Reader: A State and Community Perspective* (Vol. II, pp. 211–235). New York: The New Press.

Wilkinson, R. G., Kawachi, I., & Kennedy, B. (1998). Mortality, the social environment, crime and violence. *Sociology of Health and Illness, 20*(5), 578–597.

Williams, M. L., & Scarr, S. (1971). Effects of short term intervention on performance in low-birth-weight, disadvantaged children. *Pediatrics, 47*, Suppl2:289.

Williams, R., Haney, T., Lee, K., Kong, Y., Blumenthal, J., & Whalen, R. (1980). Type a behaviour, hostility and coronary heart disease. *Psychosomatic Medicine, 42,* 539–549.

Williams, R., & Kerfoot, M. (2005). Setting the scene: Perspectives on the history of and policy for child and adolescent mental health service. In R. Williams, & M. Kerfoot (Eds.), *Child and Adolescent Mental Health Services: Strategy, Planning, Delivery, and Evaluation.* Oxford: Oxford University Press.

Williams, R., & Richardson, G. E. (1995). *Together We Stand: The Commissioning, Role and Management of Child and Adolescent Mental Health Services: An NHS Health Advisory Service (HAS) Thematic Review.* London: HMSO.

Winkleby, M. A., Fortmann, S. P., & Barrett, D. C. (1990). Social class disparities in risk factors for disease: Eight-year prevalence patterns by level of education. *Preventive Medicine, 19*(1), 1–12.

Wolchik, S. A., et al. (1993). The children of divorce parenting intervention: Outcome evaluation of an empirically based programme. *American Journal of Community Psychology, 21*(3), 293–231.

Wolfe, D. A., Edwards, B., Manion, I., & Koverola, C. (1988). Early intervention for parents at risk of child abuse and neglect: A preliminary investigation. *Journal of Consulting and Clinical Psychology, 56,* 40–47.

Wolpert, M., et al. (2002). *Drawing on the Evidence: Advice for Mental Health Professionals Working with Children and Adolescents.* London: The British Psychological Society.

World Health Organisation. (2001). *World Health Report 2001: Mental Health: New Understanding, New Hope.* Geneva: WHO.

Wyman, P. A., Cowen, E. L., Work, W. C., Hoyt-Meyers, L., Magnus, K. B., & Fagen, D. B. (1999). Caregiving and developmental factors differentiating young at risk urban children showing resilient versus stress affected outcomes: A replication and extension. *Child Development, 70,* 645–659.

Yehuda, R., Hallig, S. L., & Grossman, R. (2001). Childhood trauma and risk for PTSD: Relationship to intergenerational effects of trauma, parental PTSD, and cortisol excretion. *Development and Psychopathology, 13*(3), 733–753.

Yeung, W. J., Linver, M. R., & Brooks-Gunn, J. (2002). How money matters for young children's development: Parental investment and family processes. *Child Development, 73,* 1861–1879.

York, A., & Lamb, C. (Eds.). (2005). *Building and Sustaining Specialist CAMHS: Workforce Capacity and Functions of Tiers 2 3 and 4 Specialist Child and Adolescent Mental Health Services across England, Ireland, Northern Ireland, Scotland and Wales—Final Draft.* London: Child and Adolescent Faculty, Royal College of Psychiatrists.

Yoshikawa, H. (1994). Prevention as cumulative protection: Effects of early family support and education on chronic delinquency and its risk. *Psychological Bulletin, 115,* 28–54.

Yoshikawa, H. (1995). Long-term effects of early childhood programmes on social outcomes and delinquency. *Future of Children, 5,* 51–75.

Zanarini, M. C., et al. (2002). Severity of reported childhood sexual abuse and its relationship to severity of borderline psychopathology and psychosocial impairment among borderline inpatients. *The Journal of Nervous and Mental Disease, 190*(6), 381–387.

Zhang, F., & Labouvie-Vief, G. (2004). Stability and fluctuation in adult attachment style over a 6-year period. *Attachment & Human Development, 6*(4), 419–437.

Zhang, T. Y., Chretien, P., Meaney, M. J., & Gratton, A. (2005). Influence of naturally occurring variations in maternal care on prepulse inhibition of acoustic startle and the medial prefrontal cortical dopamine response to stress in adult rats. *Journal of Neuroscience, 25*(6), 1493–1502.

# Index